Funding Community Initiatives

The role of NGOs and other intermediary institutions in supporting low income groups and their community organizations in improving housing and living conditions in the Third World

Silvina Arrossi, Felix Bombarolo, Jorge E Hardoy, Diana Mitlin, Luis Pérez Coscio and David Satterthwaite

Written by the International Institute for Environment and Development (IIED) in London and IIED-América Latina in Buenos Aires

Published for the United Nations Development Programme

by Earthscan Publications, London

EARTHSCAN

First published in 1994 by
Earthscan Publications Limited
120 Pentonville Road, London N1 9JN

Copyright © International Institute for Environment and Development, 1994

A catalogue record for this book is available from the British Library

ISBN: 1 85383 204 9

Typeset by PCS Mapping & DTP, Newcastle upon Tyne
Printed and bound in Great Britain by
Biddles Ltd, Guildford and King's Lynn
Cover design by Lucy Jenkins
Cover photograph by Mark Edwards, Still Pictures

Earthscan Publications Limited is an editorially independent subsidiary of
Kogan Page Limited and publishes in association with the International
Institute for Environment and Development and the World Wide Fund for
Nature.

CONTENTS

Part II: Case studies

LIST OF ILLUSTRATIONS

BOXES

TABLES

FIGURES

ABOUT THE AUTHORS

All six authors of this book work in the Human Settlements Programme which is run jointly by the Instituto Internacional de Medio Ambiente y Desarrollo (IIED-América Latina) in Buenos Aires and the International Institute for Environment and Development in London.

Silvina Arrossi is a sociologist and has a Masters in Community and Public Health from the London School of Hygiene and Tropical Medicine. She has worked with IIED-América Latina since 1987 on urban development issues, especially on the links between health and habitat conditions.

Felix Bombarolo is an architect who works in IIED-América Latina and directs the 'Programme for Institutional Strengthening and Training of NGOs' (the FICONG programme). Since 1982 he has worked on projects of research, action and capacity building for popular habitat, and since 1986 has been a member of the Argentine National Council of Scientific and Technological Research. He co-authored a recent book published in Spanish on *The Role of Non-government Organizations in Latin America and the Caribbean* (with Luis Pérez Coscio and Alfredo Stein), Ediciones FICONG, Buenos Aires, 1992.

Jorge E Hardoy was President of IIED-América Latina until his death in September 1993. He also founded IIED-América Latina and the Human Setlements Programme. Qualifying as an architect in 1950 with a Masters and PhD in City and Regional Planning from Harvard University, he has written widely on both historical and contemporary urban issues. Among his former publications with Earthscan are *Squatter Citizen: Life in the Urban Third World* (with David Satterthwaite), 1989; *The Poor Die Young: Housing and Health in Third World Cities* (edited with Sandy Cairncross and David Satterthwaite), 1990; and *Environmental Problems in Third World Cities* (with Diana Mitlin and David Satterthwaite), 1992. He was also a former President of the Inter-American Planning Society, twice a Guggenheim fellow and served on the Board of the International Development Research Centre (IDRC) in Canada. He was also President of the National Commission for Historic Monuments in Argentina and Editor of the journal *Medio Ambiente y Urbanizacion*. He was an advisor to the World Commission on Environment and Development (the Brundtland Commission), the World Health Organization and UNICEF's International Child Development Centre.

Diana Mitlin is an economist with the Human Settlements Programme (a joint programme of the International Institute for Environment and Development in London and IIED-América Latina) and managing editor of its journal *Environment and Urbanization*. With a first degree in economics and sociology from Manchester University and a Masters in economics from Birkbeck College (University of London), she has a special interest in the role of NGOs and voluntary organizations in housing and environmental action in Third World cities. She worked with David Satterthwaite in advising the

United Nations Centre for Human Settlements (Habitat) on the links between sustainable development and human settlements.

Luis Pérez Coscio is a sociologist and civil engineer working at IIED-América Latina, and coordinates the 'Programme for Institutional Strengthening and Training of NGOs' (the FICONG programme) for the Southern Cone. Before joining IIED-América Latina in 1990, he worked as a consultant for the United Nations Development Programme. He co-authored a recent book published in Spanish on *The Role of Non-government Organizations in Latin America and the Caribbean* (with Felix Bombarolo and Alfredo Stein), Ediciones FICONG, Buenos Aires, 1992.

David Satterthwaite directs IIED's Human Settlements Programme and is editor of its journal *Environment and Urbanization*. Trained as a development planner at University College London with a first degree in history, he began working with Jorge Hardoy in the joint IIED/IIED-América Latina Human Settlements Programme in 1978 and they co-authored several books and many papers on issues relating to environment, health, shelter and urban development in Africa, Asia and Latin America. He was an advisor to the World Commission on Environment and Development (the Brundtland Commission) and more recently has worked with the World Health Organization, UNICEF and the UN Centre for Human Settlements (Habitat) on the links between environment, health and development in cities.

FOREWORD

By the year 2000, half of the world's population – 3.2 billion people – will be living in cities. Seventy per cent of this urban population will be in developing countries. Eighteen cities in the developing world will have a population of more than ten million.

Although this rapid urbanization and growth in population contributes to economic growth and social development, the negative consequences are considerable. In addition to increasing urban poverty and deteriorating environment, a significant problem is the gap between demand for urban infrastructure and services and the available supply. In particular, the urban poor, who are most negatively affected, lack adequate access to affordable and secure housing, sanitation services, and education and health facilities.

As governments of developing countries increasingly lack the capacity and resources effectively to address deficiencies in the provision and improvement of infrastructure, shelter, and services, low-income groups are seeking alternatives and developing creative solutions of their own. Most new housing units and slum and squatter settlement improvements are being developed by poor individuals, households, and communities. Their efforts have been innovatively supported through funding and technical support by non-governmental organizations (NGOs) and other kinds of intermediary institutions.

This report presents an insightful analysis of the mechanisms and processes through which these intermediary institutions, based in developing countries, and often funded by national governments or international agencies, have channelled support directly to low-income groups.

Supporting community-level initiatives is at the heart of UNDP's urban strategy. Committed to a human-development approach, UNDP is seeking to enlarge people's choices by assisting in the development of their capabilities, improving their access to employment, credit, health and education, and increasing their participation in economic and social activities. To this end, UNDP is supporting institutional mechanisms for promoting equitable, participatory development, and improving the financial, technical, and management capacities of cities.

In promoting human development in the urban sector, UNDP has targeted five urgent urban challenges, which are also reflected in many of the initiatives of other national and international development agencies:

1. The alleviation of poverty by promoting income-generating activities, transforming the role of the informal sector, and encouraging the full participation of women.
2. The provision of infrastructure, shelter, and services by promoting enabling and participatory strategies that improve the poor's access to land, finance, and building materials.
3. The improvement of the urban environment by improving energy use, solid waste management and alternative transport, and by enacting laws

for environmental management and incorporating environmental issues in urban planning.
4. The strengthening of local government and administration by bolstering the capacity of local authorities to plan, manage and finance urban programmes.
5. The expansion of the role of the private sector and NGOs by encouraging private provision of urban housing and infrastructure, privatizing some urban services, and involving NGOs in development programmes.

Examples of ongoing UNDP initiatives emphasizing these priority areas and encouraging local level participatory development include the interregional Local Initiative Facility for Urban Environment (LIFE) which promotes 'local–local' dialogue among municipalities, NGOs, and CBOs; the Global Environment Facility's (GEF) Small Grants Programme which supports community-based approaches and strategies that address global environment problems; and the UNDP/UNCHS/World Bank Urban Management Programme which provides technical assistance in building local capacity at the city and country levels to address problems in municipal finance and administration, land management, infrastructure, urban environment, and poverty alleviation.

Such programmes demonstrate the significant role that UNDP and other external support agencies can play in seeking more ways to support and strengthen the initiatives of low-income households and communities. Experience has increasingly shown that supporting enabling mechanisms that target the grassroots level can significantly improve the poor's standard of living. The conclusions of this report and the illustrative case studies drawn from experiences in Latin America, Africa, and South and Southeast Asia bring to the forefront the importance of funding community-level initiatives.

It is hoped that dissemination of this report to institutions in developing countries and development assistance agencies will contribute to a better understanding and sharing of experiences in community-based initiatives.

Timothy Rothermel
Director, Division for Global and Interregional Programmes
UNDP

ACKNOWLEDGEMENTS

This report was prepared by the International Institute for Environment and Development (IIED) and IIED-América Latina (Buenos Aires) with the financial support of the Division for Global and Interregional Programmes (DGIP) at UNDP. It benefited from inputs by the Urban Development Unit at UNDP, and from discussions at a meeting of multilateral development agencies to review the report. The views presented are those of the authors and do not necessarily reflect the official views of UNDP. The authors are also grateful to the Ford Foundation for their support for work on this theme of funding community initiatives, and to friends at Earthscan for all their help in converting the manuscript into this book.

Of the six authors of this book, it was Jorge E Hardoy who first suggested that work was needed on this theme, and who initiated that work. He also had a central role in the preparation of this book, before he died in September 1993.

INTRODUCTION

There is little cause for optimism, if one reviews the achievements of governments and international agencies in Africa and in most of Asia and Latin America in reducing poverty and in ensuring basic human needs are met. But, at the same time, there are many examples of innovative schemes and initiatives involving low-income groups and their community organizations in reducing poverty and meeting basic needs. These examples are diverse in their scale, nature and organization. In many, governments and international agencies had little or no role; in others they had very important roles. It is likely that the initiatives we know about represent only a small proportion of the total number.

This book is based on case studies of NGOs or intermediary institutions which have sought to fund community-level initiatives aimed at one aspect of poverty reduction: the improvement of housing conditions and the provision of housing-related infrastructure and services. It draws mainly on documents about their work, supplemented where possible with information drawn from interviews with their staff. It is not intended as an evaluation of these experiences but as an exploration of new ways and means of working with low-income households and the organizations that they form (or could form) to improve housing and living conditions, including the provision of infrastructure (such as piped water, sanitation and drains, and paved roads) and services (such as health care and the collection of household waste).

The need for new initiatives in this area is not in doubt. Despite four decades of development planning and a growing sophistication in development assistance, the housing and living conditions of at least a third of the population of Africa, Asia and Latin America remains very poor. At least 600 million of the 1.4 billion inhabitants of urban areas in the Third World in 1990 live in 'life- and health-threatening' homes and neighbourhoods because of the poor quality of their houses and the sites on which they are built and because of the inadequacy in infrastructure and service provision. There is far less detailed information on the quality of housing in rural areas although the high proportion which lack piped, protected water supplies and sanitation gives some idea of the scale of the problem.

Low-income households have demonstrated remarkable ingenuity in finding and developing their own solutions. Despite very limited resources, low-income individuals, households and communities have been responsible for a high proportion of all new housing units and for a large proportion of all investments in the housing stock and in housing-related infrastructure and services. The scale and nature of their investments is rarely recorded and is not reflected in official statistics – perhaps not surprisingly, when so much of the investment is in illegal settlements or in structures which are termed 'temporary' or classified in other ways which greatly undervalue their scale and importance in providing shelter.

In urban areas, the homes and settlements that poorer groups have developed often contain the seeds of a model for residential development and service delivery which is far more appropriate to local climate, culture and resource availability than the official model of urban development with most of its norms, codes and preferences copied from the North. In the North, funding for housing construction and improvement, and for the infrastructure and services associated with housing and residential areas, is dependent on conditions that are absent in most Third World nations: well-developed financial markets within prosperous and often growing economies, low inflation, well-established local government with a large local tax and revenue base, and high proportions of city dwellers able to make (and sustain) regular payments for housing and basic services.

But there are limits to what low-income groups can achieve for themselves, either individually (in building or developing their own shelters) or collectively (in providing infrastructure and services) without some degree of technical support and resources. A range of intermediary institutions has developed to support low-income communities to build or improve their houses and communities. They are 'intermediary' in the sense that they make available to individuals or community organizations funding and technical advice and draw part of their capital or collateral from national governments or international funding agencies. An increasing number of case studies of such intermediary organizations (most of them Third World NGOs) show that, through providing technical, legal and financial services to low-income households for shelter construction or improvement and through working with community organizations in site improvement and service provision, it is possible to reach poorer groups with improved housing and to address the enormous backlog in infrastructure and service provision.

The main focus of this book is on funding and supporting the improvement of housing conditions and the provision of housing-related infrastructure and services in urban areas, although some consideration is also given to supporting comparable initiatives in rural areas. A particular focus is on the use of credit for housing and basic services and infrastructure investment. Lack of access to finance is a major constraint for both the communities and intermediary institutions. Through case studies of the use of innovative finance systems for both income generation and for housing and basic services and infrastructure, the authors consider the feasibility of loan-based finance for low-income housing and community development. The book seeks to draw on the experience of these case studies and on the experiences of other intermediary organizations to consider how to greatly increase the scale and effectiveness of the support given to low-income individuals and their community organizations for the improvement of housing and living conditions and the provision of infrastructure and services in residential areas.

The book is organized in two sections. The first discusses the issues, drawing on the case studies; the second provides information on each of the case studies. This introduction is intended both as an introduction and a summary of the book's main points. Chapter 1 considers the scale and extent of the need for investment in shelter, infrastructure and services. Chapter 2 discusses why the conventional responses have failed. Chapter 3 describes the growing role of non-governmental organizations in this area and Chapter 4 discusses the experiences of the case study institutions in providing credit and technical support for shelter, infrastructure and services. Chapter 5 draws some conclusions.

A number of different models, structures, processes and programme components for the successful development of housing and basic services and infrastructure have emerged from this study. While no two programmes are identical, certain similarities emerge from the experiences examined here.

Structures

A number of possible structures and relations between support agencies and communities are evident in the case studies. Most programmes involve the participation (both financial and otherwise) of key actors at a number of levels:

- at the international level, private voluntary organizations and occasionally official bilateral and multilateral donors;
- at the national level, government and sometimes separate housing finance institutions;
- at the local level, city or municipal government, NGOs and federations of community organizations; and
- communities and households themselves, sometimes organized and sometimes not.

Figure 0.1 overleaf illustrates these different actors and the most significant structural relations which link them.

Models

There are several different models for the operation of different components of the community development programme. In the case of housing, the two alternative models are individual and cooperative ownership. In the case of basic services and infrastructure, direct service provision by NGOs is complemented by NGO involvement in negotiations and pressure to ensure that better government provision (perhaps through a financial contribution) is forthcoming.

Credit systems are based on one of four models:

1. improved access to formal-sector loans (generally through the use of guarantee funds);
2. long-term integration with the existing formal credit institutions through demonstrating creditworthiness;
3. the development of alternative banking institutions to service the poor; and
4. NGO cooperation with innovative government funds.

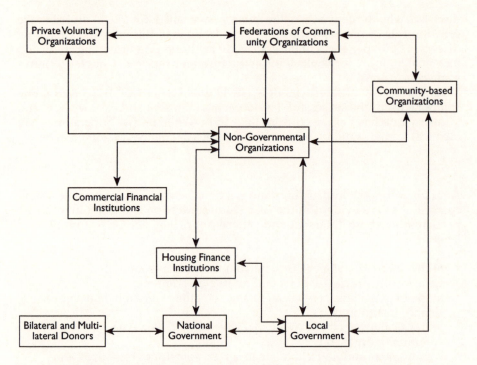

Figure 0.1 Participants and the most significant organizational relations

Relationships

Four sets of social relationships emerge as being particularly important to the successful operation of community development through intermediary institutions:

1. relations within the community and the process of community development and control of the project (design, management, monitoring and evaluation);
2. relations between the intermediary institution and the community;
3. relations between the government and the community, perhaps mediated through an NGO; and
4. in the case of innovative funding mechanisms and credit, relations with the formal financial institutions.

Programme components

A number of key elements can be identified as being included in many community development programmes for housing, basic services and infrastructure. The most common elements are:

- support for community organization and for the collective identification of mutual and individual needs;
- credit for housing and other services;
- training and technical assistance in construction skills;
- materials banks and bulk purchase of materials; and
- help in negotiating with government and private landowners to regularize the site and obtain better government services.

CONCLUSION

In most countries, a change of emphasis (and of resource allocations to shelter, infrastructure and services) is needed in the official 'model' of urban housing and residential development to one where governments and development assistance agencies work in partnership with low-income households and community organizations to make limited resources go much further in ensuring healthier, safer and more secure settlements. This change requires official support for the investments that low-income groups make (including those derived from self-help and mutual aid) and action to reduce the constraints they face in acquiring and developing their own homes and neighbourhoods. It also requires that government agencies work with low-income groups and their community organizations to ensure that infrastructure and services are provided or improved in ways which match people's priorities but which minimize subsidies and keep down per capita costs (so that limited funding can reach more people).

The means to achieve this re-orientation include ensuring the ready availability of funding and technical and legal advice to individuals, households and communities. This implies the need for intermediary institutions which can provide a continuous programme of funding and technical support to individual, community and municipal initiatives within each urban centre and district.

This channelling of support direct to low-income groups is not intended to be a replacement for government activity. Indeed, it should be seen as part of the process of building the capacity and democratic structure of local government in that it involves strong and continuous partnerships between local governments and the citizens within their jurisdiction. One of the reasons why such an approach is needed is the weakness of local governments and their incapacity to work flexibly on a large scale with low-income groups. If local authorities had the resources to ensure that all households within their jurisdiction had safe and sufficient supplies of water, adequate sanitation, drainage, roads, schools and health centres, the need for alternative models would be much less. Their relevance would be more in ensuring that agencies providing infrastructure and services were accountable to and served the needs and priorities of the local population. But in most instances, local governments lack the power and resources to address the deficiencies in infrastructure and service provision within their jurisdiction. Neither national governments nor aid agencies appear to be able (or willing) to address this.

Thus, this book offers a description and analysis of the mechanisms and processes through which intermediary institutions based in the Third World have undertaken such tasks. It also considers the ways in which such NGOs and other kinds of intermediary institution may effectively scale up the impact of community initiatives: how they can stimulate the formation of community organizations, how they can support them in their work, what the role of credit is in such initiatives and what more might be needed.

Part I

OVERVIEW

1

THE NEED FOR INVESTMENT

INTRODUCTION

By 1990, an estimated 1.4 billion people lived in urban centres in the Third World.[1] Of these, at least 600 million are estimated to live in 'life- and health-threatening' homes and neighbourhoods because of the inadequacies in the quality of the housing and in the provision of infrastructure and services associated with housing and residential areas (such as piped water supplies, provision for sanitation, garbage collection and site drainage, paved roads and pavements, schools and health clinics).[2] This implies serious shortfalls in investment in the homes and neighbourhoods of the urban population.

The speed with which urban populations have grown in Third World nations has far outpaced the institutional capacity to manage it. The Third World's urban population was under 300 million in 1950, which means nearly a fivefold increase between 1950 and 1990. During these forty years, the number of urban inhabitants in many Third World nations expanded more than tenfold. Some major cities have grown more than twenty-fold. There are dozens of cities with 500,000 or more inhabitants today which were only small urban centres in 1950. There are hundreds more with between 100,000 and 500,000 inhabitants which four decades ago had only a few thousand inhabitants or which were not urban centres at all.

However, the central characteristic of the urban problem is not the scale of population growth but the scale of the mismatch between demographic change and institutional change. This mismatch is between the speed with which population has concentrated in particular urban centres and the (often) very slow pace with which societies have developed the institutional capacity to cope with this. Most large urban centres today have city and municipal governments whose form, mode of operation and resource base have changed little in recent decades, despite enormous increases in population, resource consumption and waste generation.

Although the failure of public institutions to cope with this change is almost universal, the scale and nature of urban change, its likely extent in the future and the most appropriate means to address it will differ greatly from country to country. In some Third World countries, rapid urban growth began in the late 19th century or in the first decade of the 20th century; for a few others, it began between the two World Wars. But for the great majority, rapid urbanization has only taken place since the 1940s or 1950s. Some of the less industrialized and more rural nations have been experiencing the most rapid rate of growth in their urban population. Most of the slower growing cities are associated with countries which urbanized and developed earlier, and their urban authorities are not so pressed by the need for quick solutions. In many such cities, institutions are better developed, as is expertise, and policy makers can select from a range of different urban strategies. This is the case, for example, in Buenos Aires, Rosario and Cordoba in Argentina, Santiago in Chile, Montevideo in Uruguay, and Porto Alegre in Brazil. At the opposite end of the spectrum are the fast-growing cities of sub-Saharan Africa within countries which gained political independence one generation ago (or less) and where there are fewer traditions and limited expertise on which to call in managing rapid urban growth. These cities include Lagos, Dar-es-Salaam, Nairobi, Kinshasa and Lusaka. There are also cities with an ancient urban history, like Mexico City, Delhi, Bangalore, Bangkok and many more in Asia, which are also growing far beyond the existing capacity to plan and manage such rapid change.

The conventional model for the development of urban residential areas within market or mixed economies assumes that a considerable proportion of urban households will choose to make high levels of investment in their own shelter. This model assumes that such investment will be facilitated by long-term credit taken on by the household. It assumes that most individuals or households – whether as owners or tenants – will be able to meet the full cost of housing that has been designed by architects and constructed by building enterprises, using skilled technicians for specialist work. It also assumes that a range of public authorities and agencies will ensure the provision of infrastructure and services to all buildings and provide a planning and regulatory framework which ensures that buildings are healthy and structurally safe. While the particular form that this model takes varies amongst the nations of the North, as does the division of tasks and responsibilities between public and private sector, it remains an accepted responsibility of public authorities to ensure that all residential, commercial and industrial buildings have adequate infrastructure and services and that the buildings are structurally safe.

This conventional model was developed in the North in response to rapid urban change. Its effectiveness can be seen in the reductions in mortality and morbidity rates and in the incidence of many infectious diseases during the last decades of the 19th century and early decades of the 20th century. In the mid-19th century, levels of life expectancy were much lower and infant and child mortality rates were much higher in many of the poorer districts of cities in the North than is the case in most Third World cities today.[3] Although many urban problems remain in the North, a very high proportion of all urban citizens have shelter which protects them from the elements and which has basic infrastructure and services. However, this model of urban development took many decades to develop. Much of the urban population in the North suffered from serious deficiencies in shelter, infrastructure and services during much of the 19th century (and many people continued to suffer during part of the 20th century).

This model for the development of residential areas does not work in the vast majority of urban centres in the Third World. Government agencies in the Third World often have similar roles and responsibilities to those in the North; indeed, the very structure of the building and planning regulations and of local (municipal) government is often based on precedents drawn from the North or remains little changed from Northern models introduced under colonial rule. But the authorities who in theory are responsible for investments in infrastructure and services lack the commitment, power and resources to do so.[4] They also fail to provide the regulatory framework to ensure that buildings meet health and safety requirements. Even where such a framework is enforced, it is so inappropriate to local conditions and possibilities that the cost of the cheapest 'legal housing' is pushed beyond what can be afforded by the majority of the population.

Many reasons can be put forward to explain why the model developed in the North works so poorly in the South. Although their relative importance will vary greatly from nation to nation, the reasons include more rapid urban population growth, less well-established institutions for local government, less democratic societies with more centralized government structures, and often more inequitable distributions of income and assets, and slower economic growth (for some nations). In most cities, there are large gaps between the cost of the cheapest conventional shelter and the ability to pay of most of the urban population. What is perhaps less easily explained is the lack of examples of more appropriate models of public sector intervention for urban development.

Most investments in the built environment in all but the central districts and the more wealthy neighbourhoods come from a large and varied multiplicity of individuals and households. Most of these are unrecorded and are made outside any legal building or planning regulations. Most new housing is also built illegally. Only rarely does public policy support this investment and it may constrain or hinder it. The gap between reality and 'the conventional model' can be seen in the official statistics for the number of conventional houses constructed annually. In Third World nations, the number of conventional dwellings constructed annually is usually between two and four per 1000 inhabitants – and the actual increment in the housing stock (including all illegal and informal housing) is likely to be between 15 and 30 units per 1000 inhabitants. In many of the poorer nations, the number of conventional dwellings constructed annually can be below one per 1000 inhabitants when the population is expanding at between 20 and 35 persons per 1000 inhabitants per year and the urban population expanding at between 30 and 60 persons per 1000 inhabitants per year.

Most city or municipal governments have virtually no independent investment capacity. They also have inadequate powers for revenue-raising and lack the institutional capacity needed to plan and manage infrastructure and service provision and to recover costs. Most of their budgets are spent on meeting recurrent costs. Constrained local (and national) budgets for public works mean postponement of new investments in city infrastructure and no expansion in the number of people served. Private investment in infrastructure and services is constrained not only by low levels of demand (since most of the population have incomes too low to pay enough for infrastructure and services to be profitably supplied by private companies) but also by the difficulties for individuals or households in funding investments which can only be made on a neighbourhood or district basis such as roads, pavements, drains, sewers and piped water systems. The result is large areas within each urban centre, city or metropolitan area with no paved roads or pavements, no piped water systems or electricity supplies, no sewers or drains. Such areas also suffer serious deficiencies in services and amenities such as garbage collection, health centres, dispensaries, schools and day-care centres.

It is impossible to arrive at an accurate estimate for the proportion of the 1.4 billion urban residents who lack adequate services and infrastructure within their homes and residential areas. Case studies of specific cities show that it is common for between 30 and 60 per cent of the population to live in illegal settlements, tenements or cheap boarding houses where infrastructure and service levels range from the inadequate to the almost non-existent.[5] In many urban centres, especially in poorer African and Asian nations, the majority of the population lives in areas with major deficiencies in most or all such infrastructure and services. Most urban centres in Africa and Asia – including many cities with a million or more inhabitants – have no sewerage system at all.[6] Even in cities where investment has been made in sewers, connection to the system is often restricted to the richer areas. Garbage collection services are deficient in most residential areas; an estimated 30–50 per cent of the solid wastes generated are left uncollected.[7] The proportion of the population living with serious deficiencies in infrastructure and services may be smaller in the major cities of more prosperous nations – although in metropolitan areas such as Sao Paulo, Mexico City and Buenos Aires there are still millions suffering in this way.

There are also major problems with maintaining existing infrastructure and services. Inadequate attention to maintenance can be seen in the deterioration of bus and train services, the worsening state of roads, the poor maintenance of water, sewer and drainage systems and public buildings. In many nations, this problem has been exacerbated by foreign aid projects which provided the funds for new capital investments in roads, water and drainage systems, hospitals and health centres, schools, power stations and public transport but failed either to provide for recurrent costs or to support the development of local capacity to manage and maintain the new investments.

The quality of much existing and most new housing is very poor, reflecting the low incomes of those building, renting or buying houses. Such housing often provides the inhabitants with inadequate protection against the elements and little provision for security. In addition, there is often serious overcrowding – there are many examples of rented accommodation in urban centres where there is less than one square metre of space per person.[8] The inadequacies in the supply of many forms of infrastructure – for instance water taps and latrines – mean that these are overused and often in a poor state of repair. It is not uncommon to find 100 or more people dependent on one water tap and many households sharing a single latrine. The lack of services is evident in the local environment. There may be piles of rotting garbage, stagnant pools of water due to inadequate drainage, or pollution from factories located closeby.[9]

The neglect of the built environment and of services, through inadequate finance, affects the inhabitants in numerous ways. It can be seen in the extent of ill health, disablement and premature death within tenement districts and areas of illegal housing. A review of the literature on the links between health and development states that 'recent analyses .... show a strong association between ill health and both quantitative and qualitative shortcomings in water supply, food supply and sanitation. Inadequate shelter, poor ventilation, lack of facilities for solid waste disposal, air and noise pollution and overcrowding are also likely to have negative consequences for health.'[10] Many case studies which compare health statistics between rich and poor areas in the same city find very large differentials in such indicators as infant and child mortality or life expectancy.[11] In some urban centres in the Third World, a child born to a poor family in an illegal settlement is 40–50 times more likely to die before the age of five than a child born in the North, or a child born to a high-income family in one of the city enclaves with good quality infrastructure and services.[12]

These health problems do not arise only from diseases. They are also associated with unsafe and dangerous building structures which increase the risks of fires, building collapse and electrocution (from faulty wiring). Much of the housing stock is constructed from flammable material (wood, cardboard, plastic, canvas, straw) and the risk of fire is increased still further where open fires or mobile stoves are used for cooking. Health risks are also greatly increased in the many houses built on land prone to flooding or landslides.

In addition to working time lost through illness, inadequate infrastructure and services have direct impacts on income-earning opportunities. For instance, a considerable proportion of the urban poor in larger cities faces unnecessarily high costs in the length of time spent in travelling to and from work. Settlements are often far from the city centre owing to uncontrolled development and the fact that poorer groups can often only afford to develop housing on poor-quality land on the urban periphery. The problems are further exacerbated by poor management and maintenance of public transport and by lack of new investment, and inadequate services also inhibits entrepreneurial activities. Moreover, poorer groups often have to pay high prices for poor-quality private provision of such basic services as water supply and garbage collection while richer groups enjoy higher-quality public provision at much lower unit prices.[13]

The extent to which low-income urban communities suffer from inadequate services and the costs of providing them with the facilities they require are described below in relation to three critical areas: water, sanitation and garbage disposal. Investment is needed for much else besides: for the development of land with safe housing plots affordable by poorer groups, for adequate roads and transport facilities, for health facilities, emergency services and educational provision.

WATER

The only available estimates for water provision in urban areas in the Third World come from the World Health Organization. These suggest that in 1988

170 million urban inhabitants lacked safe and sufficient supplies of water. This is certainly an underestimate – both because of the criteria used to define what is an 'adequate' supply and because of exaggerations by governments in the figures they supply to the World Health Organization (see Box 1.1).

Inadequacies in water supply provision ensure that a high proportion of the population in most urban centres collects water from open streams and wells which may be contaminated with waste, or purchase their water from private vendors who are subject to little quality or price control. The lack of an adequate water supply affects the poor in several ways. First, they are liable to suffer from the diseases which can be carried in untreated water. Second, without water to maintain adequate hygiene, the risk of contracting disease increases. Third, the cost of buying water reduces the purchase of other essentials such as food and health care.

Of critical importance to the amount to water used by the household is the proximity of the supply to the home. Recent research has shown that consumption increases as the distance from the source of water falls but then reaches a plateau and remains more or less stable until water is available within the household plot when it rises two- or three-fold.[14]

There is an urgent need to ensure a plentiful supply of piped water of guaranteed quality. In general, more emphasis has been placed on the dangers associated with contaminated water, rather than on the risks arising from an

---

Box 1.1 The exaggerations in official statistics for water-supply provision.

Official statistics on water supply overstate the number (or proportion) of urban dwellers adequately served. One reason is the criteria used to define an 'adequate' water supply. For instance, the availability of a water tap within 100 metres of a house is often considered 'adequate', but an urban household needing to use such a standpipe is very unlikely to be able to obtain enough water to allow it to meet its needs for cooking, washing and personal hygiene. The long waiting in queues at communal water taps may reduce water consumption below volumes needed for good health. In addition, piped water systems in many tropical cities function only intermittently, for a few hours each day, which makes it especially difficult for households relying on communal taps. The water in old and leaky distribution pipes is often of doubtful quality, contaminated by groundwater and sewage. Many households and settlements judged by governments to be 'adequately served' by public systems may resort to other water sources because of these problems or may not be able to afford to purchase the water they need. Official figures for many of the poorer Third World nations claim that over 80 per cent of the urban population had access to safe water in the mid 1980s and that there was 100 per cent coverage in Nigeria and Liberia and 99 per cent coverage in Togo. Local specialists find it hard to reconcile these figures with the reality in the urban centres in which they work.

Source: Cairncross, Sandy, et al (1990), 'The urban context', in Jorge E Hardoy et al (eds), *The Poor Die Young: Housing and Health in Third World Cities*, Earthscan, London.

inadequate supply of water; however, the latter is now thought to be more important in regard to some health hazards.[15] Many low-income households in the Third World currently purchase supplies from private vendors for which they have to pay a price many times that paid by households receiving piped water. The cost of providing urban water supplies varies greatly, the single most important factor being fresh water availability. The capital cost for a private house connection in a city with plentiful water supplies can be as low as US$60 per capita whereas in a city in an arid nation it can be five times this amount. An 'average' figure for urban areas in the Third World would be around US$120 per person served. Capital costs for public standpipes are about half this, although most of the reduction in cost occurs because of savings resulting from the lower level of water use, which in itself has health implications.

SANITATION

Although the World Health Organization suggests that 331 million urban dwellers lacked adequate sanitation in 1988, this estimate also seems very low for reasons similar to those discussed in relation to water. The number of people lacking sanitation systems which are easily maintained and which ensure no contamination of food or water by faecal matter and a minimum of human contact with faecal matter is likely to be much higher. In informal and illegal settlements, provision may be no more than pits dug into the ground or buckets. It is in these often overcrowded and under-resourced areas that the health consequences resulting from a lack of sanitation can be significantly worse than in other urban or rural areas. Improving sanitation results in better health and a higher-quality living environment. It may also offer additional benefits (for example, to women, who in many cultures suffer because custom demands privacy when defecating).

There are many different methods of providing adequate sanitation at a cost significantly lower than that of investing in conventional water-borne sewerage systems. Typical capital costs for the main alternatives are given in Table 1.1 (although the complete picture requires adjustment for maintenance and operating costs). These costs are merely illustrative of the scale of investment required. Costs vary for each individual site according to the availability of water, sullage disposal, settlement density, ground conditions, and local social and economic factors.

GARBAGE

An estimated 30 to 50 per cent of the solid wastes generated within urban centres are left uncollected and are dumped on any available waste ground. The consequences impact particularly on health; piles of garbage serve as food and breeding grounds for disease vectors; rubbish blocks water courses and open drains which become stagnant pools and may overflow and in some

Table 1.1 Typical range of capital costs per household of alternative sanitation systems (1990 prices)

Type of System	US$
Twin pit pour-flush latrines	75–150
Ventilated improved pit latrine	68–175
Shallow sewerage	100–325
Small-bore sewerage	150–500
Conventional septic tanks	200–600
Conventional sewerage	600–1200

Note: Capital costs alone cannot provide a meaningful basis for determining the cost of a system since some systems are more expensive than others to operate and maintain. What must be calculated is the total discounted capital, operation and maintenance costs for each household to determine the charge that must be levied for the service and also to establish that households can afford to pay this amount. Where the monthly cost of providing sanitation exceeds 5 per cent of the family income, it might be deemed unaffordable. Most low-cost sanitation alternatives come within this limit even for the poorest of communities, especially urban communities.

Source: Sinnatamby, Gehan (1990) 'Low cost sanitation', in Jorge E Hardoy et al (eds), *The Poor Die Young: Housing and Health in Third World Cities*, Earthscan, London.

cases these may carry excreta. At times of heavy rain, the blocked drains may result in serious flooding, with loss of life and property.

The typical Northern garbage collection and disposal service is relatively expensive and beyond the means of existing urban/municipal government budgets in the South. But there are sufficient examples of alternative ways of servicing relatively poor households at affordable per capita costs to suggest that garbage collection services could be greatly improved in virtually all urban areas without high costs and with important employment-generation benefits. In addition, in recent years there have been significant changes of attitude among many professionals to the collection and processing of garbage.[16] One of these is the recognition of the need to develop local solutions which match local needs and possibilities. The reason is that conditions vary so much from city to city in (among other factors) the scale and type of refuse generation, the amount residents can afford (and are prepared to pay) for refuse collection, the type of vehicles needed to get to each building in different settlements, local possibilities for recycling or reclaiming part of the refuse, local traffic conditions, the availability of land sites for city dumps and the resources at the disposal of local authorities for the collection and management of garbage disposal. This variation usually implies solutions very different from those taught to engineers whose training is overwhelmingly based on Northern models and precedents.[17]

MEETING THE SCALE OF NEED

The costs of ensuring adequate provision for all of those in need is large, even if it is restricted to those services discussed above. If we assume that there are

400 million urban dwellers in need of new or improved water supply systems and that the average per capita cost is US$80, this implies a total cost of US$32 billion. If we assume, too, that there are 100 million urban households in need of new or improved sanitation systems, with an average cost per household of US$300, this implies a total cost of US$30 billion. Both these figures are simply for the initial capital investment: no additional maintenance or operating costs are included. In order to place these figures in perspective, we need to consider that total official development assistance from OECD members states was just under US$50 billion in 1988.[18] Much of this assistance is tied to projects which are of particular interest to the donor country. The low priority given by development assistance agencies to water, sanitation and garbage collection and to other aspects of improved housing and living conditions and basic services is discussed further in Chapter 2.

Perhaps it is wrong to view this as a problem rooted in a lack of funding. The estimates fail to take into account one key resource: the organizational and investment capacities of a high proportion of those people currently inadequately served by water and sanitation which would be released, if they were offered improvements to match their needs and priorities. This implies that the need for external funding is less. But perhaps a more fundamental constraint than funding is the lack of technical and managerial capacity within local authorities to develop appropriate local solutions with these people. It is these institutional resources which have been lacking and which present perhaps the most difficult gap to fill. Even if major additions could be made to capital investment in water and sanitation, the weakness and inefficiency of existing public-sector institutions with responsibilities for water and sanitation would severely constrain their efficient use. Developing the institutional capacity is a difficult and slow process.

THE ROLE OF RESEARCH – RETHINKING PUBLIC AND PRIVATE ROLES WITHIN THE CITY

It has long been conventional wisdom that the legal and institutional precedents from the North's experience of urbanization are usually inappropriate to conditions and trends in the South. But there have been few alternatives put forward – and even fewer tried and tested. Moreover, there are constraints on the development of alternative approaches, including serious deficiencies in basic data about the demographic, social and economic dimensions of urban change. The development of more appropriate alternatives at a national and city-wide level requires an accurate and detailed understanding of urban change with a knowledge of the social, economic and political factors which underly or shape it.

As comparative research develops, the interest in the qualitative aspects of urbanization will inevitably grow. This should replace the current picture which attracts the attention of government and development assistance agencies but which is generally too aggregated, limited and descriptive to provide an adequate basis for developing policies. There is currently a large volume of small pieces of research which lack a broad view. Meanwhile, macro-descriptions and analyses at national or international level are so aggregated that, at best, they are useful only for broad comparative perspectives. They are certainly no help in understanding the particular situations of different communities within the same municipalities. The social sciences have not received support to undertake the research necessary to understand processes and especially those taking place simultaneously.

A more useful and relevant research area is being developed by researchers who are working with people at all levels, redefining the nature of problems and the possibilities for their resolution. We have to find new ways of looking at problems. You have to be born poor in order to understand the meaning of being poor. You have to live in a squatter settlement to understand the difficulties of living without piped water, sewers, pavements and electricity – especially if you are also raising children in such circumstances. It is difficult (if not impossible) for outsiders to understand what it is like to live in a neighbourhood which is subject to regular floods and where garbage is seldom or never collected.

This raises certain basic questions. As outsiders who seek to intervene in the processes, what do we need to know if we are to help such communities overcome the worst effects of poverty and to have an impact on their future through their actions? What are the initiatives that could have an impact on existing communities and the future city? What are the crucial problems of each urban district and how are they being addressed? What knowledge is missing?

The research carried out on poverty and squatter settlements, on children on and of the street, and the like, is meant to provide the knowledge that governments and international agencies need to evaluate different options and make better decisions. More and better information should allow those who we call the policy makers to find ways to initiate the action needed to solve critical problems. But do Third World governments and international agencies understand the true meaning of building cities with minimum investments, with millions of unskilled workers and without the right type of trained personnel and weak local governments?

Life in the Third World forces those involved in urban research (whether willingly or unwillingly) to be involved in political actions. There is less and less room for the pure social science researcher. But what do we mean by political action? It does not necessarily mean membership of a political party and working through it to achieve the changes to which we aspire. Political action can also be, and perhaps in these times essentially is, being engaged in activities which question the established order and constantly challenge the way policies are being determined and implemented.

Research groups in the Third World are constantly pressurized by local and external agencies to subordinate research to policy proposals. They are asked to detect success stories for replication, as if the success of any particular project or policy is independent of culture, or of the particular social, economic and political context within which it developed, or separable from the understanding and use that people have made of legal and administrative organizations available in each nation and each city.

We are asked to postpone (or avoid using) theory in search of solutions. We sacrifice the quality of research for the sake of expediency. We delay the understanding of processes in looking for a means to solve problems that should have been anticipated with the foresight which comes from a good understanding of process. Clear and accurate thinking is critical to the development of sound perspectives of the processes we try to understand. In this context, truth becomes a rare virtue.

Why this urgency to subordinate theory to action? Can action be undertaken without the input of theory and can theory be meaningful without observing the reality that surrounds it? Can we expect to multiply the number of communities engaged in their social and economic improvement without a good understanding of how their city functions? How can communities achieve social stability in a safe environment without an understanding of the city of which they are a part? What do we know that can be put to good use and what must we learn and do to place poor communities and their needs on the political agenda of each local and national government and development assistance agency?

Most urban research in the Third World fails to contribute to developing a more effective institutional response to rapid urban change. It suffers from a short-term perspective, too narrow a focus and, often, a single-discipline approach. Most research projects are descriptive and policy-oriented, but we seldom ponder the usefulness of broad generalizations and their value to the (so-called) policy makers – a heterogeneous group of politicians and bureaucrats which includes leaders in communities, businesses, churches and trade unions. Because of inadequate funding and an emphasis on policy-relevance, most research projects are one-year efforts; some are even shorter. Longitudinal studies which are so important for understanding processes are very rare. Even basic research receives little support.

The areas of research which should be favoured by funding agencies are those which might prove useful to governments and international agencies, which address the problems of low-income groups, help to train young researchers or form the basis of networks of research institutions. In most cities, there is a great deal of information about communities but this information is dispersed. It has never been pulled together and synthesised. At present, all we have are impressionistic views and not even a good qualitative understanding of the life in a few communities. What is missing is good research and good data at the level of the community and the urban district. But the research needed for a better understanding of the social complexities of communities and the impact that outside political agents have on the lives of their members cannot be postponed indefinitely. It is at this micro level that many of the most promising initiatives to improve the quality of life for hundreds of millions of low-income people are taking place. As a result of the lack of research and understanding, decisions are made outside of these communities, which have little or nothing to do with some of their most urgent problems and priorities and which ignore the knowledge, resources and organizational capacities that these people can themselves bring to bear on their own problems.

COSTS AND INVESTMENTS

One estimate suggests that Third World societies annually invest US$150–200 billion in the construction and reconstruction of their cities. This may be a very rough estimate but perhaps not too inaccurate, as it seeks to include the value of the efforts of individuals and households, and of private businesses and public agencies, in building new houses, enterprises, public buildings and commercial centres, new schools and health centres, and in constructing, themselves, the urban environment in which they live.

Given an urban population in the Third World of around 1.4 billion today, such an amount is equivalent to US$100–133 per capita per year, a sum which can be significant if invested in a coordinated way and in the right type of project for the people in greatest need.

The real costs of building and maintaining cities is one of the least-known subjects in urban research. The information on such costs is very inadequate and fragmentary and we know of no work which seeks to synthesize information about even one particular city. While researchers in the North list several topics among those which require special attention, such as 'the efficiency of cities relative to various dimensions'; 'the influence of government on urbanization and urban economies'; 'individual cities and sub-regions as units of analysis'; and 'longitudinal assessments of social mobility, human welfare, economic interdependence, and economic growth with urban informal sectors',[19] Third World researchers are more concerned with topics such as the absence of democracy; the weakness of local social movements; poverty and its causes and the attitude of governments and social groups in addressing them; the situation of children, adolescents, and households headed by women; constraints on the access of many people to shelter and basic services; and the low productivity of urban economies. Many such topics are the concern of researchers, governments and aid agencies in the North as well as in the South but a new crop of researchers in the South is trying to join together to produce a new kind of knowledge as a tool for action by grassroots organizations. While trying to develop an accurate evaluation of where we are and of the type of knowledge which is most urgently needed, we attempt to develop a research and action agenda that will only be clear when we know where the ideas go and who will use them. In the end, knowledge and resources will be most valuable if presented in a way that it useful to communities.

US$150–200 billion per year seems a lot of money to invest in cities. Undoubtedly, it is a far larger investment than that made by Third World societies in any single sector of the economy or in resolving social problems. Much of this sum goes to produce new shelters or to expand and improve existing shelters, but key questions, such as who is investing in the cities and in what and for whom, remain unanswered.

Every day, substantial amounts are invested in most Third World cities by the central and state governments in the construction of infrastructure, in setting up and running services, in housing, in the construction of schools, health centres and hospitals, in opening new highways, and paving streets and pavements; or by the private sector in housing, shopping centres, factories and office buildings, and in building schools, clinics and clubs. But in the midst of this city-building by professionals whose projects have been approved by the municipal authorities, there are vast sections of each city being built mostly illegally in contravention of established housing, building and planning norms. The amounts invested in the legal and illegal sections of any city can only be roughly estimated. There are buildings, neighbourhoods and districts in many Third World cities that have standards equal to those in the North, while there are poor communities without water, sewers, electricity, drains or paved roads. Investment in such low-income areas makes minimum use of industrialized building materials and makes an intensive use of discarded materials. It generally draws on mostly unpaid labour.

An investment of, say, US$200 or 300 per household, used to improve sites (for instance, providing paved roads and drains) and upgrade basic services and facilities in houses, including water supplies, toilet facilities, kitchens and ventilation, could have a significant effect on the health and well-being of low-income communities. It could transform the quality of life in such settlements, whereas it would hardly be noticed in a middle class district. A considerable proportion of low-income households could afford to repay a loan of this order, if repayment of capital costs were spread over several years, and capital, maintenance and running costs were all included in the monthly payments. One such scheme is already being tried, in the municipality of El Alto, a suburb of La Paz, Bolivia. Loans of between US$200 and US$300, repayable over 10 years, are being used to cover the cost of household connections to the water network.

An investment of US$20 million could reach 100,000 families (half a million or more people, assuming 5 or more persons per household). The same sum spent on building two-bedroomed, low-cost conventional houses would benefit far fewer people – just 2,000 households, if each unit costs US$10,000.

There is very little information about the actual sums invested in the maintenance of essential urban services managed by public enterprises. However, it is generally accepted that the economic recession, the low calibre of those responsible for maintenance, and the lack of basic equipment have resulted in serious maintenance problems. Many power stations are no longer functioning or are operating well below their capacity because of poor maintenance. Water losses in the piped water systems of many Third World cities frequently represent 40–50 per cent or more of the total flow. Little is done to repair access roads, city streets and pavements. Many public telephones are out of order. Public transport vehicles are so poorly maintained that in some cities they are the cause of many accidents: the numbers of vehicles off the road increases overcrowding and delays. Of the sewers that do exist, many are 40 or 50 years old. Underground and surface water is polluted as a result of acute deficiencies in sewerage, garbage collection and treatment of waste from drains.[20]

While rich and middle-income urban residents are used to receiving all or most of the basic services and complain when they are not available, low-income groups living in illegal or informal settlements are seriously neglected. However, a modern city cannot function properly without these services. Their decay influences the movement of goods and people and the productivity of urban economies. It lowers the possibilities for income-generating activities and increases overall costs. The poorest urban communities urgently need reliable basic services – a minimum quality and quantity of water, provision for sanitation and drainage, and garbage collected and disposed of. It is for this reason that this book seeks to highlight new ways and means of using existing resources and of working with low-income communities to improve shelter, infrastructure and services.

2

THE FAILURE OF THE
CONVENTIONAL MODEL –
PUBLIC AND PRIVATE

INTRODUCTION

There is a large and obvious gap between investment needs and current investment flows into housing, infrastructure and services. Within the conventional model of urban development, both the private and the public sector have failed to fill this gap. Although an overall shortage of capital is a major problem, it is not the only one and it is important to identify the full set of reasons. This section considers the failure of four different types of institutions to contribute more to the investment needed in housing, infrastructure and services: central/provincial government; local/urban/municipal government; the private sector; and the development assistance agencies. Before considering each of these different suppliers, this section considers the nature of investment in housing, basic services and infrastructure.

CHARACTERISTICS OF HOUSING INVESTMENT

It is important to differentiate between investments such as housing which can be made on the basis of individual units and most kinds of infrastructure and services which can only be supplied cost-effectively on a settlement- or city-wide basis.

Since the capital cost of a house or apartment in most urban locations is high, relative to people's income, there is generally a need to spread the cost over a number of years. In Europe and North America, this is usually done by purchasing an already built unit by means of a long-term loan or mortgage. But for most urban dwellers in the Third World the cost of the cheapest legal shelter is too high and, for many, there is no long-term credit, allowing purchase with repayments spread over many years, available. For poorer groups, the only option is to make incremental investments in constructing, renovating or extending housing structures on illegally occupied or subdivided land (since legal housing plots are also too expensive).

Most of the urban housing stock in the Third World which has appeared over the last 40 years has been built and financed by individuals, with little use of formal banks or housing finance institutions. Many housing units remain of very poor quality, their improvement and extension limited by the inhabitants' lack of capital for investment. For those which are improved and extended, the process generally takes place over many years.

There are a variety of ways in which development programmes can support the processes by which low-income groups build or improve their own housing. These include; wholesale purchase of materials; help in obtaining a land site or legal tenure to a site already occupied; technical advice on how to reduce costs; and making available cheaper credit, or alternatives to collateral which allow households to obtain cheaper loans from existing financial sources. Cheaper credit and cheaper building materials both lower the cost and reduce the time taken to construct or improve the structure. The case study of the Housing and Local Management Unit in Chile (page 120) shows how an NGO used different methods to reduce both the cost of self-help construction and improvement (through providing households with access to building materials at wholesale prices) and the time needed for such work (through providing loans). Housing projects designed to be affordable by lower-income groups often incorporate an element of self-help in construction and improvement – reducing costs by substituting the recipients' labour for commercial builders' work. There are also many successful projects (and in some cases institutions) which have sought to make it easier for low-income households to invest in new or improved housing by making loans available.

One of the major constraints on housing improvement in many low-income communities is the fact that the settlement has developed on land whose use has elements of illegality: either the land has been illegally occupied or it has been illegally sub-divided by landowners or developers. The housing structures themselves are usually illegal, too, in that they fail to meet building and planning regulations. Such circumstances limit the extent to which the house or the housing site can be used as collateral for a loan. For this reason, initiatives to provide relatively low-income households with loans to increase investment in housing should be particularly sensitive to the difficulties that they have in producing collateral. In addition, the inhabitants of illegal settlements have little incentive to invest in housing construction or improvement if there is a threat of eviction; the risk of this is greater for those living on illegally occupied, rather than illegally subdivided, land.

Providing poorer groups with loans to allow them to acquire land and build a house or to purchase an existing unit requires loans which are relatively large in relation to income. Further problems are faced by those with irregular incomes if loan repayment conditions are too inflexible. Obviously, the longer the term over which the loan is spread, the lower each weekly or monthly repayment. However, long repayment terms delay the speed with which the lending organization can recycle their capital. An alternative is offering small loans for housing improvement and extension for those with housing units – even if these are illegal settlements – and including in the programme technical and legal support to help the inhabitant secure legal tenure.

Individual households can make limited improvements in some forms of infrastructure and services – for instance, pit latrines dug to improve sanitation or wells sunk to tap ground water sources. The costs to each household might be reduced by sharing these among more than one household – as is commonly done with wells. However, most basic services and forms of infrastructure can only be supplied at a community or neighbourhood level. Problems such as poor site drainage and unpaved roads cannot be solved by individual households. In addition, individual household solutions for water supply and sanitation are often inappropriate for urban areas, especially in high-density settlements, and unit costs per household served are usually far cheaper for community-wide solutions.

Whilst investment in housing does not usually add directly to household income, it can be an important contributor. Improvements in water systems can often provide better quality and greater quantities of water at costs well below what residents previously paid to water vendors.[1] Paved roads often bring significant improvements in bus services. Many small informal enterprises (such as the preparation of food for sale in the streets, tailoring, and running small neighbourhood stores) operate from the home, and improvements in facilities there may increase the amount that can be earned through such activities. Improvements in housing conditions reduce the incidence of illness and injury, in turn ensuring that income is not lost through time off work or spent on medical expenses. Additional rooms may be rented out, providing a further source of income. In some situations the increase in the house's value may provide an asset to secure a loan for a business investment when borrowing from conventional sources.

CHARACTERISTICS OF HOUSING-RELATED BASIC SERVICES AND INFRASTRUCTURE INVESTMENT

Investment in basic services and infrastructure generally involves significant capital investments and long depreciation periods. In many cases, the major suppliers are monopolies. The failure of public authorities to meet their responsibilities means there is either no provision or a combination of formal and informal private provision. The only types of infrastructure and services provided by private initiatives are those for which the supplier can restrict access to those who pay for it – for instance, water supplied by trucks or carts, garbage collection with fees paid on collection, and services such as schools, day care centres, buses and health care where people pay as they use the service. Many forms of infrastructure cannot be provided on this basis – for instance, sewers, site drains and paved roads – since the suppliers cannot restrict their use only to those who pay for it. It is also expensive and administratively difficult to run a piped water system where there is a high proportion of households who do not pay and have to be cut off.

The unit costs of many forms of infrastructure and services are much lower if provided to all those within a particular area – for instance, paved roads and paths, street lighting, electricity, piped water and drainage systems. In some cases, further savings can be realised through the simultaneous provision of two or more services: garbage collection is much cheaper and easier if roads are paved; drainage systems work better where garbage is collected; and piped water systems need complementary drainage systems. The costs per household of what might be defined as a minimum package of infrastructure and services (including water piped to the house yard, the cheapest appropriate sanitation system, drains, paved roads, garbage collection and primary schools and health centres) are still relatively high in comparison to the incomes and assets available to poorer groups – even when spread over a large number of families. For instance, supplying a household with water piped to its yard and the cheapest adequate sanitation system would often cost between US$500 and US$800, assuming comprehensive coverage in the neighbourhood.[2] This is several times the annual income of many low-income households.

The costs of such investment should be spread over the life of these assets and if this is done, the annual cost to users is much lower. However, this may be difficult for a number of reasons. The future of the settlement may be uncertain. Negotiation with the local government and owners of the area to secure legal tenure is likely to be an important component of developing the area. Household earnings may be irregular and uncertain and therefore it may be difficult for the inhabitants to make long-term commitments. In addition, programmes need to be particularly sensitive to establishing structures which do not penalise present residents (and benefit future residents) by requiring that capital costs are paid too quickly.

One reason why costs are higher for low-income settlements is that it is much cheaper to invest in piped water, sanitation, drains and roads during the preparation of the site, rather than after housing has been developed. Installing infrastructure and services in existing settlements is usually complex and costly. It may require some reorganization of the site to permit the installation of paved roads or to upgrade pipes and drains. Securing the agreement of residents and their representative organizations can take many years, particularly as there are financial implications. This step can require collaborative decision-making institutions and processes to be introduced. Box 2.1 describes the process for a small settlement called Hornos in Mexico City.

CENTRAL GOVERNMENT

Although central governments have not taken a major role in providing investments in shelter and associated basic services and infrastructure in urban areas, there are four particular ways in which their interventions have been important: centrally-supported housing programmes; the establishment of housing finance institutions; the establishment of banks or funds for municipal government investments; and government or parastatal companies responsible for service provision in specific areas. The first two of these are discussed below.

Box 2.1 Negotiating the redevelopment of Hornos in Mexico City

Hornos is a settlement of about 1000 families on the edge of Mexico City Metropolitan Area. It developed around the use of local clay to make bricks. Those living in the area adjacent to the settlement opposed this industry because of the pollution from oil-fired kilns. As a result, the inhabitants have been able to negotiate a regularization process supported by the local government in return for stopping small-scale brick-making. The settlement has developed in an erratic fashion on a fairly steep hillside. There is one paved road, other routes are mud tracks twisting between the houses. Between the houses are areas of waste ground and brick-making areas with ovens (only partially in use) and pits from which clay has been extracted. The paved road was constructed at the instigation of a local politician who visited the site during the rainy season and was told that the only source of water was the water tanker and this could not visit the site after it had rained.

In 1987, the regularization process began. A census of local residents was undertaken. The city council proposed a road network, necessitating the demolition of about 120 houses. Concerned about the scale of this disruption, the residents contacted a local NGO for help. The NGO worked to bring together four different community organizations active within the settlements. These included the squatter association, the brick-workers' union, a group based around the PRI (the political party which has dominated government in Mexico since the revolution) and the teachers' union. There were some differences of opinion between these different groups; the teachers' union, in particular, held views not shared by the other groups, as they represented residents who were in the more consolidated houses which were the least likely to be demolished. After about three years of negotiations, new plans were adopted, involving the demolition of about 20 houses.

The new plans involve eight residential areas which will be constructed in turn. This means that people will be able to continue living on site while its redevelopment takes place. Most people will not remain in their present location but will receive a new site. The new scheme is expected to be completed three to four years after construction begins.

The proposal is for sites and services, with a plot size of 120 square metres. Households will be allowed to build on only 60 per cent of this, one reason being to facilitate the recovery of ground water. Additional buildings include a library, a factory for brick-making, two kindergartens (both of these exist already, one run by the community, the other by the government), two children's play areas, a primary school (with a secondary school planned for phase two), a church, workshops for women and an ecological park.

Housing programmes [3]

In most nations, the first major government initiative to improve housing for low-income groups was a large public housing programme. By the 1950s, public housing programmes were underway in many nations in Latin America, Africa and Asia. During the 1960s and early 1970s, most Third World governments launched large-scale public housing programmes. There have been major problems with most of these programmes, especially in regard to the scale of the programmes relative to the number of households in need of better-quality housing and in regard to the allocation of the units (it was rare for poorer groups to receive them). High unit costs have meant that, if the cost to local residents was reduced to a level which could be afforded by low-income communities, the subsidy required was so high that relatively few units could be built. If the subsidy was reduced or removed, units were only affordable by middle- or upper-income households. An additional problem was that many of the designs and locations of public housing were inappropriate for the poorer groups. Low-income families who received public housing units often found that they were designed for small, 'western style' nuclear families and could not adequately accomodate households with more than two children and often with extended families. The design of most public housing units ignored the cultural and social needs of the groups for whom they were officially intended.[4]

Many governments changed the orientation of their public housing programmes towards serviced site schemes or core housing units. These reduced unit costs for the government since the costs of organizing and undertaking much of the building was transferred to the household who purchased (or was allocated) the site or core unit. In many instances, the number of units provided exceeded the number of public housing units built in previous programmes. However, these schemes have rarely been on a scale to make a significant difference to the number of new housing units or the scale of investment into housing within a city. During the 1970s and 1980s, many governments also undertook upgrading programmes in residential areas where there were serious deficiencies in the provision of infrastructure and services – for instance in tenement districts, squatter settlements, illegal subdivisions or peripheral, low-income legal housing developments. In many nations, these provided a much higher proportion of the urban population with improved infrastructure and services than public housing or serviced site programmes, although they tended to be concentrated in major cities. However, these have rarely done more than provide a one-off capital investment which helps compensate for previously inadequate local government investment. Without also ensuring that local government or some other body acquires the power, resources and trained personnel to maintain and extend the improvements, infrastructure and services once more deteriorate over time.[5]

Institutions for housing finance

A second strategy followed by governments has been the formation of special institutions to assist in providing housing finance. Although these aimed to fill a gap in the credit market by supplying loans for houses to lower-income groups they have not, in general, been successful. The United Nations Centre for Human Settlements notes that they have made only a limited contribution to total housing investment and have tended to favour middle-income groups.[6] They have generally accounted for less than 20 per cent of annual housing investment in countries where they have been set up.[7] Several major problems have reduced their effectiveness. They have often acted as conventional mortgage companies in richer nations, requiring lenders to have capital to pay for a proportion of the cost themselves, and to have a regular income, and only lending money for properties for which the borrower holds a legal title. As a consequence, it has been difficult for low-income households to gain access to their funds. Project-implementing agencies have tended to bypass these institutions and work directly with the beneficiaries and/or the relevant local authority. The limits of both these strategies are illustrated in the case of Tanzania in Box 2.2 below.

Box 2.2 Housing construction in Tanzania

In 1962, the Tanzanian government established the National Housing Corporation and began to clear the central area of Dar es Salaam of poor-quality housing, replacing it with single-storey houses for rent. By the early 1970s, finance was becoming difficult to obtain and the Corporation, together with other public bodies, was able to produce only just over 2000 units a year throughout the whole country. The government then adopted a policy of aided self-help. In 1972, the Tanzania Housing Bank was set up to provide low interest loans to both urban and rural low-income builders. In practice, however, the Housing Bank operated in favour of higher-income groups and reached only a relatively small number of people. For example, a survey in 1986/87 showed that only 9 per cent of house-owners had received some or all of their housing finance through the Bank (while 69 per cent relied on their own or family savings).

In 1974, an agreement was made with the World Bank to provide just under 9000 site and service plots and to improve 8000 squatter dwellings. The site and service programme was generally considered a success but a number of problems have been identified. First, it is evident that many occupants of these areas earn more than low-income households, which were the original target group. Second, there have been other problems in the programme's implementation, such as a lack of coordination in the provision of infrastructure to the serviced sites. Third, some services (especially roads and drains) have been poorly maintained.

Source: Hardoy, Jorge and David Satterthwaite (1981), *Shelter, Need and Response*, John Wiley and Sons; and Stren, Richard and Rodney White (eds) (1989), *African Cities in Crisis: Managing Rapid Urban Growth*, Westview Press, Boulder.

Although there are large variations between Third World countries, in most the development of shelter has occurred without the control of public-sector institutions and without drawing on public programmes or institutions for credit. In Tunisia, 52 per cent of urban housing constructed between 1975 and 1980 bypassed municipal development regulations, despite the establishment of a large number of different institutions.[8] The public sector was responsible for about a quarter of new housing units constructed during this period, but 75 per cent of state-aided housing was not affordable by low-income households. This is despite the fact that public-sector involvement in Tunisia in the construction, upgrading and financing of urban shelter and urban land development for shelter is much larger than in most other Third World nations.[9]

It is the failure of conventional housing finance institutions either to expand greatly the number of housing units built or to benefit poorer households which has encouraged some governments to try new approaches. For example, the Philippine government has introduced a community mortgage scheme to ensure that groups with no legal tenure and few resources are not excluded from formal credit systems (see Box 2.3).

LOCAL GOVERNMENT

It usually falls to local (urban or municipal) governments to plan and ensure the implementation of most of the provision of basic infrastructure and services within their jurisdiction, even if they are not themselves the immediate supplier. The range of tasks for which they are responsible varies greatly but in many countries it includes provision for water, sanitation, garbage collection, traffic management, emergency services, streets and street lighting, health care and schools. Local governments are also generally responsible for controlling pollution and for urban plans.

In most urban centres in the Third World, local government has failed to meet most of its legal responsibilities. This level of government often has comparable levels of responsibility for infrastructure and services to local governments in the North but with a revenue base of one hundredth (or at their most extreme one thousandth) that of local governments in the North.[10] Capacity for investment in expanding or extending infrastructure and services very rarely bears any relation to the extent of responsibilities. In some of the poorer Third World nations or the local governments in poorer urban centres within richer nations, it is common for local budgets to be the equivalent of only a few US dollars per person per year, with virtually all spent on recurrent costs. Lima's former director of planning told one of the authors that the annual capacity of the municipality to invest in projects in Lima was US$2 per capita. The central government of Peru was investing three times as much, and many people engaged in informal activities were investing around US$40 a year in reusing and rehabilitating ancient buildings. Of course, these figures do not include private-sector investment nor the multiplicity of small investments which the poor make in both time and savings in a continuous effort to provide their households with shelter and services. A former director of planning in Sao Paulo gave the annual investment capacity of the municipality as between US$6 and US$8 per capita. More recently, one of the authors of this document, while visiting Quito, was told that the annual investment capacity of that municipality was US$16 per capita. Sao Paulo and Quito are among the wealthier cities in the Third World.

One reason for this is the limitation set by higher levels of government on local government's capacity to raise revenues. Many local governments raise only a small percentage of their own finance, being dependent on transfers from central government for the remainder of their expenditure.[11] National governments usually reserve the most lucrative and easily collected taxes for

Box 2.3 The community mortgage programme

The Philippines government launched a community mortgage programme in 1988 through the National Home Finance Corporation to help poor urban households acquire title to the land they occupy and develop the site, and their housing, in 'blighted and depressed' areas. The programme provides loans to allow community associations to acquire land on behalf of their members, improve the site, develop individual titling of the land and provide individual housing loans for home improvement or house construction. Loans are provided for 25 years at 6 per cent interest.

To acquire the loan, the residents have to organize themselves into a community association. The land is purchased on behalf of the members but initially under the common ownership of the association, which is responsible for collecting monthly rentals and amortization instalments from member beneficiaries until the community loan has been individualized. Both community-based organizations and NGOs (and municipal governments) can take out loans and provide assistance in organizing member beneficiaries and informing them about loan availability.

Loans are available for up to 90 per cent of appraised value of property. Where residents were already on the site by 25 February 1986, this valuation is no longer required if an agreement has been reached between the landowner and the community association as to the value of the land – although this must not exceed ten million pesos.

As of February 1993, the programme had already assisted 208 communities (27,705 households) with a total loan value of more than 568 million pesos (US$ 22.4 million). Another 40,000 households have begun the process of obtaining a loan. An essential part of the programme is the use of an intermediary, who helps the residents form an association and supports them while they negotiate for official title to the land, apply and secure the land, and begin site development and the financial operation of the loan. Most of the intermediary institutions which have acted as originators for loans are NGOs although some of the work has been undertaken by local government units, national government agencies and financial institutions. Originators receive a small payment of 500 pesos per household from the government for this service.

One example of this community mortgage programme in operation is the loan taken by the Medel Tenants Association. Representing more than 300 families with very low incomes living on 31,000 square metres of land in Mandaluyong, Manila, the association took out a loan for 9 million pesos to purchase the land from the landowner. They then took out another loan to allow public works and site development. The association is temporarily responsible for collecting payments from its members and for keeping members' accounts.

Source: Anzorena, Jorge (1990–1), assorted reports in *SELAVIP* Newsletter; and Albert Ramon (1991), 'The community mortgage programme' in Aurelio Menendez (ed) (1991), *Access to Basic Infrastructure by the Urban Poor*, EDI Seminar Report No 28, The World Bank; Housing Finance Seminar (1993), MISEREOR/ACHR

themselves while local governments face 'a formidable list of restraints' on their taxing powers.[12] City and municipal authorities serve urban centres with hundreds of thousands or millions of inhabitants when their structures, budgets and levels of representation would be suitable for serving a few thousand inhabitants at most.

A recent study documented this process in Africa and noted that the decline in the per capita income of most countries and the subsequent shortage of resources was accompanied by an increasingly urban population.[13] As Richard Stren notes, 'By the late 1970s and early 1980s, many African countries were having severe problems maintaining an even minimally acceptable level of urban services and infrastructure'. In Dar es Salaam, for example, expenditure on services and infrastructure measured in constant currency units fell by 8.5 per cent between 1978/9 and 1986/7; when the increase in population is taken into account, this means a per capita decline of 11 per cent. As a consequence, services have deteriorated badly: central government records show that, in 1986, only 0.3 per cent of 'foul water' produced in Dar es Salaam was collected. In Tanzania's 19 major towns, the government estimated that only 24 per cent of solid waste was actually being collected by local councils. The shortage of resources has been made worse because investment in urban infrastructure often requires imported goods; devaluation of the exchange rate has frequently increased the price of goods and governments have often been particularly short of foreign reserves.

THE PRIVATE SECTOR

In most cities, the private sector has taken an important role in supplying many low-income communities with a range of basic services and (in some cases) certain kinds of infrastructure. For example, private expenditure on health care in Thailand is estimated to be four times the amount spent by government. In some cases, the private sector has moved into the market because the government is failing to provide the services. In other cases, the government contracts the private sector to supply the service rather than supplying it directly itself.

There are a number of implications of private sector provision in these areas, in terms of price and quality of service. Although it is difficult to generalise across the range of infrastructure and services, there are a few overall observations which can be made in respect of private-sector supply.

The private sector has little incentive to make a major permanent investment in a low-income area. There is no guarantee that demand for their product will continue and, if the site has been illegally occupied or subdivided, there may be the threat of eviction hanging over the settlement. Unit costs may therefore be higher than would be the case if major investments had been made. For example, the private sector will provide water through water vendors selling from tanks or carts rather than installing a piped water system (unless this is undertaken with the cooperation and encouragement of local government). Such water-vending is common throughout the Third World; one estimate suggests that 20–30 per cent of the urban population in the Third World may be served in this way.[14] Costs are likely to be several times higher than for water supplied through piped connections.[15] For example, in

Abidjan, Cote d'Ivoire, water supplied by water vendors is about five times the price charged to consumers with standard connections.[16] In addition to price, this lack of investment may also affect the quality of service offered; but for the private sector, the advantage is a low-risk investment. As a result, investments have not been made or finance has only been made available for short-term projects or for services which require a minimum of fixed costs (for instance garbage collecting trucks and water supplied by tankers) and for which payment can be received as the item or service is delivered. The result is often higher operating costs – and higher prices.

In some cases, the high cost of investment may mean that, if such investment does take place, the supplying industry may tend towards a monopolistic or oligopolistic structure, with either a single company or a small number of companies becoming dominant. With electricity, for example, the transmission and distribution network is so expensive that this is likely to be the case. The first company to enter the market is in a powerful position vis-a-vis potential competitors, and consumers may suffer as a result, being supplied at a higher price and/or with a poorer-quality service than would otherwise be the case. The only safeguard against this lack of competition is a regulatory institution which prevents consumers from being exploited.

The quality of service provided by private-sector entrepreneurs may be uncertain – especially if the local government is too weak and under-resourced to ensure effective control. For example, *matatu* drivers in Nairobi maximise their earnings by carrying as many passengers for as short a time as possible. Passengers may be put at further risk because of the need for owners to save money on vehicle maintenance and repair. In the case of particular services, such as health, the government has an important role in ensuring that those offering health care are qualified to make the right judgement. Without some effective way of setting and enforcing standards, the public may be put at risk.

There are a range of services (such as road improvement) which will not be provided by the private sector without public intervention because once the benefits are available to one member of the community they are available to all. Once a collective agreement has been made among residents to ensure payments are made, then the private sector may be interested in supplying the service, but alone they are unlikely to take the initiative. Alternatively, the public authority responsible for the provision may contract a private company to undertake this and meet the cost centrally.

If the private sector supplier has been contracted by either local or national government to provide a service, the quality of service depends on the nature of the contract and the ability of the government to enforce it. A particular problem may occur when a service which had been subsidized when run by a government agency is privatized and the subsidy is removed, imposing additional costs on low-income households which they cannot afford. There are examples of increasing proportions of low-income households disconnected from piped water systems or electricity, after privatization has occurred. In high-income areas, the private sector may be contracted to provide a range of services as the public sector becomes increasingly unable to cope. While such provision may release resources for use elsewhere in the city, it may also simply ensure that one of the most influential groups has no incentive to argue and push for improved government services.

DEVELOPMENT ASSISTANCE

In most nations, development assistance has taken a minor role in terms of the scale of funding made available for shelter and for the infrastructure and services associated with it. A very low proportion of total development assistance (both aid and non-concessional loans) goes on shelter projects (including upgrading of slum and squatter settlements, and serviced site projects), on providing housing finance, or on the infrastructure and services associated with housing and residential developments. However, although the scale of external assistance for these is very low in relation to need, in certain countries it has a considerable influence because of the enormous shortfalls in investments coming from other sources and because of the failure of governments to develop policies and programmes in this area.

In recent years, shelter projects and housing finance have attracted less than 3 per cent of the commitments of most development assistance agencies (see Table 2.1). The largest sources of external funding for shelter have come from the World Bank Group, the Inter-American Development Bank and US AID's Housing Guarantee Programme. Infrastructure and services associated with shelter receive a higher proportion from both multilateral and bilateral agencies – but very rarely do these feature as high priorities for any agency. The World Bank is much the largest donor in regard to funding for shelter and for associated infrastructure and services – both in terms of aid (through its concessional loans) and in terms of non-concessional loans. UNICEF is probably the agency which gives the highest priority to these kinds of infrastructure and services; a high proportion of its funds is spent on water and sanitation, basic education, child health and community/family health services. Non-concessional loans represent a larger source of funding for housing-related infrastructure and services and most of these loan commitments are with countries with relatively high per capita incomes.

Three qualitative changes in development assistance to shelter, infrastructure and services are worth noting. The first is a move by several of the largest donors towards funding national institutions rather than specific projects – for instance, in the case of the World Bank, a move away from shelter projects to supporting national housing finance institutions or a move away from integrated urban development projects to supporting national institutions concerned with funding municipal projects. The World Bank made 27 project commitments during the 1980s, mostly during the second half of the decade, to urban governments attempting to build their institutional and financial capacity or to institutions which support urban development. This can be seen, in some senses, as a recognition that development assistance can never provide the scale of funding needed for urban development, and that each country must develop its own capacity to fund this. One recent estimate suggests that total capital investments by sub-national governments in Latin America were more than 45 times the total volume of World Bank loans[17] – and this is despite the enormous inadequacies in the scale of such investments by sub-national governments and the fact that the World Bank's loan commitments to the region were much the largest commitments of any agency working there.

Table 2.1 Proportion of aid and non-concessional loan commitments to shelter, basic services and other basic needs projects, 1980–91

Agency	Proportion of total project commitments to					Per cent of total commitment	
	Shelter-related	Water and sanitation	Primary health care	Basic education	Poverty reduction & jobs	1980–91	1990–91
Aid (concessional loans or grants)							
International Development Association							
• Africa	1.4	3.0	2.8	4.2	1.3	12.7	21.4
• Asia	1.5	4.7	3.7	2.3	0.3	12.4	22.2
• Latin America & Caribbean	2.0	5.8	4.7	2.8	6.3	21.6	41.1
African Development Bank (1980–88)	0.7	10.5	2.2	2.4	–	15.9	–
Asian Development Fund	1.2	2.0	1.0	1.8	0.3	6.4	8.4
Inter-American Development Bank	2.6	15.9	1.4	3.0	1.3	24.1	29.5
Caribbean Development Bank	1.3	4.8	–	–	0.5	6.4	3.9
Arab Fund for Economic & Social Development	1.2	7.0	–	0.4	1.0	9.6	10.9
UNICEF	–	14.4	35.3	8.3	–	58.1	57.4
Kuwaiti Fund for Economic & Social Development	0.9	8.0	–	–	0.9	9.8	8.0
Overseas Economic Cooperation Fund, Japan (1987–91)	0.9	3.2	–	0.4	–	4.5	3.7

Table 2.1 (continued)

Agency	Proportion of total project commitments to					Per cent of total commitment	
	Shelter-related	Water and sanitation	Primary health care	Basic education	Poverty reduction & jobs	1980–91	1990–91
Non-concessional loans							
International Bank for Reconstruction and Development (IBRD)							
• Africa	2.5	8.2	1.4	0.8	0.1	13.0	12.6
• Asia	2.6	2.8	0.7	0.8	0.05	7.0	9.4
• Latin America & Caribbean	3.7	4.8	1.8	1.1	–	11.3	15.5
African Development Bank (1980–88)	0.3	7.5	0.3	0.3	–	8.5	–
Asian Development Bank	1.6	5.3	1.4	–	–	8.3	1.3
Inter-American Development Bank	1.5	6.4	0.3	0.4	0.7	9.3	12.7
Caribbean Development Bank	1.1	7.4	–	–	–	8.6	8.5

Note: Water and sanitation are part of Primary Health Care so the column headed Primary Health Care includes all its components other than water and sanitation. Basic education is taken to include primary education, literacy programmes and basic education programmes. Shelter-related projects include slum and squatter-settlement upgrading, serviced site schemes, core housing schemes, housing finance and community development projects which include housing improvement. Water and sanitation includes drainage projects to improve drainage in low-income residential areas but do not include water projects whose primary goal was not increased or improved supplies for urban dwellers (eg it does not include improved water supply for industry).

Source: Satterthwaite, David (1994) *Aid and Basic Needs*, IIED, London, Mimeo

The second qualitative change is the development of new roles in Third World NGOs. More international funding for shelter projects is now coming through international private voluntary organizations such as MISEREOR (Germany) and CEBEMO (Netherlands) or direct to Third World NGOs. It is interesting to note that in most of the 18 case studies included in this report, official development assistance agencies provided no funding or only a small proportion of the total funding. One exception is FUPROVI, since a major part of its funding came from the Swedish International Development Authority, the Swedish government's official bilateral aid agency. Funding from international private voluntary organizations was more important for many of the case studies – but perhaps what is more notable and interesting is the fact that a significant proportion of the funding in many of the case studies came from local institutions and from the population with whom the work was being undertaken (for instance through loan repayments).

The third qualitative change is an emphasis on developing the capacity of recipient governments to manage urban development and to install and maintain infrastructure and services. One reason for this may stem from a recognition of the unsustainability of many of the capital projects funded by international agencies in previous years; many projects in the 1980s were to rehabilitate urban infrastructure or services put in place only a few years before, through projects funded with development assistance. The new interest in urban management has been most evident in the project commitments of the World Bank Group (although many other agencies have recognized the importance of this subject) and, in technical assistance, in the joint UNDP–World Bank–UNCHS (Habitat) Urban Management Programme.

CONCLUSION – DRAWING ON ADDITIONAL RESOURCES

Why have central and local governments, the formal private sector and development assistance agencies failed to provide the investments for shelter, infrastructure and services in urban areas of the Third World?

First, there has been a lack of resources for investment and this has contributed to the failure of each of the institutions identified above to meet their responsibilities. But second – and perhaps as important – is the failure of central and local governments to develop responses which mesh with local people's needs and priorities and build on the resources that are available. Poorer groups with very limited resources and often limited amounts of time (because of long working hours) have been responsible for a high proportion of investments in housing and in housing-related infrastructure and services, despite the lack of support from governments and (in most instances) from development assistance agencies. The homes and neighbourhoods they develop often have the seeds of an urban development far more appropriate to local climate, culture and resources. What is needed is a change in the official 'model' of urban development to one which works in partnership with these people, supports the investment flows they make (including those derived from self-help and mutual aid), helps loosen the constraints they face, and works with them to ensure that infrastructure and services are provided or improved with very limited per capita budgets. This kind of change can address the deficits in current investment flows, without enormous changes in the scale of external investment flows.

The lack of capital investment available to governments (especially local governments) relates both to a lack of total resources, arising in many cases from the Third World's historical position within the world economic order, and a failure to prioritise investment in housing, basic services and infrastructure when determining the distribution of government expenditure. It may also relate to the low level of taxation or the inefficiency of governments' tax collection. The financial pressures on many countries have been extreme in the last decade and public expenditures have been cut as a result of the economic strategies forced on countries by the structural adjustment programmes of the International Monetary Fund. In many countries, local governments have not been a priority area for central finance, nor have they been given the powers they need to raise local taxes or local revenues from other sources. As a result, they have been unable to meet the responsibilities delegated to them by central government.

On the part of the private sector, there is both a shortage of credit for investment and a problem of incentives for making long-term investments in shelter, infrastructure and services. The problem is exacerbated in settlements where land tenure is uncertain or illegal, since any investment may be lost if the inhabitants are evicted. The shortage of credit has made it difficult for small-scale entrepreneurs, or cooperatives of residents, to raise the capital they need to develop services. The lack of permanence and aspects of 'illegality' associated with much low-income housing has reduced the time period over which a private sector entrepreneur can be confident of realising the investment.

The potential role of the private sector has been weakened by the lack of resources available to local governments. For the private sector effectively to meet many basic service and infrastructure needs of low-income residents requires a local government that is willing and able to take on a regulatory role. This would include ensuring that prices are not excessive in areas where competition is limited, offering a degree of permanence to residents and suppliers, contracting for the supply of services for 'public goods' such as street lights, and making regular checks to ensure that an adequate quality of service is maintained; and, if necessary, redistributing resources within the urban area to ensure that the basic needs of all residents are met.

The potential role of development assistance agencies is limited by a number of factors. The first is the conscious decision by many agencies to give low priority to shelter and associated infrastructure and services (because these are not seen as 'productive investments') and/or to investments in urban areas (because of a priority to rural development). The second arises from political constraints within which many bilateral agencies operate – where a significant component of their programmes is expected to generate demand for goods or services produced by enterprises in the donor country, according to which criteria investment in housing, basic services and infrastructure is often seen as unattractive. A third factor is the low priority given by recipient governments to such areas when negotiating with donor agencies. Finally, there are the administrative constraints experienced by donor agencies, most especially a lack of trained personnel working within recipient countries and a need to keep staff costs down. This often results in a bias against smaller programmes, into which category fall many housing, basic services and infrastructure projects.

Devoting more external and/or government resources to investments in shelter and associated infrastructure and services is one of the most frequently cited 'solutions'. Yet even if the scale of investments coming from these sources was multiplied severalfold, without changes in how such resources are to be used, this will also have limited impacts. What remains a higher priority in most nations is for official policies and programmes actually to respond to the needs and priorities of the individuals and community organizations who are currently responsible for most investments in shelter and infrastructure in urban areas and who generate the demand for most services – virtually all of which is outside official policy and receives little official support. This implies the need for a new strategy which centres on three aspects:

1. better use of existing, under-utilised resources;
2. increasing representation and accountability;
3. forming new partnerships in the development of low-income settlements.

The most realistic solution is a better use of existing public-sector resources to multiply and make more effective existing investment flows into shelter, infrastructure and services. This is not an acceptance of the existing inadequate level; more resources are needed, but it is difficult to see how they will realistically be increased to the scale necessary. A new strategy must consider how resources can be multiplied. The case studies considered in this book all examine innovative funding initiatives, many of them based around the use of credit in mobilizing individual and communal resources. Such programmes often effectively mobilise individual savings, and may draw on local private capital which was previously invested elsewhere. Many increase the effectiveness with which limited public-sector resources are used.

Many local communities have little control over the provision and operation of basic services and infrastructure. The role of local government in regulating and monitoring housing, basic services and infrastructure is essential and needs to remain and be developed. But it can be enhanced through the active involvement of small-scale community organizations. These have a threefold role. They can realise tangible projects, raising money and other resources to undertake work prioritized by the community. They act as pressure groups on local government, securing infrastructure and services for their members and ensuring that their interests are not forgotten. They are also important in developing the fabric of the community so that it can be an effective support for its members, many of whom suffer the extreme stresses which result from poverty.

Several new partnerships are likely to be critical in ensuring the more effective use of resources. A new strategy will necessitate the support of many small-scale community organizations by a wider network of NGOs who can provide training, advice, representation and a host of other services. It will require a new role for many local governments who will have to start working effectively with such community organizations, many of whom will be autonomous, decentralised bodies. Private-sector financiers and existing and potential suppliers of services will be needed to support such new initiatives.

3

THE ROLE OF NGOs IN COMMUNITY DEVELOPMENT

THE WORK OF COMMUNITY ORGANIZATIONS

In the previous chapters we noted the limited financial resources being invested in the development of residential areas (except for those for a relatively small proportion of middle- and upper-income group households). We also noted the lack of investment in the construction and maintenance of infrastructure and in the provision of services along with the lack of technical and institutional capacity on the part of the public authorities responsible for their provision. We also discussed the reasons why governments and bilateral and multilateral development agencies have not managed to provide effective policies and programmes to ensure adequate provision of basic services and infrastructure in most residential areas of Third World cities, and considered factors accounting for the very limited role of the formal private sector.

This suggests the need to change the conventional model of financing and managing urban development to one which not only gives a higher priority to ensuring that all urban households are reached with basic infrastructure and services but which also recognizes the 'hidden' potential in low-income areas, where limited external resources can go further if priorities and resource allocations are community-directed and supplemented by people's own resources. This requires a recognition of the importance of the inhabitants' participation in the planning, execution, maintenance and control of projects. In this respect, an important change has recently been taking place in the conception and implementation of development plans in the Third World. Traditionally, plans to deal with poverty revolved around the planning and action of central or state governments (in some cases acting together with multilateral agencies) or private institutions. Most such interventions were expensive and only reached a small number of people. Many which were in theory meant to improve housing conditions and basic services for poorer groups in reality benefited middle- or even upper-income groups or the more powerful business interests.[1] The great majority of the poor did not benefit from these plans, but had to develop their own strategies, making the most of their scarce resources.

This 'hidden' potential forms the basis for new kinds of intervention that offer opportunities to low-income groups. These new kinds of intervention, pioneered by NGOs and community organizations, have persuaded public and private institutions in many countries (including multilateral and bilateral agencies) to consider new ways to address the worst situations arising from poverty, based on support for households and community organizations. Thus, for example, the planning and construction of residential areas for the relocation of squatters (which were both expensive and required the population to be moved) has been replaced by projects to upgrade the settlements in which poorer groups already live. Proposals for industrial employment are being complemented by support for the small businesses that the poor themselves set up. Experience with both these kinds of intervention suggests that they are more successful and sustainable if residents are involved from the outset in their design and implementation.[2] In short, the idea of 'development from the bottom up' has finally gained recognition as a means of tackling urban poverty. It is the institutions that have pioneered such initiatives which are the subject of this chapter.

Although there are precedents for government support for community-action in Third World nations from many decades ago, including some under colonial governments, and certain aid agencies also promoted 'community development' in the 1950s and 1960s[3], three changes are worth noting. The first is the recognition that support for community-level initiatives is valid in urban areas; most of the earliest precedents were for rural development. The second is the recognition that 'the community' must be involved at the outset in decisions about what is needed, what should be done and how; many early community development efforts essentially saw 'the community' as a cheap source of labour, and community organizations as useful for management, liaison and conflict resolution. The third is the range of international organizations which recognize the validity of this approach. In 1987, the World Health Organization proposed that support for community organizations should be one of its priority lines of action.[4] The Inter-American Foundation, an organization set up by Congress in the United States of America to focus on development in poor Latin American countries, has as a primary objective the strengthening of community organizations through the projects and programmes that it finances.[5] The World Bank, traditionally devoted to financing large-scale projects for regional and urban infrastructure, agricultural development and social programmes, has also come to recognise the value of action on a smaller scale; it also supports programmes which involve the participation and development of community organizations and in which Third World NGOs take on a major implementation role.[6] UNICEF has also long supported a variety of basic services projects in urban areas, implemented in conjunction with community organizations and local NGOs; their urban basic services programme developed and grew in importance in the early 1970s.[7] The Swedish International Development Authority began supporting a community-based programme to improve living conditions for squatters through a Costa Rican NGO in 1988 and have since supported other initiatives in urban areas of Latin America, working with and through local NGOs.[8] In 1984, the United Nations Centre for Human Settlements (Habitat) launched a training programme for community participation.[9] Box 3.1 opposite describes the growing interest shown by the United Nations Development Programme in NGOs and community-based organizations.

Box 3.1 UNDP–NGO Cooperation

People's participation is central to UNDP's approach for bringing about sustainable human development. An analysis of 93 UNDP country programmes approved for 1992–96 shows that 86 per cent address poverty alleviation and grassroots participation in development.

UNDP began to encourage collaboration with Third World NGOs and grassroots organizations in the mid-1970s. Cooperation began to gain momentum in certain fields. For example, as community participation was deemed essential for the success of programmes undertaken in connection with the International Drinking Water Supply and Sanitation Decade (1981–1990), governments, UNDP and other donors worked with many local groups to provide safe water and sanitary waste disposal systems that communities would later maintain.

In 1986, following the decision of UNDP's Governing Council to endorse the involvement of grassroots and non-governmental organizations in the development process, UNDP took a major step to strengthen collaboration with local groups through the creation of the Division for NGOs (now the NGO Programme). UNDP cooperation with NGOs, community-based organizations and grassroots initiatives has since expanded and diversified through programmes that: support participatory, community-based development; promote dialogue and collaboration between NGOs and grassroots organizations, governments, and multilateral agencies; encourage and support NGOs and grassroots involvement in sustainable development activities; and strengthen the impact and sustainability of the development efforts of NGOs and grassroots groups.

The experience gained by UNDP since 1986 has shown that cooperation with NGOs and grassroots organizations is an asset to the efforts of UNDP in its programming cycles. This cooperation benefits both the design of upstream-oriented programmes that can draw upon the advocacy capacity of NGOs and grassroots organizations, and participatory activities that can have a direct impact on local communities. Funding support for NGO activities comes from UNDP's country, regional, and interregional/global resources, as well as its Special Programme Resources.

Some examples of UNDP–NGO cooperation include the Grassroots Initiatives Support Funds, which, with funding from UNDP country programme resources, are administered by local boards and set up in several African countries to provide small grants and loans to self-help initiatives in poor areas. The second phase of the Partners in Development Programme enables UNDP field offices to provide grants to small-scale NGO activities, including micro-enterprises and other income-generating ventures. The Africa 2000 Network is a regional programme supporting, through small grants, grassroots activities that promote ecologically sustainable development; and the Asia-Pacific 2000 Network is a regional programme that provides grants to NGOs and community groups to improve the urban environment.

With its extensive field network, UNDP is well placed to collect and disseminate information on development needs and programmes useful to NGOs. For example, its Sustainable Development Network, which was developed as a follow-up to UNCED, links governmental, non- governmental, grassroots and entrepreneurial organizations and institutions that can benefit from and/or contribute to sustainable and environmentally sound development.

UNDP is also engaged in a wide range of efforts, at the national and regional levels, to stimulate dialogue among NGOs, governments and the UN system. In Africa, a regional project based in Lomé, Togo, has, over the last two and half years, provided services to governments, NGOs, and UNDP field offices in 33 countries, as well as providing management support to eight national and regional associations of African NGOs. In several regions, national workshops and seminars have been organized to discuss participatory development issues and relations between NGOs and the UN system.

Several of the funds associated with UNDP have also developed active partnerships with NGOs and grassroots organizations. For example, under the United Nations Volunteer Programme (UNP), support for capacity-building for NGOs and community-based organizations has been provided in the Asia-Pacific and Africa regions through the Domestic Development Services (DDS). At the end of 1992, 247 DDS Field Workers were working with local communities in 27 countries in Africa, Asia and the Pacific. Other funds include the United Nations Development Fund for Women (UNIFEM), the United Nations Capital Development Fund (UNCDF), and the United Nations Sudano-Sahelian Office (UNSO).

Source: Urban Development Unit, UNDP, New York, 1993.

There are also a growing number of case studies documenting how community organization by low-income residents has led to an improvement in the living conditions of members through a better use of their own resources and cooperative efforts. In many instances, the reinforcement of such organizations has also strengthened the ability of these people to negotiate with government and non-governmental organizations to secure support and resources for their development.

The growth and consolidation of community organizations, often encouraged by the democratization process which grew in strength in many Third World nations during the 1980s[10], has led to new forms of planning and support for programmes dealing with poverty. The development of 'participatory planning' is one of the most obvious changes in focus. Coordination between different social organizations and institutions (the state, financing agencies, NGOs, community organizations, private business, universities, churches, political parties, etc) is now considered to be one of the most effective mechanisms for implementating development programmes. Less emphasis is being given to large-scale national and regional plans while concepts of 'local development' and 'micro-regional development' have emerged.

With more importance being given to the role of communities and to community participation, there has also been an increase in the number of non-governmental institutions encouraging and supporting low-income groups. These NGOs fulfil an increasingly important role, growing and becoming stronger along with the new concepts of development.

THE GROWTH OF NGOS

Various public and private institutions in the world, national as well as bilateral and multilateral, have tried to quantify the growth of NGOs. Some have produced national, regional or sectoral directories of NGOs. In Latin America, the Inter-American Foundation noted about 11,000 NGOs working in the region (although some of these may be community organizations).[11] A study in Bangladesh found 11,044 voluntary organizations which were registered with the government, although this includes thousands of very small voluntary organizations which receive no foreign funds.[12] The World Bank is compiling a directory of current NGOs in its 154 member countries, and in most it has noted hundreds of institutions of this kind. One estimate suggests the number of international NGOs (including trade and professional associations) grew from 2300 to 24,000 between 1970 and 1989.[13]

The increase in the number and the importance of NGOs in the Third World is, in part, associated with the worsening economic, social and political crisis experienced by many Third World countries in recent decades and governments' inability to find viable development alternatives. Government and state institutions and enterprises remain unpopular in the current orthodoxy and strategies of influential bilateral and multilateral donors. Many bilateral aid programmes have also greatly increased the scale of funding channelled through Northern-based private voluntary organizations working in development; many of these private voluntary organizations also work with or through Southern NGOs.[14] In some instances, channelling official bilateral aid through private voluntary organizations is considered a more effective use of aid than conventional government-to-government bilateral aid programmes. Donor policies to improve market efficiency and the medium- and long-term strength of the economy favour commercial enterprises which have neither a mandate for, nor interest in, meeting the needs of the poor. Cuts in government spending on social programmes, infrastructure and basic services, combined with economic recession, have resulted in increasing problems for the poor. As Third World governments have reduced social expenditure, those unable to afford the costs of commercial services have increasingly had no alternative but to go without, or use the voluntary sector, where available. It has long been recognised that private voluntary organizations are particularly suited to working with the poor.[15] In response to this, some donors are actively exploring and promoting the actual and potential roles of private voluntary organizations in both the North and the South. In some countries, a combination of local NGOs and international voluntary organizations has become as, if not more, important than government in certain areas of social policy and in the delivery of certain services.

Other reasons for the growth of NGOs can also be identified. In Latin America, the non-representative, usually military governments forced many professionals or academics out of government and universities. Some found new employment within the NGO sector where they gained an appreciation of its work; some also set up NGOs to permit them to continue with their work. With the return to democracy, some of these professionals have returned to or entered government employment, bringing with them their experiences from working with NGOs.[16] A third reason is an increasing social awareness on the part of both professionals and non-professionals who find that working with NGOs provides the means to act on this awareness. A lack of conventional employment opportunities has also encouraged some professionals to initiate community development projects.

The term NGO came into use for the first time at the end of the 1940s and refers to a wide range of organizations or institutions whose only common feature is the fact that they are not part of any area of government and their primary purpose is not maximising profits. Many organizations which today would be called NGOs existed in both the North and the South well before the 20th century and had important roles in social provision and humanitarian relief, although generally with only a local focus. International private voluntary agencies such as OXFAM, CARE, MISEREOR, CEBEMO and the various Save the Children associations whose present primary role is to fund development projects in the Third World have become a distinctive group within the voluntary sector. Their origins can be seen in the international philanthropic organizations set up in Europe and North America who sought to attend to the needs of those wounded or dying in wars and of prisoners of war.[17] After the end of World War I, there was a growing interest in expanding these humanitarian concerns beyond those suffering from war. Their number and strength expanded considerably during and after World War II. Their role further expanded during the 1970s and 1980s as an increasingly large amount of government bilateral aid came to be channelled through them; by 1989, grants from these organizations to the Third World totalled over US\$ 4 billion.[18]

In many nations in Asia and Africa, the struggle for independence either initiated or strengthened the role of indigenous NGOs – and their role was further reinforced by support from some Northern private voluntary organizations and a few government bilateral aid programmes. In Africa, indigenous NGOs in general are still weak, although their importance and the scale of their activities is growing.[19] Where they do exist, they are mostly service providers with a welfare orientation. In Asia, there is a greater diversity among NGOs. A number of different types have developed in common with other parts of the world.[20] In most Latin American countries, NGOs also have a long and varied history. The number working in the field of housing and basic services increased considerably during the 1960s and 1970s. Part of this expansion was the result of new NGOs formed by university professors and researchers expelled from their universities by military dictatorships; their concentration was mainly in research and training, although many also developed action programmes working with low-income groups.[21] Another part of this expansion was new NGOs which concentrated on providing technical assistance and, on occasion, financial help to poorer groups. In most countries of the South, umbrella or network NGOs are now growing in importance and pioneering new forms of lobbying for change and new ways of exchanging information and advice within and between countries.[22]

DEFINING NGOS

The increasingly large and diverse role of NGOs and of international private voluntary organizations has stimulated a growing interest in their work.[23] However, there has been some confusion with the-term NGO being used to include institutions as diverse and dissimilar as research organizations, political parties, union organizations, sports organizations and charities. International corporations or particular groups of commercial interests also set up 'NGOs' for specific purposes. The private organizations who are involved in supporting and carrying out development projects within low-income communities have also sometimes been called NGOs.

Based on the fact that they are not administered directly by the state, NGOs are sometimes seen as 'private' institutions. NGOs have been described as Private Development Associations,[24] Private Associations for Collective Management,[25] or Private Institutions with Social Interests.[26] In other instances, no definitive judgement has been given as to whether or not NGOs are private, and they have been classified instead as 'institutions of the third type' (ie neither public nor private)[27] or as autonomous organizations[28] or they have been differentiated as 'private with social interests'. Definitions reflect these varied perspectives: Box 3.2 includes some definitions of voluntary organizations drawing on the literature about such organizations in both the North and the South.

The number of definitions, in particular those relating specifically to the Third World, are indicative of the growing interest in NGOs and their role in society. There are evident similarities in the definitions included in Box 3.2. The key characteristics of such organizations appear to be that they are:

- formal organizations;
- involved with public interest issues and concerns;
- independent from government and state institutions;
- non-profit making; and
- self-governing with an independent decision-making body.

A number of people have sought to categorize NGOs into different types. Some typologies distinguish them according to the focus of their work – for instance whether it is primarily service- or welfare-orientated or whether it is more concerned with providing education and development activities to enhance the ability of poorer groups to secure resources and gain greater control of their own lives. Such organizations are also classified according to the level at which they operate, whether they collaborate with self-help organizations (ie community-based organizations), whether they are federations of such organizations or whether they are themselves a self-help organization. They can also be classified according to the approach they undertake, whether they operate projects directly or focus on tasks such as advocacy and networking. One book on NGOs working in the South[29] proposed that they be divided into six categories:

Box 3.2 Definitions of voluntary organizations or NGOs.

Northern organizations

'The definition of a voluntary organization is essentially a statement of an ideal type ... key elements of this ideal type are that a body should have a formal organization, constitutionally separate from government, be self-governing, non-profit-distributing ... and of public benefit.' *Brenton (1985), p 9*

'... a non-profit organization (is) a body of individuals who associate for any of three purposes: (1) to perform public tasks that have been delegated to them by the state; (2) to perform public tasks for which there is a demand that neither the state nor for-profit organizations are willing to fulfil; or (3) to influence the direction of policy in the state, the for-profit sector, or other nonprofit organizations.' *Dobkin Hall (1987), p 3*

'voluntary association ... forms of behaviour that are organized and that are directed at influencing broader structures of collective action and social purpose ... for the purpose of advancing an interest or achieving some social purpose. Theirs is a clear aim toward a chosen form of 'social betterment.' *Van Til (1988), p 8*

Southern organizations

'... are non-governmental (private), tax-exempt, non-profit, agencies engaged in overseas provision of services for relief and development purposes.' *Gorman (1984), p 2*

'Non-profit organizations, established and directed by private citizens, with a stated philanthropic purpose that included providing emergency relief and longer-term assistance to developing countries.' *InterAction (1985), p 2*

'... groups and institutions that are entirely or largely independent of government and characterised primarily by humanitarian or cooperative, rather than commercial, objectives.' *World Bank (1989) quoted in Korten (1991), p 21*

'... (NGOs) are, in general, private non-profit organizations that are publicly registered (ie have legal status), whose principal function is to implement development projects favouring the popular sectors, and which receive financial support.' *Padron quoted in Landim (1987), p 30*

'The non-governmental organizations (NGOs) or private voluntary organizations (PVOs) ... are non-profit-making organizations ... whose principle aim is to contribute to the alleviation of human suffering and to development in poorer countries ... we do not mean either the large private foundations or the private firms in search of profits ... (w)e mean voluntary, private organizations that mobilize the enthusiasm and commitment of volunteers to the objective of the relief of suffering, and of development.' *Streeten (1988), p 1*

'... non-governmental organizations are any of those organizations which are not part of government and which have not been established as a result of an agreement between governments. NGOs can be research institutions, professional associations, trade unions, chambers of commerce, youth organizations, religious institutions, senior citizens' associations, tourist bodies, private foundations, political parties, zionist organizations, funding or development, international and indigenous agencies, and any other organization of a non-governmental nature.' *Padron (1987), p 70*

'The term NGO embraces a wide variety of organizations. They include voluntary organizations that pursue a social mission driven by commitment to shared values. Public service contractors that function as market-orientated non-profit businesses serving public purposes. People's organizations that represent their members' interests, have member accountable leadership, and are substantially self reliant. Governmental non-governmental organizations that are creations of government and serve as instruments of government policy.' *Korten (1990), p 2*

'Voluntary Development Organizations (VDOs) represent a distinct class of organizations that depend on energy and resources given freely by their members and supporters because they believe in organizational missions ... Exactly how the voluntary differs from its government and commercial counterparts becomes clear in answering two questions: What is the organization's central concern? How does it mobilise resources and human energy?' *Korten and Brown (no date) p 1*

Northern and Southern organizations

'... organizations included under the term non-profit sector have the following basic characteristics: ... (1) to provide a useful ... public or semipublic good or service and serve a specified public purpose of weal ... (2) they are not allowed to distribute residual income ... (3) created, maintained and terminated based on voluntary decision and initiative by members or board ... (4) value rationality ... which implies a deeply rooted set of values...' *Anheier (1990), p 372*

'Five structural/operational features: formal (ie institutionalized), private (ie institutionally separate from government), non-profit distributing (ie nor returning profits to owners and directors), self-governing (ie equipped to control their own activities) and voluntary (ie involving some meaningful degree of voluntary participation).' *Salamon and Anheier (1992), p 11*

'A voluntary agency is an organization established and governed by a group of private citizens for a stated philanthropic purpose and supported by voluntary individual contributions ... the-term "NGO" may include profit-making organizations, foundations, educational institutions, churches and other religious groups and missions, medical and commercial associations, cooperative and cultural groups, as well as voluntary agencies.' *OECD (1988), p 14*

Sources: Brenton, M (1985), *The Voluntary Sector in British Social Services*, Longman; Dobkin Hall, Peter (1987), 'A historical overview of the private non-profit sector' in Powell, Walker W (ed) *The Non-profit Sector: a Research Handbook*, Yale University Press, New Haven and London; van Til, J (1988), *Mapping the Third Sector: Voluntarism in a Changing Social Economy*, Foundation Center; Gorman, Robert F (1984), *Private Voluntary Organizations as Agents of Development*, Westview Press, Boulder and London; Interaction (1985), *Diversity in Development*; Korten, David C (1991), 'The role of non-governmental organizations in development: changing patterns and perspectives' in Samuel Paul and Arturo Israel (eds), *Non Governmental Organizations and The World Bank*, World Bank, Washington DC; Landim, Leilah (1987), 'Non-governmental organizations in Latin America', *World Development* Vol 15 supplement, Pergamon Press; Streeten, Paul (1988), 'The contributors of non-governmental organizations to development' *Asian Institute of Economics and Social Studies* Vol 7, No 1, pp 1–9; Padron, M (1987), 'Non-government development organizations: from development aid to development cooperation', *World Development* Vol 15 supplement, Pergamon Press; Korten, David C (1990), *Getting to the 21st Century: Voluntary Action and the Global Agenda*, Kumarian Press, Connecticut; Brown, L David and David C Korten, 'Voluntary development organizations: what makes this sector different?', Institute for Development Research; Anheier, Helmut (1990), 'Themes in international research on the non-profit sector', *Nonprofit and Voluntary Sector Quarterly*, Jossey-Bass Inc, pp 371–391; Salamon, Lester M and Helmut K Anheier (1992), 'In Search of The Nonprofit Sector 1: The Question of Definitions', Johns Hopkins Comparative Nonprofit Sector Project, Working Paper 2 Johns Hopkins University Institute for Policy Studies; OECD (1988), *Voluntary Aid for Development: the role of Non-Governmental Organizations*, Organization for Economic Cooperation and Development, Paris.

1. *Relief and welfare agencies:* such as missionary societies and Catholic relief services.
2. *Technical innovation organizations:* organizations that operate their own projects to pioneer new or improved approaches to problems, generally within a specialist field.
3. *Public service contractors:* NGOs mostly funded by Northern governments that work closely with Southern governments and official aid agencies. These are contracted to implement components of official programmes because of advantages of size and flexibility.
4. *Popular development agencies:* both Northern and Southern NGOs that concentrate on self-help, social development and grassroots democracy (most of the organizations included in the case studies would be within this category).
5. *Grassroots development organizations:* Southern locally-based development NGOs whose members are poor and oppressed themselves, and who attempt to shape a popular development process (these often receive funding from Popular Development Agencies).
6. *Advocacy groups and networks:* organizations without field projects that exist primarily for education and lobbying.

Some authors (especially Latin Americans) have begun to use the concept of 'civil society' to refer to the complete set of organizations and activities which have a public purpose or concern but which are not organized by government. Within this term are included trade unions and associations and self-help groups.[30] The advantage of such a concept is that it enables the term NGO to be reserved for a specific type of organization while at the same time recognising other types of institutions which do not fall neatly into either the government or commercial sectors and which share some of the concerns and interests of NGOs. The term has emerged from the years of dictatorship and reflects a perceived need to strengthen a broad range of institutions which favour democracy and political pluralism.[31]

NGO–STATE RELATIONS

The fact that most NGOs are both involved with public interest issues and concerns but independent from government and state institutions establishes an immediate tension in much of their work. The relationship between NGOs and government is often difficult because, in choosing to work on public-interest issues, NGOs often try to work within the same arena as government. Government attitudes and policies influence much of the work that they are able to do; Box 3.3 describes some of the ways in which government influences the work of an NGO involved in improving a squatter community.

Box 3.3 The impact of government on the work of NGOs

An NGO working with the inhabitants of a squatter settlement which developed on government land may be subject to any or all of the following government policies and regulations.

- **NGO-related regulations**

Registration: Government legislation will establish the basis on which the NGO and any community organization formed within the settlement are legal entities. The degree of independence of the judiciary may affect the extent to which non-governmental organizations have freedom to meet the needs of their members.
Currency regulations: These may affect the ability of NGOs to raise money from external donors or obtain goods which have to be imported.

- **Site-related regulations**

Land ownership: The government sets the terms and conditions for the occupation of the site – from one extreme of demanding and implementing a forced eviction with no provision of compensation or an alternative site through to setting the terms and conditions under which the ownership or right of use of the site is transferred to the settlers (individually or as a collective).
Basic infrastructure and services: The responsibility for providing most forms of infrastructure and many services (for instance, schools and health care) will fall to national, state or municipal agencies. Their failure to provide most or all of these may be the result of an explicit policy not to provide these in illegal settlements or may simply reflect their incapacity and lack of resources. In most instances, there will be official norms for infrastructure, service buildings and internal and external facilities which NGOs and community organizations may be expected to meet if they take on the responsibility for their provision. Where public agencies provide some forms of infrastructure or services, they usually determine the size of any capital subsidy, the net cost of services and the quality of service provided.
Housing and site development: Site layouts and buildings are likely to be subject to a wide range of norms and controls through building, planning and zoning regulations.

- **Non-sectoral policies with consequences for the settlement**

Financial regulations: These may stipulate the type and form of organizations able to offer loans and effectively debar most NGOs from providing credit facilities.
Macro-economic policies: These are likely to impact directly on the income of the poor, affecting their capacity to pay for services or repay loans.
Land development policies: Governments will influence the amount of land available for residential use and its location. They are also in a position to influence other land use policies which may affect conditions in the settlement and therefore the need for specific forms of housing, basic services and infrastructure investment (for example, land-use upstream may influence the

intensity and frequency of floods; industrial policy may influence the proximity of dangerous industries).

Urban transport policies: These will affect the amount and location of land accessible to the poor for a given expenditure on transport. Transport costs represent a significant proportion of the total expenditures of many poor households which can only find housing, or land on which to build housing, in distant, peripheral locations.

Privatization policies: These will affect the cost and range of services provided to the poor. They may also affect the size and location of land held by the state which may be available either for illegal settlement or for allocation to the urban poor.

Relations between the voluntary sector and the state reflect both differences in state ideology and underlying social and economic factors such as the distribution of wealth in society and the extent of political pluralism. Some governments may consider that they have a monopoly over the public arena and public interest issues. In such cases, NGOs are operating in a territory perceived by government to be its own; and the extent to which they can exist depends critically on the attitude of government. As noted by Berger and Neuhaus (1977), in a totalitarian state, the extension of the state may be such as even to close down the space open to the family.[32] Under such conditions, voluntary organizations may be difficult to run and the work they do in the 'public interest' may reflect more what the government permits than the organization's own priorities. This concern with state intrusion in the affairs of voluntary organizations including NGOs may mean that organizations which receive 100 per cent (or some substantial percentage) of their funding from government are defined as not belonging to the voluntary sector.[33] While voluntary organizations in the North may argue for additional state funds, similar organizations in the South may prefer to look for alternative sources. Implicitly, the requirement for self-governance is believed to necessitate a greater degree of financial independence from the state than is often the case in the North.[34]

In some cases, NGOs may be closely allied to political movements. In the North, many voluntary organizations work with and for specific minority groups. Improved access to resources and increased recognition of the rights of such groups can never be obtained through voting power. Thus, the role of the organization remains to provide services directly and to help the community obtain access to state resources. But many NGOs in the South are working to improve the opportunities for the poor majority and therefore achieving state power is a (potentially) realistic strategy to attain their objectives. In some cases, community-based self-help groups may develop a close relationship with the state, serving almost as local councils in the areas for which they are responsible. Organizations which began as a self-help groups to improve local conditions may become drawn into acting as state institutions. In some cases, the group itself may press for greater incorporation.[35]

DISTINGUISHING CBOS FROM NGOS

One of the biggest problems with defining the voluntary sector in the South is the diversity of groups within it. This is shown by the confusion over the use of the term NGO. NGO is used both as a general term to refer to all non-state, non-profit making organizations and as a specific term for indigenous and/or Northern-based organizations which support self-help groups, people's organizations and individuals in need.[36] A broad distinction is generally made between two types of voluntary organizations: self-help, grassroots, community or people's organizations; and intermediary or service organizations who further their cause. The latter are often further divided into three types: federations of people's organizations, Southern-based organizations and Northern-based organizations.[37] Another distinction sometimes made is between non-governmental development organizations (NGDOs) and NGOs; this is to distinguish those whose main focus is on development from those involved in another activity such as cultural affairs.[38]

The characteristics of self-help groups are, in general, significantly different from those of the intermediary institutions which support them. Verhagen (1987) defines self-help as 'any voluntary action undertaken by an individual or group of persons which aims at the satisfaction of individual or collective needs or aspirations. The distinctive feature of a self-help initiative or activity is the substantial contribution made from the individual's or group's own resources in terms of labour, capital, land and/or entrepreneurial skills'[39]. He goes on to say 'A self-help organization is a membership organization which implies that its risks, costs and benefits are shared among its members on an equitable basis and that its leadership and/or manager are liable to be called to account by membership for their deeds.' Korten (1990) cites similar characteristics (mutual benefit, democratic structure, self-reliance) for groups he terms people's organizations.[40] In this book, such groupings are referred to as community organizations or community based organizations (CBOs).

The origins of some self-help groups in the South bear a close resemblance to the origins of organizations now within the commercial sector in the North. For example, in many countries in the North, mutual benefit associations earn and distribute profits for their members. In their present form, they may be virtually identical to commercial organizations within the same industry and are generally excluded from definitions of the voluntary sector in the North.[41] But in their origins they share some characteristics with some small self-help organizations in the South. For example, the Nationwide Building Society in the UK began with eight individuals in 1883 who met to 'talk about ways of encouraging thrift and of making a small contribution to the fight for better living and working conditions'.[42] They decided to establish a group to offer loans to its members and registered it under the Building Societies Act. One hundred years after their inception, the Nationwide Building Society has 4000 staff, three million savers, 500,000 housing loans and assets of over £7 billion. There are numerous small self-help groups in the South which raise capital through both savings and loans to assist their members in a manner that is very similar to the small group that set up the Nationwide Building Society.

While many definitions of the Northern voluntary sector exclude cooperatives because most are profit-making, this is not true of much of the literature on the Southern voluntary sector.[43] Even though most cooperatives are profit-making, they are also a means by which low-income individuals can raise their incomes and challenge the existing distribution of resources. In a traditional society where investment and capital are controlled by a small number of people, such initiatives by the poor both raise their income and increase the size of the domestic market to allow for further economic growth. While the inclusion of cooperatives within the voluntary sector does not deny their essential profit motivation, it stresses that such organizations may be considered to be broadly developmental, creating opportunities for low-income individuals and communities. In terms of the definitions in Box 3.2 above, the promotion of cooperatives falls within a 'public interest' activity and is therefore included in the voluntary sector.

THE WORK OF NGOS IN THIRD WORLD HOUSING AND BASIC INFRASTRUCTURE AND SERVICES

Traditionally NGOs have concentrated on such areas as low-income housing, community development, support for micro-enterprises, preservation of the environment, popular education, health care and health-related education, and services for mothers, infants and children as well as projects for research, training and information dissemination. Some NGOs are well established institutions with considerable experience, including some which have had active work programmes over twenty or more years. Others are institutionally weaker; many were only formed recently and many have undertaken only small-scale projects. There has been a growing diversity and heterogeneity in the areas in which they work and in the methodologies that they use, as each seeks to deal with the particular social, economic and environmental problems faced by the low-income households in the neighbourhoods in which they work.

It is difficult to generalize about NGOs which work in housing and basic infrastructure and services; the form, content and scope of their work differs so much, as it is shaped by the particular circumstances of each continent, region, country and neighbourhood, the different institutional forms the NGOs take and the different objectives they have. However, there is evidence of the increasing quantitative and qualitative impact that NGOs can have. One example of this is the growing number of networks, federations or coalitions of NGOs within cities, nations or internationally. The expanding role of NGOs in addressing problems of housing, service and infrastructure provision, income generation and community development in Third World countries was emphasised by the attendance at an international seminar in Limuru (Kenya) in 1987, of representatives from 46 Third World NGOs and various international private voluntary agencies and official aid agencies.[44] This group of NGOs also had a central role in changing the nature and expanding the scope of Habitat International Coalition, the umbrella NGO which helps link and coordinate the work of NGOs and NGO federations working on housing and basic services issues at local, national and continental levels. Among the most important changes were a more democratic structure, a more active role in regional and global campaigns, especially that promoting housing rights and stopping forced evictions, and a much increased role for Third World NGOs on its Board and in its work programme.

Although the work of NGOs is now established in many Third World societies at a level which has achieved international recognition, only rarely have NGOs been able to work at a scale which has a significant impact in terms of poverty reduction. Only within a few nations or cities have particular NGOs or groups of NGOs reached a significant proportion of poorer groups – for instance, the experience of FUNDASAL in the urban centres of El Salvador, the credit programmes for small businesses carried out by the Carvajal Foundation in Cali (Colombia), the Grameen Bank and the Bangladesh Rural Advancement Committee in Bangladesh, and the work of the Orangi Pilot Project in Pakistan.

At present, there is considerable debate about the role that NGOs should take in Third World development. The definition of this role is closely connected to the different positions which NGOs adopt in relation to other social organizations and institutions. In many countries, where NGOs grew and developed work programmes within societies ruled by dictatorships (and where most such work programmes were undertaken without official approval and included some in direct opposition to government), the relationship with the state has changed with the emergence of or return to democracy. In a growing number of countries, NGOs are working in collaboration with or as counterparts to the state in many different programmes dealing with poverty. Cooperative links have also been developed between NGOs and churches, universities, trade unions and political parties. At the same time, there has been an expansion of joint projects between NGOs and community organizations, and few dispute the importance of this work in programmes of social development.

In some Third World countries, the increase in the number of NGOs is being encouraged by governments. One reason for this is the recognition of the large and often growing volume of funding being offered to NGOs or to NGO–government partnerships by some international development agencies. At present, there is an increasing willingness on the part of most multilateral and bilateral agencies to acknowledge the role of NGOs. There is a chapter on the future role of NGOs, in achieving all aspects of sustainable development, in Agenda 21, the document agreed by governments at the Earth Summit (the UN Conference on Environment and Development) as the guidelines for their future policies. Although the real impact of NGOs' work is still difficult to evaluate, various aid organizations, both bilateral and multilateral, seem prepared to agree on a strategy whereby NGOs become important channels for funds, to complement (or in some instances replace) government action in carrying out or administering development projects such as those to improve housing and provide services. For instance, the report of the World Commission on Environment and Development, *Our Common Future*, stresses in its chapter on 'the urban challenge' the importance for both governments and international agencies of channelling funds direct to community-based organizations and the NGOs which can support their work. It notes that 'non-governmental and private voluntary organizations are springing up in many countries to provide cost-effective channels for assistance...' and that 'a much larger proportion of assistance should be channelled directly through these organizations'.[45] It also recommends a large increase in the aid that goes directly to community groups for improvement of shelter, infrastructure and basic services, using intermediaries such as national or international NGOs.[46] The World Bank, for its part, has clearly set down that the work of NGOs should be encouraged within compensatory programmes to reduce the social costs of structural adjustment policies promoted by the World Bank and the International Monetary Fund. In this way it has supported health and family planning programmes in Kenya and the provision of infrastructure and education in Togo, in both cases with the joint participation of both the state and community NGOs.[47] However, as noted in Box 3.4, important questions have also been raised about the role which NGOs can take in aid or development assistance programmes that are official agreements between governments and official development assistance agencies. Although some official multilateral and bilateral agencies promote the role of NGOs, the projects or programmes they support must receive the support of the recipient government. There is also the issue of the extent to which the procedures and working practices of official development assistance agencies permit an increased role for NGOs. Box 3.4 includes some of the recommendations made by a group of NGOs working in Guatemala to the World Bank to enable the development of a more effective working relationship.

There is little consensus on the possible roles for NGOs working in housing, basic services and infrastructure. Different authors have sought to define these roles and have put forward a range of possibilities. These are not necessarily contradictory and can be complementary. But there can be substantial differences in approaches at a community level between one group of NGOs which are essentially delivering projects or programmes planned by professionals and another group which focus on advising and supporting a community-driven approach. The different roles undertaken by NGOs can be summarised under the following headings:

Work at the community level

- To give technical and financial support to low-income households and communities to carry out development projects.
- To design and carry out programmes and projects aimed at supplying basic services to low-income groups (for instance carrying out housing programmes or providing health care, popular education, etc).
- To act as 'consciousness raisers' for low-income groups, working with communities in carrying out activities to encourage the political mobilization of the population in support of its own interests (including the 'conscientization' approach which developed from the work of Paulo Freire which means working in communities with a combination of political education, social organization and grassroots development[48]).

Box 3.4 World Bank–NGO relations

The World Bank began an official programme of cooperation with NGOs in 1981, although NGOs had been involved in many projects prior to this. The number of contacts with NGOs has grown considerably in recent years; by 1990, about 20 per cent of World Bank projects involved NGOs to some degree. The World Bank has identified six possible roles for NGOs:

- advising on development issues;
- advising on project identification;
- advising on project design/designing projects;
- co-financing projects;
- implementing projects; and
- monitoring and evaluating projects.

Between 1973 and 1988, the main use made of NGOs was as implementors (58 per cent), even though it has been recognised that, in some cases, NGOs act very much as commercial contractors. Just over a quarter of Bank contacts with NGOs (27 per cent) involved the NGOs acting as advisors in some aspect of the project. NGOs were involved in project design in 12 per cent of contacts. Co-finance roles for NGOs were infrequent, as were evaluator roles. All co-financers and over three quarters of NGOs used in an advisory capacity were international (ie Northern-based) NGOs, not Southern-based organizations. The Bank itself recognizes that '... NGOs' most valuable contributions to development – their vision and grassroots-level experience – have been overlooked in many of the Bank–NGO interactions'. The Bank acknowledges the need to develop a greater understanding of NGOs, increase their contribution to project design, and collaborate with borrower governments to 'create an enabling environment in which NGOs may operate to their fullest potential'. But it also notes that:

- governments may perceive NGOs as a political threat and the Bank should be sensitive to such concerns; and
- Bank-operating procedures may make NGO participation difficult.

NGOs have also identified some problems in working with the World Bank. A group of NGOs working with both the Bank and the government of Guatemala to develop a Social Investment Fund drew the following conclusions from their relations with the Bank:

- While the Bank can encourage governments to be more receptive to NGOs, it is ill-suited to taking on the role of mediator, especially in conflict situations.
- The Bank needs to devote more time to preparation, gaining a greater appreciation of what degree of NGO participation is being proposed and which NGOs are to be approached, before sending a full mission. Involving NGOs proved difficult within the time scale of the Bank – the average Bank project takes eight person-weeks to plan.
- The scarce resources of NGOs make it difficult to resolve conflicts. It would help if there were small matching grants or earmarked funds to cover the costs of NGO participation.
- To be more effective partners, NGOs must prepare themselves by improving their organization, adminstration and relations with the government.

Sources: Salmen, Lawrence F and A Paige Eaves (1991), 'Interactions between Non-governmental Organizations, Governments and the World Bank' in Samuel Paul and Arturo Israel (eds), *non-governmental Organizations and The World Bank*, World Bank, Washington DC; and PACT (1990) *Steps Toward a Social Investment Fund*, PACT, New York.

Influencing policy

- To develop and promote a new social model to other social actors (including residents, the state, political parties and international agencies) which differs from the one in force and which includes the creation and promotion of social practices such as participation, democracy and cooperation.
- To disseminate information on problems related to poverty to governments and other national or local groups (for example, business circles, the media) and to international groups (for example, aid organizations and financial institutions).
- To act as coordinators between different local and national institutions (residents' organizations, government organizations) and international institutions (official aid agencies and private voluntary organizations) in the development, execution and evaluation of aid policies and programmes.
- To serve as institutions for the analysis and improvement of technology for use in different areas related to the reduction of poverty – which includes working as consultants or advisors on the problem of poverty and making proposals for solutions.
- To form technical teams to work with the state on issues such as public administration, and the execution and evaluation of local development projects.
- To analyse and evaluate developments in the state and civil society and, in particular, those directly related to the causes and effects of poverty, and the deterioration of the environment and people's quality of life.

ANALYSIS OF CASE STUDIES

The NGOs whose work is considered in this book (see Box 3.5) have carried out a wide range of programmes and projects to address poverty in the Third World. Despite their different origins and perspectives, and the very different social and political contexts within which they work, all have a strong emphasis on support for the development of community organizations and an interest in new strategies for dealing with the problems of poverty.

The case studies presented in this book offer various examples and describe and analyse some novel initiatives which have achieved a certain degree of success. They have been selected for a variety of reasons; some are particularly innovative, others are good examples of programmes whose characteristics are frequently replicated. Five of the case studies are from Asia, two from Africa, nine from Latin America and two are international. They can be classified in a number of ways.

- *According to scale of impact* The case studies vary widely in terms of the scale of their programme: very small-scale such as La Esperanza or the Koperasi Kredit Borromeus, which affect only a specific group within the given locality; projects with a settlement or neighbourhood-wide approach such as Barrio San Jorge; those within a municipality, such as CUAVES, the Carvajal Foundation and the Catholic Social Services; those within a provincial or metropolitan area, such as the FVC and Uvagram; those with a regional impact, such as Microfund; those with a national impact, such as the Housing Cooper-atives in Ethiopia, the Bangladesh Rural Advancement Committee or FONHAPO; or international programmes such as RAFAD.

The work of all these organizations serves to demonstrate the import-ance of community-level approaches for both national and international agencies and emphasizes the ability of families and organizations from poor communities to obtain resources and repay loans. The dissemination of experiences, such as that of CUAVES in Peru and UVAGRAM in Sri Lanka, serves to demonstrate to national and international financing organizations the ability of the poor to save and to be creditworthy.

- *According to sectoral focus* The programmes include those that are directed towards dealing with the problem of poverty in both rural and urban areas. They include the following subjects:
  - improvement of habitat/living environment: Housing Cooperatives in Ethiopia, FUPROVI, Housing and Local Development Unit;
  - support for people running small businesses: Microfund, Kenya Rural Enterprises Programme (KREP);
  - development for women: Bangladesh Rural Advancement Committee;
  - an integrated mix of development activities which incorporate environment/housing, health and work programmes: FVC, FUNDASAL, CUAVES.

- *According to the beneficiaries* Different programmes target different groups of beneficiaries: in Microfund, they are the small-scale entrepreneurs who were previously dependent on the informal credit sector; in Uvagram, the low-income rural communities in the Province of Uva, Sri Lanka; in KREP, NGOs (in the NGO programme) or small entrepreneurs (in the credit programme for individual businesses). In the Latin American cases, the beneficiaries are generally the poor communities living on the periphery of large cities.

- *According to services provided* Cases are described which concentrate on training, technical support and financing in communities such as Barrio San Jorge. There are also those which provide credit for the inhabitants of these communities: KREP, Koperasi Kredit Borromeus and Fondo de Microproyectos, FVC. In some cases, for example that of the Bangladesh Rural Advancement Committee, the programme has developed into a comprehensive programme of community support. Finally there are those whose main focus is technical and financial support for NGOs which work with community organizations: for example, RAFAD and FONHAPO.

The focus of the following chapter is on financial services and, in particular, the use of credit by the case study organizations.

Box 3.5 The NGO case studies*

1. Bangladesh Rural Advancement Committee (BRAC), Bangladesh.
2. Barrio San Jorge-IIED-America Latina, Buenos Aires, Argentina.
3. Catholic Social Services, Pakistan.
4. Comunidad Urbana Autogestionaria de Villa El Salvador(CUAVES)/Villa El Salvador Self-managed Urban Community, Lima, Peru.
5. Cooperativa de Vivienda Consumo La Esperanza/La Esperanza Housing and Consumer Cooperative, Buenos Aires, Argentina.
6. Cooperative Housing In Ethiopia.
7. Equipo de Vivienda y Gestión Local (EVGL)/Housing and Local Management Unit, Chile.
8. Fondo Nacional de Habitaciones Populares (FONHAPO)/National Fund for Popular Housing, Mexico.
9. Fundación Carvajal, Cali, Colombia.
10. Fundación Promotora de Vivienda (FUPROVI)/Housing Promotion Foundation, Costa Rica.
11. Fundación Salvadorena de Desarrollo y Vivienda Minima (FUNDASAL)/ Salvador Foundation for Development and Basic Housing, El Salvador.
12. Fundación Vivienda y Comunidad (FVC)/Housing and Community Foundation, Buenos Aires, Argentina.
13. Kenya Rural Enterprise Programme, Kenya.
14. Koperasi Kredit Borromeus, Bandung, Indonesia.
15. Local Initiative Facility for the Urban Environment, UNDP.
16. Microfund, Philippines.
17. Research and Applications for Alternative Financing for Development (RAFAD).
18. Uvagram Foundation, Sri Lanka.

* In some case studies, the focus is on a particular project rather than the work of the NGO as a whole.

4

INNOVATIVE CREDIT SCHEMES

INTRODUCTION

The value of innovative programmes to supply credit to low-income individuals and groups has been recognized in recent years. Most such programmes have provided credit for income generation schemes, although a few have been orientated to other areas such as housing. This chapter seeks to draw on these experiences for a better understanding of the potential for new financing systems to support the provision and improvement of housing, infrastructure and services. Reports and evaluations of such schemes have identified a number of different issues related to the operation of credit programmes. Many of these issues are also relevant to the use of credit for housing and infrastructure and basic services. This chapter draws on the case studies and documentation on other credit schemes (and related publications) to outline the major issues and, where possible, draw some conclusions. The conclusions are not definitive in any sense. The case studies and documentation from other projects or programmes are a partial, non-representative sample. But they are drawn from many different countries and cultures – and have a considerable diversity in institutional structure as described in Chapter 3.

THE RELATIONSHIP OF CREDIT SCHEMES TO OTHER FORMAL AND INFORMAL LOAN INSTITUTIONS

Innovative funding schemes offering access to credit are necessary because of the inadequacies of existing formal and informal credit institutions. Formal credit institutions are operated by commercial organizations or the government. They act as intermediaries between those from whom they take deposits and those to whom they give loans. Exclusionary eligibility criteria and unnecessary bureaucratic procedures often mean that credit from these financial institutions is inaccessible to a high proportion of individuals and households. Common problems include the insistence on regular repayments with little flexibility according to income (despite the often high proportion of the population with variable incomes), an unrealistically high minimum size of loan or deposit, fixed time periods for the loan and a demand for collateral which a high proportion of households cannot provide.[1] Generally, no account is taken of the viability of the investment for which the loan is requested. Rather, emphasis is placed on the borrower being able to guarantee repayment from other sources – and this works against poorer groups. In addition, there may be practical problems such as branches being concentrated in the richer areas of a few cities, which may mean that the majority of the urban and rural population cannot easily visit them, and the use of complex forms requiring a high degree of literacy to fill in. Finally, such institutions may specifically exclude sections of the population such as those in the informal sector or women from receiving credit. Some of their weaknesses are evident in the case study on cooperative housing in Ethiopia, a government-sponsored programme involving the Ethiopian Housing and Savings Bank.

Informal credit may be supplied either by friends or relatives or obtained through a professional money lender. Two common problems with such credit are the restricted availability of funds and the high costs of repayment. In the case of loans from family or friends, repayment obligations may be complex and involve further exchanges. Loans from a professional money lender are often associated with high interest rates that may make it difficult for the borrower ever to repay the debt. The terms of such loans may include other restrictive conditions; for example, in agricultural areas, additional demands may include the sale of crops at below market prices to the money lender.

An important issue in setting up a credit programme is the relationship between existing formal and informal institutions and any new credit scheme. All three may coexist happily; they often service different needs with only limited competition between them. A number of case studies refer to the shortage of sources of credit in low-income communities, suggesting that the introduction of a new source of funds is unlikely to threaten existing lenders.

Three broad models emerge from the case studies examined here. Implicit in each is a different hypothesis as to the ability of the formal sector to service the needs of the low-income groups. First, there are those credit schemes which provide an alternative lending institution in the short term but have as the long-term objective the integration into the formal sector of the low-income groups who take part. Second, there are schemes which facilitate the immediate integration of low-income groups into the formal sector. Third, there are schemes which involve the establishment of an alternative institution, implying special provision for low-income groups which will continue in the future. These options are further discussed later in this chapter.

In some cases, the credit schemes have been set up to promote the long-term integration of low-income groups into the formal credit system. The case of FUPROVI, for example, involves a credit system that is dependent on a large number of households transferring their loans to the National Financing System for Housing, thereby allowing FUPROVI to recover their capital and to extend credit to other households. However, this degree of integration with a formal credit institution in unusual in the case studies, and in other project reports. Most credit schemes which see themselves as facilitating the integration of low-income groups into the formal sector have this only as a long-term goal, or have a more tentative and tenuous link.

An alternative model is for the immediate integration of the low-income groups into the formal financial sector; for example, through the use of loan guarantees. In a few cases, NGOs have established loan guarantee schemes to provide the collateral that low-income households need to obtain credit from formal sector credit institutions, ie to permit this integration to take place before trust and confidence in the ability of low-income groups to repay loans has developed in the commercial sector. In such schemes, the NGO takes on the risk of loan default and relies on the formal sector institution to provide the loan. The Housing and Local Management Unit (EVGL) is one example of an organization which has operated such a guarantee successfully, persuading a commercial bank to commit its own money. The case study of RAFAD shows how such a guarantee fund can work at an international level. RAFAD provides loan guarantees to support a range of different NGO initiatives within the Third World. RAFAD's experience suggests that, once its funds have been used to establish a relationship, the NGO then finds it possible to raise funds without the guarantee. Another method of facilitating the integration of low-income groups into the formal sector is shown by the Fundación Carvajal which offers training in self-build techniques and a materials bank with the loans being provided by a formal bank. The case of the Villa El Salvador Self-managed Urban Community (CUAVES) illustrates a further possible relationship. In this case study, credit was received from the formal sector but conditions imposed by this institution became too onerous for the community after an economic crisis in Peru. The NGO helped negotiate a more acceptable solution.

An example of a more autonomous approach to meeting the credit needs of low-income groups is Microfund which developed without any specific relationship to formal-sector institutions. Microfund is seeking to meet all the credit needs of participants through innovative funding strategies, even though it does not attempt to meet them all from its own finance. Other experiences also suggest that the formal financial sector is unable to meet the needs of low-income groups, who have to look for alternative means; the Grameen Bank is one particularly well-known example.[2]

A relatively small number of credit schemes belong to a fourth model, exemplified here by FONHAPO. In such a model, the government provides finance for small loans to communities for individual and community investment. NGOs support the successful use of credit by the communities, developing financial awareness and the ability to manage loan finance and providing technical advice. This model has been used by the Community Mortgage Programme in the Philippines and is being followed in the development of a Fund for the Urban Poor in Thailand.[3]

The relationship between any innovative credit scheme and the formal sector clearly depends on the particular strategy chosen. There are no obvious lessons emerging in respect of whether one strategy is more successful than another. Some schemes have successfully managed to integrate low-income groups into the formal sector; others have been less successful. Some attempts to set up alternative institutions have worked; others have not. The necessary conditions for success are dependent on the particular context within which the scheme is operating.

SUBSIDIES AND LOAN FINANCE

Subsidies may be offered on one or more of five broad categories of goods and services provided by donors to a community project which involves the provision of loans or grants for housing. These five categories are: grants to cover direct housing costs; grants for direct infrastructure and basic services costs; subsidized loan repayments, mainly through reduced interest rate charges; local support services provided free or at reduced cost (eg community development, construction training, legal assistance); and other services (such as management and technical advice) from international funders provided free or at reduced cost. The major problem with all such subsidies is that credit programmes cannot continue when the funds which paid for the subsidy run out. National and international finance is not available on a scale commensurate with need if grants are made and none of the costs recovered. This section focuses particularly on issues related to subsidies to cover part of the cost of loan repayments.

A number of credit schemes described in the case studies involve (or have involved) an element of subsidy in the loan. It is these experiences, together with others reported in the literature, which are examined here. Subsidies in the form of grants for housing and infrastructure and basic services are not discussed. The financing of an additional programme to facilitate and support the operation of the credit scheme specifically and the area's development in general is discussed on page 58.

There is a general, although not universal, consensus in income-generation schemes that subsidized credit should be avoided. A number of reasons are offered for this. It is not evident that low-income groups require reduced rates – access to finance is a bigger constraint than the cost of finance. Low income groups often pay substantially more than open-market interest rates when they borrow in the informal market. It has been argued that the demand for credit is not particularly sensitive to the interest rate and lowering the interest rate does not greatly affect the demand for loans.[4] This evidence therefore suggests that repayment at market interest rates is not a major burden, and that schemes charging market rates will not find it difficult to secure the involvement of poorer groups. A second reason given is that subsidized credit has offered an incentive to richer groups to appropriate a scheme initially intended for low-income groups, and thus cheap credit simply becomes another way in which the rich can receive government aid. Third, subsidies may encourage the people receiving support to become dependent on that support and delay their integration into conventional sources of credit (if this is an aim of the scheme). Fourth, the cost of subsidies reduces the possibility of extending the credit scheme to reach more people.

However, some observers specifically limit this conclusion on the need to avoid subsidies in the provision of credit to loans for income-generation projects.[5] While many projects have been successful without subsidies, this does not necessarily mean that projects with subsidies have been unsuccessful (although the World Bank argues that subsidized borrowers have been less reliable than unsubsidized ones[6]). Government credit programmes for housing may offer a subsidy to those able to join such programmes; under such circumstances it is hard for NGOs to charge more to groups whose members are significantly poorer than those receiving government loans. It is also evident that low-income communities require substantial assistance to pay for housing, basic services and infrastructure.[7] Nevertheless, a continuing problem is securing an inflow of funds to cover the cost of the subsidy.

Diversity in practice is evident from the case studies included in this analysis. There are three patterns evident:

1. organizations which subsidize interest rates, offering beneficiaries below-market rates (eg Catholic Social Services, FONHAPO);
2. organizations which offer rates equal to or exceeding market rates (with the additional amount collected financing costs related to the project and/or covering an insurance payment) (eg BRAC, KREP); and
3. organizations which do not lend directly but simply facilitate access to national housing funds (eg CUAVES, EVGL).

None of the case studies which lend for housing charge market rates, although this experience is not universal.[8] In some high-inflation countries, the subsidy (or at least its magnitude) is determined inadvertently as the real interest rate is not maintained, as is evident in the case study of Villa El Salvador (CUAVES). This is likely to be a particular problem if the interest rate is fixed over the repayment period.

All credit schemes which make use of subsidies face the difficult question as to whether or not the resources spent on subsidizing the loans might be better spent on alternative project support; for example, directly meeting part of the project costs such as in the provision of support services, or paying part of the capital investment required or targeted to help the poorest members of the community. Few credit schemes appear to have explicitly considered the relative merits of offering an interest rate subsidy or providing other support. For instance, where a grant is available to support the upgrading of a low-income settlement, charging individuals or households market rates for loans to upgrade or extend their housing can allow more funding to be allocated to infrastructure and service improvement or to providing the initial capital for the bulk purchase of building materials.

CONDITIONALITY

A number of credit schemes and some formal credit institutions are designed to offer credit or support in particular sectors – for instance, those which provide credit for agricultural activities only. Such schemes normally impose conditions on the recipient's use of the credit. While the conditions attached to loans are obviously necessary for credit schemes aimed at particular sectoral development, a number of authors emphasize that such practices may not be helpful.[9] Credit schemes which leave the recipients free to determine how best to invest resources are believed to be more successful. In addition, there may be practical problems in ensuring that the credit is used as required by the scheme and not used to purchase other goods. These practical problems obviously increase, the larger the number and the smaller the size of the average credit.

The advantage of sector-specific credit schemes is that they can enable the NGO to provide very focused support and training. They also offer an opportunity for cheaper inputs through bulk purchase, and the provision of specialist marketing services.

Despite the caution of several authors in regard to conditional credit, several such schemes are operating successfully. Housing often appears to be treated as a special case with subsidized loans being available for housing investment which cannot be used for income-generation activities. For example, the Grameen Bank operates a housing loan scheme which lends members the equivalent of several hundred dollars over a period of about ten years. This scheme includes the purchase of a package of house building materials produced by cooperatives supported by the Bank (see Box 4.1). Moreover, the case studies include a number of examples which show how other housing and basic services projects have used credit successfully with a sector-specific focus.

Box 4.1 Grameen Bank housing loans

Although the Grameen Bank's main focus has been on providing credit for income-earning activities to poor rural households, it has also developed a housing loan programme which has been in operation since 1984. Members of the Grameen Bank who are borrowing to finance income-generating activities, have met loan conditions and are up to date with repayments are also eligible for housing loans. The average loan made in May 1990 was US$298. The annual interest rate is 5 per cent and the period of the loan is about 10 years, although borrowers are advized to try to repay more quickly. Up to May 1990, just under 80,000 loans had been disbursed, over 80 per cent to women. This programme is integrated into the Bank's other credit programmes, in which those seeking loans must form themselves into groups of five, and several groups then come together to form a Centre. All group members and the elected Centre Chief must approve a loan made to any of their members. The housing loan package includes four reinforced concrete pillars, two bundles of galvanized iron sheets, one sanitary latrine and additional material for the walls and roof. Some of this material is produced by manufacturing units supported by the Bank.

Source: Anzorena, Jorge (1989–91), assorted *SELAVIP* papers. Some additional information about the Grameen Bank comes from UNCHS (Habitat), *IYSH Bulletin* Tenth Issue, July 1987.

ADDITIONAL MEASURES AND SUPPORT

Many innovative credit schemes include a package of additional measures to supplement and enhance the provision of credit. Some are multi-faceted community development programmes within which credit provision plays a small part; others are primarily for the provision of credit, with some small-scale extra support services being offered. The kinds of additional measures include the provision of infrastructure appropriate to the activities for which credit is extended and training either in particular activities or in financial/business management.

Some of the more ambitious credit schemes use group development techniques to establish a structure through which borrowing can take place. In many cases, the group also provides a guarantee of repayment. In such cases, it may be several years before credit can be provided. Major social changes may need to be initiated within the community before credit is made available and this may take some time and much support to be implemented effectively. The Bangladesh Rural Advancement Committee estimates that it takes about four years after first starting work in an area before credit can be extended without subsidized support.

Other new skills may also be required by those receiving credit. For example, entrepreneurs may need help in marketing their products or, if money is being lent for cooperative development, support may be needed for developing effective methods of group-working. In the context of housing, the Housing and Local Management Unit (EVGL) in Chile developed a number of other activities to enhance the effectiveness of their credit scheme. On a simple level, they set up a materials bank and offered technical assistance to improve the quality of housing development. However, they also encouraged households to work in groups in order to extend the use of mutual help within the community, and set up a network to support these groups.

In regard to training, some of the organizations included in the case studies suggest that NGOs involved in the provision of credit and associated programmes are also likely to need specialist training for their staff.

In general, there is a consensus in favour of some measure of additional support being incorporated into credit schemes. However, an alternative view is given in the case study of Kenya Rural Enterprise Programme which argues that minimalist credit schemes are the most successful within the context in which this organization is operating. This programme found that, in their situation, the provision of additional services was not necessary; it did not ensure a greater probability of financial success by the individual entrepreneurs and delayed the distribution of funds.

The full cost of these additional measures and services is rarely charged to the community but is met through project support from donors. In some cases, such as the Bangladesh Rural Advancement Committee, an additional charge is made to cover community initiatives within each specific community but this does not cover the services provided by the intermediary institution. In another case study, FUNDASAL recovers some of its administrative costs from the community although subsidies are offered through low-interest rate loans, basic services and infrastructure being provided at no charge.

SAVINGS AS A COMPONENT OF CREDIT PROGRAMMES

Many credit schemes (including many of those considered in the case studies) involve the generation and use of recipients' savings as an integral component. Saving is believed to help develop and encourage a sense of financial responsibility among recipients. Borrowers may have to maintain savings at a certain level for a specific period of time before they are able to obtain a loan. In some cases, their savings can be invested in the same project as their loan; in others, they must retain the savings with the lending organization to provide a minimal form of collateral. The willingness to turn income into savings is often seen as an important indicator of the ability of the household to maintain loan repayments in the absence of any form of collateral. Completion of a successful savings programme indicates that a proportion of income is uncommitted and thus can be made available for loan repayment.

Some innovative credit systems are based on rotating savings and credit associations (often given the acronyn ROSCAs). These are autonomous groups of people with each person agreeing to save a given amount within regular periods of time. Each period's savings are then allocated to one or more members of the group to use in turn. Interest rates (if used) are agreed collectively, as is the system for allocating the fund. Such associations offer members access to a capital sum without using financial resources from outside the community. While the scale of credit available is obviously constrained as many communities have little surplus available, such small-scale traditional savings schemes have been used successfully as the basis for more ambitious credit schemes.

RISK AND REPAYMENT

Overcoming and reducing the risk of loan default is a critical element of NGOs' work in the area of credit. It is the lack of collateral that is often the most important single factor excluding low-income groups from access to formal credit institutions. In some cases, through the use of guarantee funds, NGOs' intervention in this area is simply to take on some of the risk and thereby open up access to formal credit institutions. However, NGOs are often directly involved in managing the credit, gaining expertise in developing systems to ensure effective loan recovery.

There are several generally accepted conclusions in regard to the characteristics of credit schemes that are successful in securing high rates of repayment and these are described in the paragraphs below. However, it is important to note that repayment rates are usually measured as simply the amount of loans repaid on time or within a specific period. They do not always take into account the resources spent on developing an appropriate support mechanism to ensure repayments are made. In some cases, these costs are charged against the loan but in others they are met by external grants or internal funds which the organization has raised.

The use of group guarantees has been made famous by the Grameen Bank and has been used (albeit with slight variations) in many different credit schemes throughout the world. The basic strategy is to organize individual entrepreneurs into small groups of about five people. Each individual is eligible for loans but the granting of each loan is staggered over a specific period of time. Repayments by all members must be up to date to permit the next person to receive a loan. The group is collectively responsible for ensuring that each individual member continues to make repayment contributions. Similar conditions apply for all future loans. This group structure may also be used for further community development activities.

The administrative costs of such programmes are high. The Grameen Bank estimates that its expenses equal 16–25 per cent of the value of outstanding loans for new branches, although this falls to six per cent after three years. Attaching the programme to an existing group structure may offer an effective method of reducing costs; for example, the Zimbabwe Agriculture Finance Corporation lends only to established groups and has reduced costs to one per cent of loan capital.[10]

An alternative option to stimulate good repayment records is to provide only small loans, with further loans being conditional on successful repayment. The effectiveness of this procedure relies on the scarcity of the available credit to provide an incentive for borrowers to maintain repayments. The small amounts (together with the fact that market interest rates are charged) generally ensure that only those on low-incomes are interested; richer individuals borrow elsewhere. Once individuals have successfully repaid several small loans they are allowed access to larger loans.

In some cases, those operating credit schemes have kept losses to a minimum by lending only to a small group of people whom they know very well, or who have received a reference from someone well known to the organization. For example, Koperasi Kredit Borromeus offers loans to only employees of a given organization. While this method has been successful, it obviously greatly reduces the potential growth of the credit scheme.

The challenge to those operating credit schemes for low-income communities is to reduce the costs incurred on each individual loan, such as the costs of chasing up those who default and the administrative costs associated with the scheme. Generally people with low incomes only want to borrow small amounts and so individual transaction costs are high relative to aggregate lending. This is one of the reasons why such lending is unattractive to the formal sector. If interest rates are not to exceed market interest rates and credit schemes are to remain viable, the NGOs have to ensure high repayment rates with only limited additional expenditure on overheads. Where this is not possible, donor funds may be used to cover some of the adminstration costs. The evidence from many different projects is that, if the projects are carefully designed, high repayment rates can be secured and have been secured in many different situations and cultures. One factor which has helped is that credit has often been scarce and therefore high rates of return can be earned by those able to invest in entrepreneurial opportunities. Obviously, high repayment rates can only be secured if the large majority of investment projects are successful.

As well as establishing mechanisms which (through whatever means) offer a strong incentive for the individual borrowers to maintain repayments, credit schemes generally examine applications for funds to assess the viability of the individual projects for which investment is required. In some cases this process is built into the group structure; in others, staff belonging to the organization are trained to undertake the task.

In housing projects (which may include the provision or improvement of infrastructure for individual housing units), there are a number of special characteristics relevant to issues concerned with risk and repayment. The large capital cost and slow depreciation of the capital asset mean that repayments are often spread over an extended period. In some of the case studies which involve housing projects, loan periods are significantly longer than is common for loans for income-generating activities. For example, those participating in FUPROVI and Koperasi Kredit Borromeus programmes repay their housing loans over 15 years. However, in many other cases, much shorter periods are used; for example, Catholic Social Services requires their borrowers to repay the loan in three years. For the household, the shorter the period of repayment the higher the monthly repayments and the smaller the loan which can be afforded. But longer loan periods raise the amount of capital needed by the NGO to reach a given number of people.

A second characteristic is that housing construction or improvement does not usually add directly to household income (although for the reasons discussed earlier, it may indirectly increase the size and stability of income). In general, the investment does not generate additional funds to help meet the costs of repayment. For this reason, the requirement that participants save at a rate equivalent to their future repayments for a period before obtaining a loan may be particularly important to ensure that households who cannot afford the repayments do not participate. The organizations in several of the case studies would only lend money to households which have successfully completed a savings programme.

A third characteristic is that the money may be invested in a property for which the residents lack legal tenure. In most urban centres, projects which offer loans only to those households with legal tenure of the house site will not reach a high proportion of low-income households. It is common for between 30 and 60 per cent of a city's population (and a much higher proportion of the low-income population) to live in illegal settlements. For this reason, the intermediary institution may also need to assist participants in obtaining legal tenure. In several case studies – for instance that of Barrio San Jorge – the intermediary institution is working with the inhabitants to secure the transfer of tenure to the inhabitants. The case study on FUPROVI is interesting in this respect because the organization offers possibilities to those who cannot achieve legal status. In other cases, the land may be legally owned but the housing design may infringe building regulations. The NGO may have to support the community in negotiations with the municipal council.[9]

A fourth characteristic occurs in much infrastructure and basic services provision where the investment is, by necessity, provided to the community as a whole. The provision of credit for investment in infrastructure or services which benefit a group of households or a community clearly has different characteristics from the provision of credit for individuals. Certain services – for instance, bulk purchase of building materials to ensure their availability on site – may be funded through charges made to residents as they use the service. Other services for which there is a constant demand – for example, childcare centres and the collection of garbage – might also be financed in this way. Loans for larger, more capital-intensive schemes which depend on regular repayments from most or all inhabitants in a settlement may be more problematic, although there are case studies of settlement-wide piped-water supply schemes which have had good records of cost recovery. Certain forms of infrastructure, such as roads and site drains, can present particular problems in terms of recovering costs from all beneficiaries since their use cannot be denied to those who do not pay. There may be little incentive for individual households to repay once the investment has been made. One possibility, evident in some slum and squatter-site upgrading schemes, is a regular payment levied on all households to recover costs for an integrated package of infrastructure and service improvements. Although costs per household can be kept down, especially where all inhabitants are prepared to contribute to the improvements, such integrated schemes for whole settlements or neighbourhoods will still demand relatively large amounts of capital up front, with repayment having to take place over a number of years. If cost recovery is sought from such integrated schemes – or from the more capital-intensive aspects such as piped-water systems – the inhabitants must be fully involved in discussions about what should be done and the cost implications of different options. Consensus reached within low-income settlements as to what should be done and its cost implications for each household are obviously more likely to produce good cost recovery.

WOMEN

Women are discriminated against in many development processes and the supply of credit is no exception. In some formal institutions, women are unable to borrow money without the support of a husband or a male relative. In many traditional communities, they may also have more limited access to informal credit systems. In most societies, women take on most or all responsibilities for child care and household management and therefore have fewer opportunities to develop income-earning activities. In most instances, they also face discrimination in the education system and in access to training to acquire the entrepreneurial skills they need to make their use of credit successful.

Women are a high proportion of borrowers in many credit schemes. In some cases, this is deliberate; the Bangladesh Rural Advancement Committee focuses on the particular needs of women and, as a consequence, a majority of members and loan recipients are women. In others, as discussed in the case study of Microfund, this has simply evolved due to women's greater willingness to participate in the credit scheme.

With regard to making credit available to women, several authors have noted the particular importance of some of the issues discussed elsewhere in this book. Training may be necessary because women have traditionally been excluded from acquiring certain skills. Particular support may be needed if the scheme encourages women into taking on new social roles. One seminar which examined the International Fund for Agricultural Development's experience with rural credit schemes concluded that government credit schemes have isolated women as a group in need of charity. Schemes which linked women with formal financial institutions offering loans on a commercial basis were to be preferred. The seminar also noted that women have a better record of repayment than men.[12]

Access to new sources of credit may be particularly important for women. Women often work in the informal sector because it provides the flexibility they need to allow them also to meet child care and domestic responsibilities and because they are excluded from many formal-sector jobs (either for lack of education and training or for other reasons). Formal-sector financial institutions are often reluctant to lend money to informal-sector enterprises although credit offers women a chance to develop small-scale trades, such as the small retailing and marketing operations in which many are involved. Many female heads of households have a particular need to develop income-generating activities as they have to combine a role as the main income earner with child care and household maintenance. Even within households with both male and female income-earners, the income earned by the woman may be of particular importance to the children's health and nutritional status.[13]

Women generally have particular needs with regard to housing. For example, a women who is the sole or main income-earner for the household (with additional responsibilities for child care and household maintenance) may have less possibility of self-help.[14] This triple role – often combined with gender discrimination in employment markets – also means lower incomes and thus lower capacity to repay. However, women may also be prepared to pay a higher proportion of their income towards credit repayment, if they can acquire the kind of housing which meets their needs and priorities.[13] In respect of infrastructure and services, it is generally women and children who suffer most from the inadequacies since they spend most of their time in or near the home and they generally have responsibility for fetching water and fuel, disposing of rubbish and looking after the house. Improved provision for water supply, sanitation and garbage collection and disposal brings many advantages to those responsible for such tasks. The adults who take responsibility for child care (again mostly women) are also those who benefit most from such services as health centres. Good provision for day-care centres, pre-school groups and schools also provides more time for these adults to earn incomes. In settlements where women are important income-earners – or where there are untapped possibilities for them which are restricted by their responsibilities for household management and child care – there may be a considerable potential demand from women for certain kinds of improved infrastructure and services. The scale and nature of these needs may not be apparent in consultations with community organizations in which women are not fully represented.

CONCLUSIONS

Some of the characteristics of different types of investment in shelter and associated infrastructure and services are summarized in Table 4.1 on page 66. The table identifies a number of key areas in which such investments differ: the recipient of the loan, the size of the loan, the different sources for realising loan repayment, the repayment term, the potential for self-help to reduce costs, and possible sources of collateral. It is evident from the table and from the case studies that generalizations about investment in shelter and associated infrastructure and basic services are difficult. The particular needs of a credit scheme depend not only on the social, economic and political environment of the community receiving support, but also on the type of investment required by the community.

The lessons from credit schemes for income-generating activities are clearly important to the establishment of effective schemes in other sectors. However, the issues and conclusions from credit schemes which have concentrated on income-generating investment cannot necessarily be applied to credit schemes for housing, infrastructure and services. For instance, in the case of credit to support the acquisition or construction of new housing, the time scale is much longer, and the size of the loan needed by a household generally much larger. For credit for many forms of infrastructure and services, the capital investment is much larger and it is not cost-effective for it to be made on an individual basis.

But as the case studies on credit schemes for housing and basic services indicate, many of these issues remain relevant. Credit can be used effectively to increase access to housing, basic services and infrastructure. There are also more specific experiences which are useful. For example, the type of additional support required may be similar; and similar methods of securing repayment may be effective. This is especially so for loans to individuals to purchase, build or improve their own housing. Loans for infrastructure and service provision or improvement for a large group of households probably need different techniques and may depend on the existence (or development) of a representative community organization which can facilitate management of the credit.

Thus, the lessons from the experience in credit schemes to date need to be examined on a case-by-case basis to see if they are applicable to any particular project. The experience to date is important in helping identify likely issues and in understanding many of the pressures and stresses on such communities as they seek to improve housing and living conditions and the provision of infrastructure and services through the use of credit.

Table 4.1 Characteristics of different types of borrowing for individual or community initiatives in shelter and related infrastructure and services

Type of investment	Borrower	Capital required	Cost per household	Source of loan repayment	Repayment term	Comments on investment	Potential of self-help to reduce costs	Collateral
Housing improvement or upgrading	Individual	Can be initiated with modest capital; short-term loans allow rotating funds	Flexible; often small loans required	Income and savings	Typically 1–5 years	Potential savings on future repair costs	High	The shelter itself although problems if the shelter is illegal. Group guarantees
Housing purchase	Individual	Generally large	Medium to large	Income and savings	Long, especially where land and house prices are high	–	–	The shelter itself although problems if the shelter is illegal. Group guarantees
Housing construction	Individual or small group	Generally large, except in rural areas. Serviced site can reduce initial cost	Medium to large	Income and savings	Long, especially where land prices are high	Reduced capital if incremental construction	High	The land – although problems if it is occupied or sub-divided illegally
Land acquisition	Individual or community	Medium to large in urban areas, especially larger cities	Medium to large	Income and savings	Medium to long	–	None	The land
Building material bulk purchase	Community, enterprise, NGO	Large up front. Reduced if credit from wholesalers	Small to medium (flexible)	Payment for materials by user	Short to medium	May only need capital for a short time once repayment record established and credit offered	Limited	Building material stock
Water supply, individual household*	Individual	Medium to large, depending on site and water delivery system	Small to medium (usually $50–500 per household)	Income and savings	Short to medium	Often a more capital intensive project serving a large group of people is more cost-effective and may have lower	Some	Shelter

Table 4.1 (continued)

Type of investment	Borrower	Capital required	Cost per houshold	Source of loan repayment	Repayment term	Comments on investment	Potential of self-help to reduce costs	Collateral
Water supply, settlement*	Community or NGO	Large capital costs, small recurrent costs	Small to medium	User charges; sometimes some capital from connection charges	Medium to long term	Major economies of scale if all households in the settlement are connected; user charges can be set to cover repayment of capital and recurrent costs	Limited	Reputation of community organization or NGO undertaking the installation
Health centre*	Community, NGO	Medium capital, large recurrent costs	Low	User charges or group insurance scheme	–	Recurrent costs difficult to cover	Some in construction; some in use of community volunteers	Reputation of community organiz-ation or NGO setting up and running service
Garbage collection*	Community, group, individual entrepreneur	Small to medium, flexible depend-ing on tech-nology chosen and site	Low but regular	User charges, waste re-use and recovery	Dependent on technology used	Individual household payments have to cover capital and recurrent costs	Some – in recycling & reclamation	As above
Surface water drains*	Community, NGO	Medium to large	Low	Regular payment–difficult to collect	–	Capital cost best met through regular monthly charges over a number of years, integ-rated into charges for water or other services	Medium	–

Table 4.1 (continued)

Type of investment	Borrower	Capital required	Cost per household	Source of loan repayment	Repayment term	Comments on investment	Potential of self-help to reduce costs	Collateral
Sanitation: individual household system	Individual	Medium to large, depending on technology chosen	Low to medium depending on system used	Income and savings of individual household	Short to medium	Often a more capital-intensive project serving large group of people is more cost-effective in urban settlements	High, although technical advice often needed	–
Sanitation: community system	Community, NGO	Medium to large, depending on technology chosen	Medium	User charges; connection charges	Medium to long	–	Low	–
Paving roads	Community	Medium to high (depending on settlement)	Relatively low	User charges difficult to collect	Medium to long	Capital cost best met through regular monthly charges over a number of years, integrated into charges for water or other services	Medium to high	–
Child care*	Community group, entrepreneur	Medium capital investment (unless done in existing building)	Medium (low but regular repayment required)	User charges	Long-term recovered through user charges	–	Some in construction considerable recurrent cost savings by use of volunteer staff	–
Small-scale business	Individual or small group	Flexible	Small to medium	Increased incomes for beneficiaries	Short to medium	–	–	Savings, value of household or business assets

5

CONCLUSIONS

INTRODUCTION

The greatest challenge that Third World countries face at the beginning of the 1990s is to end the poverty which affects over a quarter of their population. The solution requires both the mobilization of additional resources and the better use of existing resources.

Additional resources are obviously needed. The scale of poverty and deprivation is too large to be tackled only by the better use of existing resources. Although poverty is rooted in the inequitable distribution of economic power both within and between nations, the political changes needed to instigate a significant redistribution rapidly are unlikely to occur. The projects which are included in the case studies all involve the use of additional resources but perhaps the key to their success is their better use of under-utilized resources (both financial and human).

In developing the scale and scope of community-level initiatives, such resources need to be identified and tapped. There are three main kinds of unutilized or underutilized resources which successful projects employ:

1. *Technical and organizational skills.* For the individual household
   building or improving their home, technical advice can help improve
   health and safety standards and reduce costs – for instance in avoiding
   the over-use of cement and other expensive materials. Technical and legal
   advice can also help those living in illegal settlements negotiate more
   secure tenure or even the acquisition of ownership or tenure rights.
   Technical advice can also ensure the best possible use of local resources –
   for instance the harvesting of rainwater where the cost of other water
   sources is high, making best use of local springs or aquifers and devising
   the cheapest means to improve the environment, for instance to improve
   site drainage.
2. *Financial resources.* A good match between low-income households'
   credit needs and their capacity to repay can permit relatively modest
   sums of money to mobilize people's own financial contributions.
   Guarantee schemes can provide the means by which both individuals and
   groups who have been excluded from the formal financial sector can
   obtain credit, and can help develop a more permanent relationship

between these two groups. The use of material banks and bulk purchasing of construction materials, fixtures and fittings can help lower building costs and also lessen the difficulties that self-builders face in obtaining and transporting materials to their house site. Supporting the process by which illegal settlers become legal settlers with shelters (which they can themselves develop through self-help construction and incremental improvement) also helps poorer households acquire substantial capital assets, as well as safer and healthier places to live. Some projects train local people in building and construction skills both to enable them to work on community improvements and to improve future employment prospects.[1]

3. *Productive capacities.* In many low-income settlements, there is an important synergy between improving services and job creation – as in nurseries, community kitchens, day-care centres and other community services set up there which employ some local staff and also make available time for mothers to earn incomes. Supporting individuals or groups to build, extend or improve housing is also likely to generate demand for many goods and services which can be supplied locally – building materials, fixtures and fittings, furniture and the services of plumbers, electricians, builders and other skilled or semi-skilled labour.

Aid agency and NGO projects, particularly those involving community initiatives, appear in this context as mobilizers of an enormous reserve of resources (financial, technical and human) which can be central to reducing poverty and improving the quality of life for low-income groups. This new means to confront poverty also recognizes that the main actors in social transformation must be the inhabitants themselves; outside agencies (whether NGOs, aid agencies or municipal authorities) can mobilize, support and advise but it is the low-income groups and their community organizations which direct the process. The case studies considered in this book demonstrate that there are ways to address poverty successfully, without large subsidies. The methods used in the case studies are generally far more cost-effective than those of traditional development projects which tend to have a relatively small impact in relation to the scale of their investment.

The experiences presented in the case studies demonstrate that intermediary institutions can provide support for individual and community initiatives in which poorer groups and their community organizations retain control of what is done and how it is done. They demonstrate that it is feasible to carry out initiatives which, based on a variety of approaches, achieve real improvements in the quality of living. The case studies analysed cover a whole spectrum of different possibilities for intervention: working with different types of people, with different degrees of independence from the state, with different organizational objectives, and with different forms of finance. Both in these and in other case studies, the impact (and success) must be assessed in the national social context from which each case has developed. But all have implicit lessons or principles which can be used in other initiatives to develop new lines of action. These lessons are discussed further below.

REINFORCEMENT OF COMMUNITY ORGANIZATION

Several of the case studies note that a consolidation of community organizations took place through the resolution of specific problems (housing, health, income generation and others). In some case studies, one objective was to form or consolidate an organizational structure which serves as a nucleus for the inhabitants of a certain district or sector and to stimulate and enhance their ability to resolve some of their basic problems. On this subject, some points can be drawn from the cases studied.

There is a need to increase the collective capacity of poorer groups for negotiation and management when they deal with other groups – government as well as NGOs and international agencies. The capacity that each community has to understand that it has rights for which it is worth struggling and negotiating with the state and with other powerful interest groups is key in avoiding permanent dependence on external projects. Work with communities should include a reinforcement of the population's awareness of their basic rights as citizens and their collective strength as a community.

The strengthening of community organization is also a good means of optimizing and multiplying the financial resources invested in a project. Projects such as Barrio San Jorge, La Esperanza and CUAVES are all examples of the strengthening of neighbourhood organization albeit on different scales. Each of these communities has been able to negotiate with the municipality, with NGOs and private employers for the provision of different kinds of support (human, material and financial) to help them improve their living conditions.

Another conclusion drawn from the case studies is that, whether for housing or for income generation, successful projects are not simply about providing finance. They also involve the provision of additional measures of support. The case study of the Kenya Rural Enterprise Programme is an exception but this organization is unique among the case studies included here. This suggests that it is inappropriate only to consider new ways of financing community initiatives to provide improved housing and associated basic services and infrastructure. Attention should be given to the package of resources and the ways in which this can be made available to the individuals and community organizations which need it. Among the additional resources commonly included are training (which may be specific to the project or involve more general business or financial development) and community development skills. In some projects, the promotion of community organization is given an even higher priority with the establishment of groups for collective work and/or decision-making.

WORK WITHIN COMMUNITIES

Low-income groups are generally not only poor in a financial sense. The health burden of being poor, the continuing struggle for resources and the stress associated with providing for themselves and their dependents all have other costs. A strong and effective local community can be a way through which many of the multiple deprivations suffered by poorer individuals and households can be tackled. The informal support of neighbours (who often have similar experiences) and community organizations can help individuals to take a more active role in addressing their own problems and in discovering a greater sense of their own self-worth. Such contacts may be important in enabling individuals to take the necessary action to improve their current and future lives, and in supporting them in the personal and political challenges which they face.

There are an increasing number of community organizations which take a central role in the redesigning or upgrading of their own settlements to make them more attractive, healthy and secure. They often guide their members in how to maintain the buildings in which they live and the areas which they share; they organize and implement changes and ensure coordination and continuity in the projects they carry out. Perhaps one of the best measures of success for any programme of support for community organizations lies in the extent to which it leads to a strengthening of internal social relations – this being a means not only to achieve physical improvements but also of reducing the levels of psycho-social health problems suffered by the inhabitants, and achieving a greater social stability in a healthier environment.

Community organizations need access to capital to function effectively and to make the investments required by their members. Providing such capital for investment may seem a high risk in circumstances where income is insufficient and uncertain but supporting investments by and through community organizations can enable people both to obtain resources at a lower unit cost and to increase the value of their own resources. As such, it helps reduce their vulnerability to adversity. The provision of credit may itself be a source of income for community activities if an additional small charge is made on each individual loan. The case studies show that capital can be made available for individual and community investments with a minimal risk to those lending the money and can even be profitable for the private sector. Without such risks being taken (and many of the case studies show that the risks can be minor), it will be difficult to reduce the level of poverty.

COMMUNITY PARTICIPATION

Community participation is one of the key features in NGO projects directed towards the development of poor communities. Although much has been said and written in recent years on the importance of participation, it must be emphasized that the term 'participation' can be used in different ways. In many instances, external agencies view participation as a means to reduce the cost of projects; 'the participation of the community' provides cheap labour for health, education, and (in particular) environmental programmes and a means of mobilizing support. A very different understanding of participation is one which encourages the community to become involved in the process of decision-making in the project and to influence how resources are used, choices made about what should be done and the role that external agencies take. It is this kind of participation which has been gaining acceptance in recent years, based on a recognition of the increasing importance of the role which communities take in solving their own problems and their capacity to design, manage, execute, control and evaluate the projects which aim to develop their settlements.

Many case studies suggest that the population's participation in this kind of project has brought with it an improvement in the self-esteem of individuals and households. Although it is clear that the increases in the standard of living, the improvement in health and the quality of life, and the social status of the individuals, are contributory elements in reinforcing the families' potential to develop, this is an aspect of community development which remains poorly understood. More detailed analyses of the results of greater participation are still needed to clarify this.

However, it is essential that the different roles of the various groups and individuals involved in any project are clear, so a specific level of participation for each of them can be defined. Participation does not mean complete access to all areas of the project in which everyone participates independent of their function. Experience shows that this lack of definition brings with it serious conflicts between technical staff and residents as well as delays in the carrying out of the projects.[2]

SCALE OF THE PROJECTS

One of the lessons that emerges from community-based projects is the importance of working at an appropriate scale. Some projects have involved a large number of participants but nearly all also group participants into small units within which members can more easily cooperate with each other. A concentration on supporting the projects of small groups does not mean a small-scale impact if a great number of small groups projects are supported. Working in small groups has secured the success of many credit initiatives. Two main advantages have been identified: the group has helped secure the loan repayments of individuals, and group members have supported each other in undertaking their initiatives. What is required for large scale impact is that the managing organization establishes an appropriate network within which small groups can operate successfully. The incorporation of small-scale interventions and theories based on concepts such as that of 'development on a human scale' (reinforced in the 1980s), have been fundamental in the process of changing the scale of community development projects.[3]

It is now accepted by some governments and bilateral and multilateral agencies that most large, centrally-organized projects bring few (if any) benefits to most low-income groups. But the reverse problem is also evident. For much of the 1970s and 1980s, there was a proliferation of so called 'pilot projects' in the Third World. For instance, in Latin America, it is very common to find NGOs working with low-income communities on the construction of a few dozen housing units.[4] The need to change the scale of the impact is one of the challenges currently facing those who, working for community development with the micro project concept, try to carry out programmes which will reach the greatest number of people without losing the qualities of a small-scale project. Because of the advantages of working at the small-scale, one of the keys is to seek ways of supporting a large range of small-scale projects. In some cases, small-scale projects can be realized even within large projects by giving much autonomy to small groups. Some of the points emerging from the case studies are noted below.

- The organizations which carry out credit programmes have noted that work in small groups has been one of the important factors in the success of their programmes. Among other advantages, this has allowed the authorization of credit, providing more flexible mechanisms for the accreditation, control and guarantees than are normally required by the formal financial sector. In most cases, the rate of repayment has been between 90 and 100 per cent. Repayments have been made within the time specified. In the few cases where there were failures to meet payments, this was due more to technical issues (lack of material delaying project completion, for example) than to a lack of willingness to repay.
- Work in small-scale groups has made it possible to have a continuous financial assessment, with ongoing contact between the staff and the beneficiaries of the project. This itself allows decisions to be made jointly between the staff and the inhabitants, strengthening people's confidence in their own abilities. It has also permitted a greater degree of community participation and project control. Participation and a broadening of decision-making which takes place in a small group may slow down the processes necessary for carrying out the project. This is one reason why more work must be undertaken to develop methodologies which, while maintaining the level of participation in the project, allow the programmes to be carried out within the agreed timetable.
- Although there is a consensus in public, private, national and international organizations about the desirability of working with small groups of inhabitants, there is a tremendous need for professional training that goes with this kind of project. Methodologies for passing from small projects to large ones or greatly increasing the number of small projects which succeed seem to be critical in making this kind of intervention more effective.
- One of the most serious disincentives to community participation and activity is discontinuity in projects and programmes. The feeling that the efforts which have helped to initiate a project might be discontinued discourages residents who may simply withdraw their support. It is very common for external agencies to fund one intervention in a low-income settlement, providing only a very partial solution to problems there, and then move to fund another project elsewhere. It is hardly surprising that low-income groups feel discouraged, and even view with some hostility some other external agency which suddenly promises 'another project'. If

there are resources – human and otherwise – which can be put to the service of the communities so that they can develop their initiatives, another of the challenges to be met is to ensure the continuity of the projects and the community processes associated with implementation, however modest in scale. In every low-income settlement lacking basic services and infrastructure and with poor-quality housing, the inhabitants want a continuous process of improvement, not a series of individual projects with no certainty that the forthcoming project will be acceptable to donors.

THE COORDINATION AND PARTICIPATION OF DIFFERENT GROUPS

The need for better coordination between the different organizations, groups and individuals carrying out community projects has long been recognized. More recently, such coordination, combined with a better match between existing community and external resources, has been judged to be of prime importance for policies which are more effective at reducing poverty. The importance of these two factors is heightened further by the crisis in government evident in most Third World countries, the (usually advancing) democratization processes, the consolidation of NGOs which support communities in carrying out projects and, most importantly, the increase in community participation in the projects. The 'models' of project management in which coordination and more careful matching of resources are central are still sufficiently new for it to be impossible to make categorical judgements about how effectively they function. However, it is possible to suggest some conclusions arising from the use of such models:

- Careful attention to coordination has allowed the efforts of different social groups to be effectively combined in certain development projects. This can be seen in the case studies of Barrio San Jorge and the work of the Carvajal Foundation. Agreement on project strategies has made it possible to avoid the imposition of one action on top of another and to establish clearly the responsibilities of each institution within the project.
- The combined effort and participation of different people and institutions in the resolution of problems has given rise to many varied, creative and novel alternatives. This can be seen in the tremendous innovation and diversity within the case studies both in technical solutions and in financial measures.
- There are certain important characteristics in the role taken by the different groups in the field of coordination:
  - There has been a greater degree of commitment from government organizations when they 'jointly' participate with community organizations, NGOs, and other actors in devising and executing the social development projects.
  - Private enterprise can have a role in these projects, as can be seen in the case of the Fundacion Carvajal. Such organizations can provide

important support in carrying out social development projects. Richer groups may also contribute if sufficiently attractive projects are put forward.[5]

– The community often gains a greater influence when decisions are taken within a coordinated project but it also makes a greater commitment through being more involved. The NGOs have generally taken on the role of managers and coordinators in these kinds of initiatives, as well as offering technical support for the projects.

• On occasions, other institutions, such as the church[6] or university[7] or technical training centre have also taken an important role. The inclusion of all those who are willing and able to contribute their resources is important.

INTERNAL FINANCING SYSTEM OF PROJECTS

The possibility for all development programmes and projects to include a credit component (for individual loans for housing or to support small businesses, or develop community infrastructure and services) is essential to enable the population to achieve an improvement in the quality of living. The exclusion of the poor – both individually and as a group – from the formal credit markets is not necessarily due to the fact that they cannot pay the rates of interest the market requires or to the inability to make repayments within the periods agreed. Some of the problems are the lack of experience in dealing with different aspects of finance, the insecurity which this causes, the inaccessibility of banks' branches, and a lack of sufficient guarantees and incomes for their applications to be accepted.

Several conclusions can be drawn from the case studies included in this book.

• The scale of support needed to introduce effective credit schemes is not large. Successful schemes have drawn on a number of other sources of funds such as local banks, participants' own savings, government support (either local or national), and participants' labour or other goods in kind. Successful credit programmes are those which use external credit as a catalyst to draw in or mobilize other resources.

• In the cases studied here, repayment has not been a major problem. This clearly has been a problem in some other cases and there is a need to think carefully how to ensure that money can be repaid for any activity undertaken which is financed by a loan. There are several lessons which emerge in regard to establishing successful schemes: use of social pressure to ensure repayment through establishing small groups with some degree of collective responsibility for repayment, providing small loans for a relatively short period of time, and penalties for those who do not repay.

• Analysis of the case studies of housing and infrastructure projects shows a large variety of different schemes with differing characteristics. For instance, there is a considerable variety in the project timescale, the amount invested, and the type of investment (for example, it may be for shelter improvement, partial construction or new developments). This obviously reflects both the needs and resources of participants, and those of the initiating and supporting organizations. It is difficult to generalize as to a model for the 'right kind' of project since the model will be one which differs from case to case, to reflect different circumstances.

- Participants in credit schemes are rarely allowed to choose to divide the money, allocating part to housing and part to income-generation needs. Most organizations concentrate on meeting one kind of credit need, although a few have separate, specific programmes for each. Generally, more favourable terms are offered for housing investment with subsidies provided by supporting organizations or government.
- One feature common to successful projects is that they are based around the more efficient use of resources, with a particular focus on investment so that the community is better able to make use of existing resources. For example, they involve the training of participants to help them use their energies and resources more effectively. Community development is included to enhance the efficiency of collective activities. Effective community organization also offers greater political power; lobbying and negotiating becomes possible. Many projects encourage the formation of new partnerships in order to enable more activities to be undertaken. Credit opportunities enable household income to be turned into a capital asset. In making such investments, the role of NGOs is often critical. There are limits as to what individual community organizations can achieve by themselves.
- A number of serious limitations are also evident from the case studies. First, it may be hard to reach the very poor through credit – some case studies identify this as a problem, others do not. Many of the poorest individuals and households live and work in locations with less possibility of community organization developing – or less possibility of collective action and organization being able to address their problems. Second, there remains a question in regard to the replication of successful experiences. Some of the case studies involve projects which are very neighbourhood-specific. The extent to which even some of the processes used can be replicated elsewhere remains unclear. Third, many of the housing, infrastructure and basic-service projects identified in the case studies involve a financial subsidy (either in the provision of credit or grants or through the full costs of administration and support not being charged back to participants). This means that it is hard to replicate such projects on a large scale without substantial grant-funding.

EFFICIENCY AND EFFECTIVENESS IN UNDERTAKING PROJECTS

Development programmes and projects suffer in many cases from a lack of efficiency and effectiveness. Lack of 'efficiency' is reflected in inadequate provisions for technical and administrative support and/or in poor management of the programmes' funds. Programmes and projects have also, on occasion, been 'ineffective', in that they have failed to achieve their objectives (technical, social, financial). The institutional management of organizations (public or private) that is responsible for promoting development programmes and projects is often weak and conveys this weakness both to those in other organizations and to those working in the programmes.

From the cases that have been studied, it has been possible to draw some conclusions on this:

- Efficient and effective projects require the inhabitants' participation in the design, management, and evaluation of programmes and projects.[7]
- Poor management and a lack of appropriate methodologies to carry out these kinds of processes have, in many cases, led to longer periods being needed for implementation. The different systems and methods for designing, developing and implementing the kinds of projects discussed here have not been systemized and evaluated. The lack of professional training, and of the development and dissemination of methodologies, represents one of the main obstacles to be overcome. This lack of knowledge leads to wastage in the organizations that participate in projects and often causes serious financial difficulties.
- The lack of technical training among staff from the NGOs and, above all, government organizations, to carry out participatory projects, is a serious barrier to realizing such projects. Certain institutions have been seeking to develop appropriate techniques and methodologies – for instance the German agency GTZ, the International Union of Local Authorities (IULA) and the Massachusetts Institute of Technology, USA. Such institutions have identified the difficulties underlying the design and implementation of participatory projects for local development. At present, they are trying out these methodologies in various countries. They offer different training programmes for NGO professionals and civil servants who work on developing and implementing projects dealing with poverty in the Third World.[9] Donors may also be willing to support Southern institutions to provide training to enhance housing and neighbourhood development programmes. For example, the Asian Coalition for Housing Rights has just begun a three-year training programme for Asian NGOs and community organizations.
- The use of commercial and administrative practices in carrying out local development projects is gaining wider acceptance. Established and agreed criteria for participation and community development is being brought together with efficient production methods both to consolidate the structures and informal practices used by low-income communities and to incorporate these communities into the formal sector.[10]
- Efficient and effective methods for undertaking projects are usually stipulated fairly clearly in programme and project objectives. But it remains necessary to place a strong emphasis on the need to evaluate the extent to which these objectives are met. Two different sets of objectives can be identified:

  1. Technical objectives. Projects dealing with urban poverty should aim at a high quality of product, be this a house, an enterprise, improved

infrastructure or some other item. The fact that this is 'for the poor' does not necessarily mean that costs can be saved by lowering quality; on many occasions, the importance of quality is underestimated. It is common to see, for example, low income districts constructed cheaply which reveal serious technical problems that are difficult or impossible to resolve within a short time of being built.[11] In addition, where communal infrastructure or services are being provided, it may be that the intensity with which they will be used and the need for local management and repair justifies higher quality standards of provision.[12]

2. Social objectives. It is very difficult to measure the social impact of projects and initiatives such as those included in the case studies: for example, the extent to which the objective of developing the community and achieving self-management in the community organizations has been realized. The analysis and evaluation of the real impact of projects in terms of strengthening the self-esteem of the inhabitants and their capacity for self-organization, negotiation and management of funds must be included, together with a commitment to developing the methodology for such analyses.

6

Notes and references

THE NEED FOR INVESTMENT

1   This is the figure for the Third World's urban population given by a draft of the 1992 estimates of the United Nations. The latest published estimate is 1.5 billion, in United Nations (1991), *World Urbanization Prospects 1990; Estimates and Projections of Urban and Rural Populations and of Urban Agglomerations*, United Nations, ST/ESA/SER.a/121, New York.
2   Cairncross, Sandy, Jorge E. Hardoy and David Satterthwaite (1990), 'The urban context', in Jorge E. Hardoy et al. (eds), *The Poor Die Young*, Earthscan Publications, London.
3   See for instance McKeown, Thomas (1988), *The Origins of Human Disease*, Basil Blackwell, Oxford and New York.
4   See for instance Cochrane, Glynn (1983), *Policies for Strengthening Local Government in Developing Countries*, World Bank Staff Working Paper No. 582, The World Bank, Washington DC; Stren, Richard E (1989), 'Urban local government', in Richard E. Stren and Rodney R. White (eds), *African Cities in Crisis*, Westview Press, Boulder; and special issue of *Environment and Urbanization* on 'Rethinking Local Government: Views from the Third World', Vol. 3, No. 1, April 1991.
5   Hardoy, Jorge E. and David Satterthwaite (1989), *Squatter Citizen*, Earthscan Publications, London.
6   Ibid.
7   Cointreau, Sandra J. (1982), *Environmental Management of Urban Solid Wastes in Developing Countries: a Project Guide*, Urban Development Technical Paper, No. 5, The World Bank, Washington DC.
8   Aina, Tade Akin (1989), *Health, Habitat and Underdevelopment – with Special Reference to a Low-Income Settlement in Metropolitan Lagos*, IIED Technical Report, IIED, London; and Murphy, Denis (1990), *A Decent Place to Live – Urban Poor in Asia*, Asian Coalition for Housing Rights, Bangkok.
9   See *Environment and Urbanization* (1989), Vol. 1, No. 1, (special issue entitled 'Environmental Problems in Third World Cities').
10 Cooper Weil, Diana E., Adelaida P. Alicbusan, John F. Wilson, Michael A. Reich and David J. Bradley (1990), *The Impact of Development Policies on Health: A Review of the Literature*, World Health Organization, Geneva.
11 Stephens, Carolyn, Trudy Harpham, David Bradley and Sandy Cairncross (1991), *A Review of the Health Impacts of Environmental Problems in Urban Areas of Developing Countries*, Paper prepared for the Panel on Urbanization of the WHO Commission on Health and the Environment, London School of Hygiene and Tropical Medicine, London.
12 Belmartino, Susana, Carlos Bloch, Jorge E. Hardoy and Hilda Herzer (1989), *Urbanization and its Implications for Child Health: Potential for Action*, World Health Organization, Geneva.
13 See for instance Adrianza, B.T. and G.C. Graham (1974), 'The high cost of being poor: water' *Architecture and Environmental Health* No. 28, pp. 312–315; and World Bank

(1991), *Urban Policy and Economic Development: an Agenda for the 1990s*, The World Bank, Washington DC.
14   See note 11.
15   Esrey, S. A. and J. P. Habicht (1986), 'Epidemiologic evidence for health benefits from improved water and sanitation in developing countries', *Epidemiologic Reviews*, Vol. 8, quoted in Cairncross, Sandy et al. (1990), 'The urban context' in Hardoy et al. (1990), op. cit.
16   See note 7.
17   Flintoff, F. (1976), *Management of Solid Wastes in Developing Countries*, WHO (SEARO), New Delhi, quoted in Cointreau (1982), op. cit.
18   OECD (1989), *Development Cooperation: Efforts and Policies of the Members of the Development Assistance Committee – 1989 Report*, Organization for Economic Cooperation and Development, Paris.
19   Kasarda, John D. and Edward M. Crenshaw (1991), 'Third World urbanization: dimensions, theories and determinants', *Annual Review of Sociology*, Vol. 17, pp. 467–501.
20   Hardoy, Jorge E. and David Satterthwaite (1991), 'Environmental problems in Third World cities: a global issue ignored?', *Public Administration and Development*, Vol. 11, pp. 341–361.

THE FAILURE OF THE CONVENTIONAL MODEL

1   Cairncross, Sandy (1990), 'Water supply and the urban poor' in Jorge E. Hardoy et al. (eds), *The Poor Die Young: Housing and Health in Third World Cities*, Earthscan Publications, London pp. 109–126.
2   Ibid; and Sinnatamby, Gehan (1990), 'Low cost sanitation' in Hardoy et al. (1990), ibid, pp. 127–167
3   This draws on evaluations of 31 Third World governments' housing, land and settlement policies undertaken by IIED's Human Settlements Programme in collaboration with research teams in Argentina, the Sudan, Nigeria, Kenya and India as well as other published material on this subject. See Chapters 3 to 5 in Hardoy, Jorge E. and David Satterthwaite (1989), *Squatter Citizen*, Earthscan Publications, London, for a more detailed summary.
4   See case studies and chapters by editors in Moser, Caroline O.N. and Linda Peake (eds) (1987), *Women, Housing and Human Settlements*, Tavistock Publications, London and New York.
5   Hardoy and Satterthwaite (1989), see note 3; see also Silas, Johan (1992), 'Environmental management in Surabaya's Kampungs', *Environment and Urbanization*, Vol. 4, No. 2, October.
6   UNCHS (1987), *Global Report on Human Settlements 1986*, Oxford University Press, Oxford.
7   Ibid.
8   Renaud, Bertrand (1981), *National Urbanization Policies in Developing Countries*, Oxford University Press, Oxford.
9   Hardoy and Satterthwaite (1989), see note 3.
10   Editorial in *Environment and Urbanization*, Vol. 3, No. 1 (special issue entitled 'Rethinking Local Government – Views from the Third World').
11   Stren, Richard and Rodney White (eds) (1989), *African Cities in Crisis: Managing Rapid Urban Growth*, Westview Press, Boulder.
12   Bird, Richard (1978), *Inter-Governmental Fiscal Relations in Developing Countries*, World Bank Staff Working Paper No. 304, The World Bank, Washington DC.
13   Stren and White (1989), see note 11; see also papers in *Environment and Urbanization*, Vol. 3, No. 1 (special issue entitled 'Rethinking Local Government–Views from the Third World')
14   Cairncross, Sandy (1990) 'Water supply and the urban poor' in Jorge E. Hardoy et al. (eds), *The Poor Die Young: Housing and Health in Third World Cities*, Earthscan Publications, London, pp. 109–126.
15.   See table in World Bank, (1988), *World Development Report 1988*, Oxford University Press,

Oxford. See also Roth, Gabriel (1987), *The Private Provision of Public Services in Developing Countries*, Oxford University Press, Oxford.
16   Stren and White (1989), see note 11.
17   Guarda, Gian Carlo (1990), 'A new direction in World Bank urban lending in Latin American countries', *Review of Urban and Regional Development Studies* Vol. 2, No. 2, July, pp. 116–124.

THE ROLE OF NGOS IN COMMUNITY DEVELOPMENT

1   See for instance: Asian Coalition for Housing Rights (1989), 'Evictions in Seoul, South Korea', *Environment and Urbanization* Vol. 1, No. 1; Hardoy, Jorge E. and David Satterthwaite (1989), *Squatter Citizen: Life in the Urban Third World*, Earthscan Publications, London; Stren, Richard E. (1989) 'Administration of Urban Services', in Richard E. Stren and Rodney R. White (eds), *African Cities in Crisis*, Westview Press drawing from: Dieng, Isidore, M'Baye (1977) *Relogement de Bidonvillois a la Peripherie urbaine*, ENDA, Dakar, 1977; and Portes, Alejandro (1979), 'Housing policy, urban poverty and the state: the favelas of Rio de Janeiro', *Latin American Research Review* No. 14, Summer 1979, pp. 3–24 and *Revista Interamericana de Planificacion* No. 13, March 1979, pp. 103–124.
2   See, for instance, Silas, Johan and Eddy Indrayana (1988), 'Kampung Banyu Urip' in Bertha Turner (ed.), *Building Community, a Third World Case Book*, Habitat International Coalition, London.
3   Moser, Caroline O.N. (1989), 'Community participation in urban projects in the Third World', *Progress in Planning* Vol. 32, No. 2, Pergamon Press, Oxford.
4   World Health Organization (1987), 'Housing and Health, a Programme for Action', Geneva, Switzerland. See also World Health Organization (1990), *Environmental Health in Urban Development* – report of a WHO Expert Committee, Technical Report Series 807, Geneva.
5   Inter-American Foundation (1991), *1990 Annual Report*, Washington DC.
6   World Bank (1991), *The World Bank and Non Governmental Organizations*, Washington DC. Some World Bank loans have supported NGO housing programmes, as in the loans to FUNDASAL (El Salvador), or have supported programmes in which NGOs took a major role, as in the support for upgrading in Lusaka (Zambia). World Bank loans have also been provided to government funds which support community-based projects – for instance in the World Bank loans to FONHAPO in Mexico; see case study 8 for more details.
7   Cousins, William J. (1989), *Unicef in the Cities: a History of Urban Basic Services Programme*, Monograph, UNICEF, New York, December. See also UNICEF (1988), *Improving Environment for Child Health and Survival*, Urban Examples No. 15, UNICEF, New York; and UNICEF (1983), *UNICEF and Non-Governmental Organizations* – a Report by Martin Ennals, United Nations Economic and Social Council document no. E/ICEF/NGO/209, New York.
8   SIDA (1990), *Development Cooperation; Sida Infrastructure Division*, Stockholm, and Sevilla, Manuel (1993), 'New approaches for aid agencies; FUPROVI's community based shelter programme', *Environment and Urbanization* Vol. 5, No. 1, April, London.
9   UNCHS (no date), *The UNCHS (Habitat) Community Development Programme*, Nairobi
10   Tensions can also arise within community organizations during a transition to multi-party democracy which limit the scope of community-based actions; see for instance Cuenya, Beatriz, Diego Armus, Maria Di Loreto and Susana Penalva (1990), 'Land invasions and grassroots organization: the Quilmes settlement in Greater Buenos Aires, Argentina', *Environment and Urbanization* Vol. 2, No. 1, April, London.
11   See Inter-American Foundation (1990), *A Guide to NGO Directories*, Virginia.
12   Hasan, Samiul, George Mulamoottil and J.E. Kersell (1992), 'Voluntary organizations in Bangladesh: a Profile', *Environment and Urbanization* Vol. 4, No. 2, October, London.
13   Private correspondence from Paul Ghils, Union of International Assocations, quoted in Samuel Paul and Arturo Israel (eds) (1991), *Non Governmental Organizations and The World Bank*, World Bank, Washington DC

14 OECD (1988), *Voluntary Aid for Development: the role of Non-Governmental Organizations*, Organization for Economic Cooperation and Development, Paris.

15 Gorman, Robert F. (1984), *Private Voluntary Organizations as Agents of Development*, Westview Press, Boulder and London.

16 Landim, Leilah (1987), 'Non-governmental organizations in Latin America', *World Development* Vol. 15 supplement, Pergamon Press, Oxford.

17 Black, Maggie (1986), *The Children and the Nations: The Story of UNICEF*, UNICEF, New York.

18 OECD (1990), *Development Cooperation: Efforts and Policies of the Members of the Development Assistance Committee*, Organization for Economic Cooperation and Development, Paris.

19 SINA (1987), *NGOs and Shelter*, Settlements Information Network Africa, Mazingira Institute, Nairobi.

20 PRIA (1989), *NGO–Government Relations: A source of life or a kiss of death?* Delhi.

21 Hardoy, Jorge E. and David Satterthwaite (1987), 'Laying the Foundations: NGOs help to house Latin America's Poor', *Development Forum*, October (part 1) and November (part 2), New York.

22 See, for instance, the work of Habitat International Coalition and the Asian Coalition for Housing Rights in an NGO profile in *Environment and Urbanization* Vol. 2, No. 1, April 1990 and the work of HIC Women and Shelter Network in an NGO Profile in *Environment and Urbanization* Vol. 3, No.2, October 1991.

23 For example, see: Mendez, Lopezllera (1988), *Sociedad civil y pueblos emer-gentes*, PDP Mexico; Godofredo, Sandoval (1988), *Organizaciones no Gubernamentales de Desarrollo en America latina y El Caribe*, UNITAS, Bolivia; Padrón, Mario (1982), *Cooperación al Desarrollo y Movimeinto Popular: las organizaciones privadas de desarrollo*, DESCO, Peru; and, World Bank (1991), *Cooperation between the World Bank and NGOs*, World Bank, Washington DC.

24 Padron (1982), see note 23.

25 See note 23.

26 CEDOIS (1989), *Directorio de Institutiones Privadas de Interés Social de la République Dominica*, Editorial CENAPEC, Santo Domingo, Dominican Republic.

27 See Turner, John F.C. (1988), 'Introduction' and 'Issues and conclusions' in Bertha Turner (ed.), *Building Community, a Third World Case Book*, Habitat International Coalition, London.

28 Mendez (1988), see note 23.

29 Clark, John (1991), *Democratizing Development – The Role of Voluntary Organizations*, Earthscan Publications, London.

30 Salamon, Lester and Helmut K. Anheier (1992), *In Search of the Nonprofit Sector 1: The Question of Definitions*, Working Paper 2, Johns Hopkins Comparative Nonprofit Sector Project, Johns Hopkins University Institute for Policy Studies, Baltimore.

31 See note 16 and Garcia-Guadilla, Maria Pinar and Jutta Blauert (eds) (1992), 'Environmental social movements in Latin America and Europe: challenging development and democracy', *International Journal of Social Policy*, Vol. 12, Nos 4–7, Hull.

32 Berger, Peter L. and Richard John Neuhaus (1977), *To Empower People: The Role of Mediating Structures in Public Policy*, American Enterprise Institute for Public Policy Research, Washington DC.

33 The UN System of National Accounts defines organizations which receive half or more of their income from government to be a part of government regardless of other characteristics. This is discussed in Salamon, Lester and Helmut K. Anheier (1992), *In Search of the Nonprofit Sector 1: The Question of Definitions*, Working Paper 2, The Johns Hopkins Comparative Nonprofit Sector Project, Johns Hopkins University Institute for Policy Studies, Baltimore.

34 Ingersoll, T.G. and P.W. Ingersoll (eds) (1990), *Towards Partnership in Africa*, Interaction and FOVAD, Massachusetts.

35 Ba, Hassan with the collaboration of Cristophe Nuttall (1990), 'Village associations on the riverbanks of Senegal: the new development actors', *Voices from Africa* Issue No. 2, NGLS, pp. 83–104.

36 Jorgensen, Steen, Margaret Grosh and Mark Schacter (1992), *Bolivia's Answer to Poverty, Economic Crisis and Adjustment: The Emergency Social Fund*, World Bank, Washington DC.

37   Many authors discuss distinctions between different types of NGOs. For example see the publications in notes 13, 14, 29 and 40.
38   Theunis, Sjef (ed.) (1992), *Non-governmental Development Organizations of Developing Countries: And the South Smiles*, Martinus Nijhoff, Dordrecht.
39   Verhagen, Koenraad (1987), *Self-help Promotion: a Challenge to the NGO Community*, CEBEMO/The Royal Tropical Institute, Amsterdam.
40   Korten, David C. (1990), *Getting to the 21st Century: Voluntary Action and the Global Agenda*, Kumarian Press, Connecticut.
41   See note 30.
42   Cassell, Michael (no date), *Inside Nationwide: One Hundred Years of Cooperation*, Nationwide Building Society, London.
43   Dichter, Thomas W. (1988), 'The changing world of northern NGOs: problems, paradoxes and possibilities', in John Lewis (ed.), *Strengthening the Poor: What have we Learned?*, Transaction Books, New Brunswick.
44   The Limuru Declaration – Declaration by representatives of 45 Third World NGOs and 12 international NGOs after a seminar in Limuru in April 1987, published in Bertha Turner (ed.) (1988), *Building Community, a Third World Case Book*, Habitat International Coalition, London.
45   The World Commission on Environment and Development (1987), *Our Common Future*, Oxford University Press, Oxford, p.251. In a meeting called by the United Nations Development Programme to study future strategies for sustained development and the environment in Latin America and the Caribbean, a key role was once again assigned to the NGOs.
46   World Commission on Environment and Development (1987), see note 45.
47   Paul, Samuel and Arturo Israel (eds) (1991), *Non Governmental Organizations and The World Bank*, World Bank, Washington DC
48   Clark (1991), see note 29.

INNOVATIVE CREDIT SCHEMES

1   Renaud, Bertrand (1981), *National Urbanization Policies in Developing Countries*, Oxford University Press, Oxford.
2   For example, see Patel, Sheela and Celine d'Cruz (1993), 'The Mahila Milan crisis credit scheme: from a seed to a tree', *Environment and Urbanization*, Vol. 5, No. 1, London.
3   Housing Finance Workshop (1993), MISEREOR/ACHR
4   Schmidt, R. H. and Erhard Kropp (1987), *Rural Finance: Guiding Principles, GTZ and DSE*, Bonn, Eschborn and Berlin.
5   Hurley, Donnacadh (1990), *Income Generations Schemes for the Urban Poor*, Oxfam, Oxford.
6   For example, see: McLeod, Ruth and Diana Mitlin (1993), 'The search for sustainable funding systems for community initiatives', *Environment and Urbanization*, Vol. 5, No. 1, London.
7   See note 3
8   World Bank (1990), *The World Development Report 1990*, Oxford University Press, Oxford.
9   See note 3 above; and Remenyi, Joe (1991), *Where Credit is Due*, Intermediate Technology Publications, London.
10   See note 6.
11   See note 5.
12   IFAD (1988), *International Seminar on Credit for Rural Women*, Rome.
13   See for instance Oruwari, Yomi (1991), 'The changing role of women in families and their housing needs: a case study of Port Harcourt' in *Environment and Urbanization*, Vol. 3, No. 2, London.
14   Moser, Caroline O.N. and Linda Peake (eds) (1987), *Women, Housing and Human Settlements*, Tavistock Publications, London and New York.
15   See for instance: Falu, Ana and Mirina Curutchet (1991), 'Rehousing the urban poor: looking at women first', in *Environment and Urbanization*, Vol. 3, No. 2, London.

CONCLUSIONS

Part of this text draws on an earlier document prepared by the authors: *Reaching Summit Goals in Urban Areas: New Means and New Partnerships*, Unicef Urban Examples No. 18 (forthcoming).

1   Housing Finance Workshop (1993), MISEREOR/ACHR
2   See for instance Silva, Mauricio (1986) 'La participacion comunitaria en Programas Sociales', *Revista Interamericana de Planificacion*, SIAP.
3   Put forward by, amongst others, M. Max-Neff, Elizalde, A and Hopenhayn, M (1986), 'Desarrollo a escala humana, una opcion para el futuro', CEPADUR, Santiago de Chile. This concept has also been influenced by such studies as 'El Hilo Conductor', edited by FUNDASAL in El Salvador in the 1970s.
4   Particularly in Latin America, NGOs have drawn a large part of their support from these kinds of projects. For instance, a research project undertaken by the IIED-AL on the role of the NGOs analysed nearly 150 projects in Latin America and found that in the last two decades, the average number of housing units constructed by NGO projects was not more than 80, in projects which lasted on average more than two years. For more details see IIED-AL (1991), 'El rol de las ONGs en America Latina', mimeograph, Buenos Aires, Argentina.
5   The Fundacion Carvajal has been able to channel a large amount of financial investment from large Colombian businesses to develop social programmes. This business capital generally exists in Third World countries but it is not exploited or sought by NGOs and public organizations to contribute to community development projects.
6   In Latin America, Christian churches have been the initiators of a large number of development projects in communities. For example, they have had a crucial role in: (a) the creation of NGOs (such as FUNDASAL in El Salvador or la Fundacion Vivienda y Comunidad – the Housing and Community Foundation–in Argentina); (b) providing financial support for projects (the World Council of Churches and large church-directed funding institutions such as MISEREOR in Germany or CEBEMO in the Netherlands have all financed a large number of projects of this nature); and (c) providing other support for projects (for example, contributing land for urban development in San José de Costa Rica, Lima or Buenos Aires).
7   One among many examples is the Faculty of Architecture in the University San Simon in Cochabamba, Bolivia, which provided assistance with the analysis and evaluation for the Bolivian Social Emergency Fund. Another example is the work of the Faculty of Architecture in the University of Buenos Aires, Argentina, working with the municipality of the city of Campana, with technical and financial support from the Swiss Federal Government's official bilateral agency (DDA) and IREC of Switzerland. Working with other local groups, a complete programme for local development has been worked out in the peripheral areas of the municipality.
8   There have been cases which clearly reflect the value of the community's control, such as the Roofing Programme, carried out by the Republic of Argentina's National Mortgage Bank between 1985 and 1989. The programme involved approximately 50 local development projects throughout the country with community participation. In an evaluation of this programme, a reduction in costs and an improvement in completion time was noted in those cases where the communities took on a greater role in project management and development.
9   For instance, there are the following manuals: Reinhard Goethert and Nabeel Hamdi (1987), 'La Microplanificacion. Un proceso de programacion y desarrollo con base en la comunidad', developed in MIT, USA and used in recent years in poor urban and rural municipalities in Chile, Sri Lanka, and other countries in the region; GTZ (1988), 'Planificacion y Gestion de Proyectos de Mejoramiento Urbano', prepared by the German Agency for Technical Cooperation, GTZ, based on the ZOPP methodology developed by the same institution and used in various countries in the Third World; Hector Sanin (1989), 'Manual de Administracion de Proyectos de Desarrollo Local', prepared at the request of the IULA Latin American office and CELCADEL, Latin American Centre for Training and Development of Local Government, used in Latin American countries such as Colombia, Peru, Costa Rica and Ecuador.

Since 1991, IIED-Latin America, with the support of the Economic Development Institute of the World Bank (EDI), have been carrying out a training programme for NGOs and civil servants in 'Developing, Executing and Evaluating Programmes and Projects Dealing with Poverty in Latin America.' This Programme has a regional focus and is expected to train technicians in about 600 public and private institutions over its three year duration.

10   Institutions such as International Action have recently introduced very specific criteria for business efficiency when offering technical and financial support to poor communities with the establishment of small businesses. International Action is a private, non profit making institution in the United States of America, set up to provide technical and financial support for small business projects in Latin American countries. It is presently working with a network of NGOs located in almost all the countries in the region.

11   Differences can be observed, for example, between the districts established by the projects included in the ATEPAM programme (Self-construction Programme with Technical Assistance, Individual Effort and Mutual Assistance) undertaken by the government of the Province of Buenos Aires, Argentina, in the 1960s and 1970s and the units of housing established by the Programmes carried out by the Uruguayan Cooperative Centre, CCU, in the same period. With the same criteria for community participation, self-construction and district organization, better technical results were achieved in Uruguay than in Argentina. See Balista, Jose (1981), 'La participacion en los programas de autoconstruccion con asistencia tecnica en la Provincia de Buenos Aires' CONICEYT-SVOA, Buenos Aires, Argentina; or CCU (1985), 'El cooperativismo y la ayuda mutua en el Uruguay', in *CCU Journal*, Montevideo, Uruguay.

12   See for example, Gakenheimer, Ralph and C.H.J. Brando (1987), 'Infrastructure standards' in Lloyd Rodwin (ed.), *Shelter, Settlement and Development*, Allen and Unwin, Boston.

Part II

CASE STUDIES

1

Bangladesh Rural Advancement Committee (BRAC), Bangladesh

6 Mohakhali Commercial Area
Dhaka – 1212
Bangladesh

INSTITUTION

Background

The Bangladesh Rural Advancement Committee is a non-governmental voluntary organization which works with rural landless communities, with a special emphasis on women's development. The organization began work following the Bangladeshi war of liberation and, since its inception in 1972, has adopted poverty alleviation as a key objective. Its main focus is now to develop viable organizations for the rural landless and to extend credit facilities to improve their socio-economic conditions.

Programme and activities

The Committee began work on its Rural Development Programme in 1986, and is now working in 3664 villages in 26 districts of Bangladesh. Just over 7000 village organizations have been formed, 60 per cent of which are women's organizations. Total membership is 398,830 and the organization has a staff of about 4000. Total expenditure in the year ending 31 December 1990 was 348 million Tk (just under US$10 million).

The Rural Development Programme is the major integrated, multi-sectoral programme of the Committee. The Programme involves four main components: institution building, credit operation, income and employment generation, and support services. Work in new areas starts with the implementation of such a programme. After an average of four years in a village, the necessary institutional framework has been established to initiate credit activities without the subsidized support considered necessary for the Rural Development Programme itself. Each Rural Development Programme includes about six regular staff, and 10 to 12 part-time staff, and involves some 50 villages with a total membership of 6–7000.

From inception to the end of 1990, the Bangladesh Rural Advancement Committee had distributed 68 million Tk (US$1.9 million) through its credit programme, 62 per cent of which has been advanced to women. The recovery rate for loans repayable to date is 98 per cent. The largest number of loans (both in terms of numbers of loans and amount allocated) has been for rural trading activities.

THE RURAL DEVELOPMENT PROGRAMME AND ITS CREDIT COMPONENT

Introduction

The credit component is well integrated into the Rural Development Programme. The basis used for distributing the credit is established through the institution-building work; and the credit scheme itself supports some of the income-generation activities. The support services complement the operation of the credit programme both directly, by monitoring its work, and indirectly, by facilitating the operation of the other programme components.

The particular objectives of the credit programme are to:

- stimulate employment and income both for men and women;
- mobilize underutilized and unutilized local resources; and
- diffuse technology and promote better health care.

Credit is mainly given for income-generation projects.

The Committee considers that institution building is fundamental to the successful operation of its Rural Development Programme. The institution-building component is centred around Village Organizations which are formed of between 50 and 70 people, members being divided into small groups of between five and seven people. Each small group appoints a secretary and the Village Organization chooses a management committee of between seven and ten members from these secretaries.

Projects and activities

Financial aspects, both credit and savings, are a major focus of the weekly meetings of each small group. All group members are encouraged to participate in a savings programme and are each expected to save 2 Tk (US$0.06) every week. The aim of the fund is both to encourage the habit of saving, and to provide a fund which is available in emergencies. Up to December 1990, 103 million Tk (US$2.9 million) had been saved by individual members. A further 20 million Tk (US$0.6 million) is currently being held in the group fund, to which contributions are made when loans are disbursed (see below). During 1990, an insurance policy was introduced for members. To join the policy, members must have been with a group for more than one year, and be less than 54 years of age. An insurance benefit of 5000 Tk

(US$143) is payable to a designated individual on the demise of the insured person. Members do not pay a premium. The fund is generated by a compulsory 1 per cent deduction from loan disbursements. In the six months to December 1990, just over 4 per cent of the membership had joined.

Training is considered to be a vital component of the Rural Development Programme; this training supports community development, the activities undertaken through credit, and the management of the finance itself. It is divided into two kinds: Human Resource Development Training, which includes courses in functional education, consciousness-raising, leadership development and project planning and management; and Occupation Skills Development Training, with courses in poultry-raising, agriculture, fish culture, sericulture and social forestry, both to develop existing expertise and to help with the acquisition of new skills appropriate for income-generation projects. To date, more than 200,000 members have undertaken one or more Human Resource Development courses, and about 75,000 members have attended a course in Occupation Skills Development.

There are few opportunities for many of the landless poor in traditional job markets and therefore the Bangladesh Rural Advancement Committee has undertaken activities to directly support income and employment generation. The Committee sees only limited possibilities for employment in farm activities and stresses the importance of the non-crop agricultural sector such as the ownership of agricultural equipment or irrigation assets (eg shallow or deep tubewells). The main income- and employment-generation projects which receive support are: irrigation, poultry and livestock, fisheries, sericulture and ericulture, rural transport and small-scale industries, and a new programme, social forestry. The provision of credit is often critical in enabling landless households to join these programmes.

There are two activities undertaken by BRAC within their Support Services Programme which are integrated into the credit programme: the income-generation scheme for particularly vulnerable groups and a programme to examine different alternative forms of rural enterprise.

Income-Generating for Vulnerable Group Development is a collaborative programme undertaken by BRAC and three other agencies: the World Food Programme, the Government's Directorate of Relief and Rehabilitation and the Department of Livestock. The objective of the programme is to improve the income-earning potential of destitute women. These women are given a monthly allocation of 31.25 kilograms of wheat, in addition to skills training in poultry-rearing and other support over a period of two years. The programme has been well received and has now been expanded so that it currently involves about 80,000 women.

The Rural Enterprise Project was started in 1985 with external funding. The purpose of the first phase of the project was to develop new and innovative income-generating activities for the landless poor. A second phase of the project has recently been initiated. The activities considered during 1990 were: shrimp-rearing, integrated farming, pigeon-rearing, horticulture projects, small carp hatcheries, agro-forestry, sugar cane developments, goat-rearing, restaurants, paddy-fish culture, carp polyculture, nilotika monoculture and new activities associated with poultry-rearing.

In October 1988, a monitoring unit was established to assist in developing an effective monitoring and management information system for the Rural Development Programme. Two years later the unit was upgraded and renamed the Monitoring Department. Its responsibilities now include monitoring the institution-building process through a participatory methodology involving 30 separate indicators. A detailed monitoring system has also been provided for the credit operation in order to assist management in meeting targets for disbursement and for recovery rates, including those for outstanding debts.

Operational details

Loans are disbursed through the small groups of members established through the institution-building programme. In order to qualify for a loan, members must have completed the compulsory part of the Functional Education training, and must have actively participated in the group to which they belong. They must hold an amount of personal savings equivalent to 5 per cent of the first loan requested, this figure rising to 10 per cent for the second loan and 15 per cent for all further loans.

Loan requests have to be presented to the group for approval and a majority of members must be present in order for a loan to be approved. Much stress is placed on group participation and responsibility. After approval, the proposals are submitted to the area manager. The loan is given to the recipient in the presence of the management committee for the group.

Priority is given to projects which have the potential to be economically and socially profitable. No collateral is required but loans are subject to continuous monitoring and supervision. Ten per cent of the value of the loan is immediately deducted in an attempt to 'bring the borrowers under the framework of certain credit discipline' (Annual Report, page 12). Of this 10 per cent, 5 per cent is deposited in the compulsory savings fund, 4 per cent in the group fund and 1 per cent allocated to the insurance fund. Borrowers pay 16 per cent interest calculated on the reducing balance and repayable in weekly instalments.

There are three types of loans: short-term loans which must be repaid within the year, medium-term loans which run for three years, and long-term loans whose duration depends on the type of project being undertaken. All loans are between 500 and 8000 Tk (US$14–228).

Up to the end of 1990, 686 million Tk (US$19.6 million) had been loaned to 264,378 group members for 140 different types of income- and employment-generating activities. Sixty one per cent of the total funds have been loaned to women. A large proportion (73 per cent) of these funds was for short-term loans, 17 per cent was for medium-term loans and the remainder for long-term loans.

Forty three per cent of loans was for activities in the rural trading sector; 20 per cent was for activities related to the keeping of livestock; food processing, 12 per cent; irrigation, 8 per cent; and rural industries and agriculture each equalled 6 per cent. All other activities accounted for less than 5 per cent of the total number of loans.

Assessment

There are three main reasons why BRAC follows a group-based lending system to operate its credit programme. First, such a strategy has been successful in securing high repayment rates. Second, it is easier to encourage and monitor savings through the groups and BRAC believes that this is an essential component of its programme. Finally, groups are seen as supporting its work in changing the mentality of the landless poor, and in particular overcoming their fatalism and assisting them to increase their opportunities.

The success of their system in securing repayment is evident. Cumulative repayment shows an upward trend, rising from 95 per cent in December 1989 to 98 per cent the following year. (These figures allow for one extension period on each loan which has not been repaid within the time originally allotted.) One weakness is that the savings are held on deposit in local banks, but the banks have not often used these funds to lend back to those depositing the money, preferring instead to lend to the formal sector which is often located in urban areas.

In respect of loans for some income- and employment-generation activities, the recovery rate has been low. For example, irrigation projects have suffered from problems caused by mechanical failures and inadequate supplies of essential inputs. The recovery rate on fish culture projects has also been low, partly accounted for by problems associated with unexpected floods. However, in general, high recovery rates have been achieved, indicating the success of the projects and the mechanism used for disbursing funds.

Sources: BRAC Annual Report 1990; Remenyi, Joe (1991), *Where Credit is Due: Income-generating programmes for the poor in developing countries*, Intermediate Technology Publications, London.

2

Barrio San Jorge, IIED–América Latina, Buenos Aires, Argentina

Piso 6, Cuerpo A
Corrientes 2835
1193 Buenos Aires
Argentina

INSTITUTION

Background

IIED-América Latina is a research NGO which has been in operation for over ten years. Based in Argentina, it undertakes research and policy work on sustainable development, with a particular focus on urban issues. It is also concerned with developing participatory ways of working with low-income groups in designing and implementing projects to improve housing and living conditions, and with increasing the capacity of Latin American NGOs and municipal governments to work with low-income groups and their community organizations.

Programmes and activities

The research programme has varied considerably since IIED-AL's inception. Key programmes at present include the following:

- *Rethinking the Latin American city* draws on a large network of researchers to review what has been learnt about urbanization and its causes, and what this suggests for more effective policies and actions. The principal aims are to identify the obstacles which prevent the poorest urban dwellers in the region from meeting their basic needs and to identify the main institutions and resources which might be mobilized in order to overcome deficiencies in basic services and infrastructure.
- *Local government in intermediate-size urban centres* is a joint project with partner institutions based in Bolivia, Brazil, Colombia, Chile, Ecuador and Peru which examines the capacity of municipal authorities in 21 urban centres to meet the needs of their citizens.

- *Sustainable development in Argentina* is a report compiled with assistance from other Argentine organizations. This report is one of a series which formed part of IIED's preparations for the 1992 UN Conference on Environment and Development.
- *A study of historical centres in Latin America* has also been completed. This examines how such centres might be best preserved whilst also meeting the needs and priorities of many of the low-income groups which live there.
- *Funding Community Level Initiatives* is a joint programme with IIED's London office. This book is a component of the programme.
- *Technical assistance* has been provided to many national and international organizations on urban planning, housing and health, development and the environment.
- *Capacity-building* is being undertaken through a three-year programme of workshops and seminars both for government officials and for the managerial and technical staff of non-governmental organizations.
- *The Barrio San Jorge project* is a long-term programme of support for a low-income district in the suburbs of Buenos Aires.

PROGRAMME OF SUPPORT FOR BARRIO SAN JORGE

Introduction

Most case studies of community action to improve housing and living conditions report from settlements in which a community organization has already been formed. This case study is unusual in that it describes an example of outside support helping the development of a representative community organization.

Barrio San Jorge is located in San Fernando, one of the municipalities on the periphery of Buenos Aires metropolitan area and some 35 kilometres north of the city centre. It covers a site of less than ten hectares located in the middle of a neglected environment of flat lowlands with few trees or shrubs. The Barrio is surrounded by vacant land plots (some of them subject to seasonal flooding), garbage dumps, polluted soil, factories and some isolated houses, and is close to an industrial area. The Reconquista river, which marks the northern boundary of the Barrio, is polluted by untreated industrial and household wastes which have been illegally deposited there. Two narrow streams, which form the east and west boundaries, are full of garbage – much of it put there by local residents because of the inadequate garbage collection service. The smell from the stagnant waters and untreated rubbish and the constant presence of flies, mosquitoes and rodents are depressing; the animals, insects and garbage dumps are also sources of infection, injury and disease. According to a census of the Barrio undertaken by IIED-América Latina in December 1990, there were 630 households and 2926 inhabitants. Forty-eight per cent of the population is female. As is usual in this type of settlement, a high proportion of the inhabitants are infants, children and adolescents and there are few elderly people.

Projects and activities

The mother and child centre

In 1987, after almost seven years of meetings with residents and with members of the local parish (Nuestra Senora del Carmen), a decision was reached to build a mother and child centre in the Barrio. The leader of the IIED-AL assistance group was asked to plan and coordinate the construction of the centre. With initial financial support from Caritas San Isidro – a branch of Caritas Argentina – the construction of a first stage of the centre (covering a surface of 68 square metres) began in September 1987. The centre received its first group of children in April 1988. The second and third stages, including a playground, were completed between 1989 and 1990.

Since 1990, the mother and child centre has been self-financing. It is run by a group of mothers whose children attend the centre. A successful campaign to obtain one scholarship for each child (US$120 per year) was launched in early 1990 and in two weeks contributions were obtained for all children from Argentine donors. In addition, the family of each child contributes the equivalent of four litres of milk per month and many mothers make a direct input to the centre. The staff of the mother and child centre includes a director, three teachers and a cook.

The women's workshop

In July 1989, 24 women from the Barrio, most of them linked to the mother and child centre, began a sewing and knitting workshop. This is both to train the women and to help them develop a permanent source of income. The products of the workshop are sold in the Barrio at very low prices and also to private customers in the locality. A teacher has now been hired. This programme was launched with support from the German Embassy in Argentina.

The house of the Barrio

In the winter of 1989, the programme purchased the right to use a lot with a derelict building on it. This building is situated in front of the chapel and close to the mother and child centre along one of the main access streets. Soon after the purchase and repair of the building, the women's workshop, a workshop for training adolescents, and a small community library began to use it. The 'House of the Barrio' is now also used for neighbourhood meetings and for a cloth and building-materials fair. In late 1990, a project for the expansion and reconstruction of the house was started with the help of residents.

The employment exchange

For more than two years, an employment exchange was run from the house of the project leader because there was no telephone in the Barrio. It was only after a long delay that it proved possible to have a telephone installed in the Barrio. Finally, in August 1990, a telephone line was installed in the 'House of the Barrio' from where the labour exchange now operates. Although it is a slow process, several women and young men have obtained employment – mostly short-term – in service activities, or in jobs such as gardening or bricklaying.

This telephone line was the first in the Barrio. Before it was installed, the inhabitants of San Jorge had to walk more than two kilometres to the nearest telephone in cases of emergency.

Improvement of streets and pavements
In 1989, several streets, covering around 30 per cent of the Barrio's layout, were selected for improvement. The work was done by the inhabitants, using waste from a nearby factory mixed with salt, cement and water.

Bulletin
In 1989, the different organizations working in Barrio San Jorge began to meet to exchange experiences and to coordinate their work with the community. As a result of these meetings it was decided to publish a bulletin. Since 1989, this has been published every two months with the help of residents. It includes local news and is used to report on the progress of different initiatives, and to outline future activities. It also contains useful information about health care, and environmental improvement.

Initiatives to strengthen the organization of the community
When the head of the IIED-AL assistance group – a woman architect and business manager by training – began the construction of the mother and child centre in September 1987, only 16 people in San Jorge (mostly women) were interested in community activities. The great majority of the population looked upon the construction of the centre with scepticism. In late 1989, residents became more interested in the activities being introduced in the Barrio. Attendance at meetings increased; so too did participation in decisions about work priorities. But few people were prepared to contribute to building tasks unless they received payment.

During the first half of 1990, the consolidation of a community organization really began. In August 1990, elections were held in the Barrio to choose representatives from the community to join a commission which was to develop a long-range plan and a programme for the improvement and integrated development of the Barrio. This commission included representatives from the government of the province of Buenos Aires, the municipality of San Fernando and IIED-AL.

Operational details

The total budget for 1990/91 was just under US$70,000, double that for the previous financial year. About 17 per cent of funding was raised by voluntary work both inside and outside the Barrio. A further 6 per cent was income received from a variety of activities including the retailing of meat purchased through a wholesaler. The remainder was made up of external donations from a variety of organizations; these include both public (the municipality, the provincial government, the university) and private (IIED-AL, FLASCO, Parroquia), and national and international (the German government, Dutch Save the Children Fund, UNICEF). Local businesses have also supported the project with money or goods in kind. The largest single donation in 1990/91, US$17,000, was from government sources.

To date, there has been no savings or credit component in the programme of support. The high rate of inflation in Argentina and the declining value of money has led to a distrust of savings. The loss of trust in saving has been made worse by the collapse of several financial institutions. A new project for which support is currently being sought is a materials bank which would assist the people in making improvements to their homes. It is possible that a savings and credit scheme might develop from such a project.

Assessment

The Barrio San Jorge programme has taught the supporting team at IIED-AL several lessons. First, there must be a change in attitude away from the paternalistic approach of government agencies, political parties and some charities which reduces the population of a squatter settlement to simple recipients of 'public charity'. This means overcoming the mistrust that many government agencies and politicians have of community organizations and NGOs. The conclusion is that provincial governments and municipalities should be partners with community organizations in well-defined roles within a comprehensive institutional effort to improve the quality of life of poor individuals, families and barrios.

A second lesson of the San Jorge programme is the importance of working through small, diverse and well-coordinated projects and programmes with communities, even in settlements in which there is no organization representative of the majority of the population. Most low-income settlements in Argentina (and in Latin America) lack a representative community organization. This type of intervention encourages the participation of neighbours and the development of such an organization.

A third lesson is that most external agencies fail to understand that each community is different. For each, these differences are shaped by their particular history and the specifics of their social and physical environments. In the case of San Jorge, the inhabitants of both the old and the new part of the Barrio have been used and manipulated by political and religious leaders. They have been threatened, expelled from a different site and frequently subjected to harassment. They never express their political views openly. Nor do they take positions about their lives under democratic or dictatorial regimes. They have learnt to survive. Their future plans are measured in days or, at most, in weeks. Their contacts are mostly in the locality and they socialize only with the settlers of their own community and of similar communities in the vicinity. They do not have a broad view of their city, of its size and problems or opportunities. Their view is purely local.

Even today, people do not like to dissent openly. Time is needed to allow new ideas to mature and it is only in a second or third round of discussions that comments and suggestions from individuals are made and that informal chats with the elected representatives from the community or from the province or from IIED-AL take place. Some good initiatives have been aborted because they were presented by a representative from an outside agency –

even an experienced representative – who asked for a direct answer to a very concrete proposal. This representative could not understand that the group of women to whom the initiative was presented were not ready to give an answer. Failures are almost inevitable, when outsiders try to impose their points of view. Such attitudes have often puzzled foreign agency staff who have visited the Barrio and have proposed a new initiative. They have left the Barrio convinced that there had been a warm response to their initiative yet without understanding how the minds of this particular group of people worked.

The most important lesson learnt is the need for permanence. The continuous presence of the team in the Barrio is fundamental. It is an active and regular presence, able to listen and to undertake activities step by step, small and irrelevant as many of these things may appear to outsiders.

The Barrio San Jorge project is gradually becoming the project of the Barrio, not the project of an outside agency or a political party or a charity. All agencies talk of neighbourhood participation and of co-management: participation, decentralization and co-management have become necessary for the credibility of political leaders and agencies. But how do you measure participation? How is participation achieved? What structures do participatory organizations require? There is no blueprint for these. As noted already, each community is different and the only way to help their members is to listen to the voices of the Barrio, both the individual and the collective voices. Time, patience and continuity must be given by any outside agency to allow the inhabitants to develop and express their thoughts.

For many, such an approach may appear time-consuming – a wasteful use of human resources. But all community work is labour-intensive, much more so if the advisory team is patient and maintains a continuous presence in the settlement. Can the timing of such an initiative be accelerated and deepened?

Sources: Barrio San Jorge, Annual Reports 1989/90 and 1990/91, Buenos Aires; and Hardoy, Ana, Jorge Hardoy and Richard Schusterman (1991) 'Building community organization: the history of a squatter settlement and its own organization' *Environment and Urbanization*, Vol 3, No 2, London.

3

Catholic Social Services, Pakistan

P O Box 7457
Old Illaco Building
Zaibun-Nisa Street
Karachi
Pakistan

INSTITUTION

Background

Catholic Social Services organizes cooperative groups to provide housing loans for low-income communities in Karachi. Between 1981 and 1992, 830 loans were disbursed, of which 483 have now been settled. The revolving fund for credit was set up after the society had been approached by some people who had been evicted from Benaras Colony in Karachi. The revolving fund was first used for those who had been evicted to provide them with money to rebuild their houses in resettlement areas. Later, the group eligible for housing loans was extended to those who had land but no other resources, and to households which still needed to secure a plot. Additional programmes have also developed to support the Housing Loan Programme.

Programmes and activities

In addition to the Housing Loan Programme described below, Catholic Social Services operates a Community Workers Training Programme which aims to increase basic awareness about the problems faced by low-income communities. It has five main objectives:

1. conscientization of the people;
2. empowering the powerless with tools of analysis;
3. organizing the unorganized groups;
4. undertaking critical analysis at a micro and macro level; and
5. understanding the power structures.

With people based in the community, the Community Workers Training Programme establishes small groups of men and women (two women workers coordinate these separate groups) who are interested in identifying and resolving some of the problems that they face. Meetings are held weekly and mostly informal training is given. A more formal training programme is being developed which will include sessions on group dynamics and the principles of organization. In many of the communities in which the Programme is working, there are some established community organizations which focus on particular concerns, for example youth groups or political parties, but the purpose of the Programme is to bring all these interests together. A sewing centre and adult education programme have also been initiated.

Through the process of coming together to understand and work for their common interests, several communities have been successful in improving their circumstances. For example, one community negotiated with the local government council to install a sewerage line, while another is negotiating with the Karachi Municipal Council to have its land regularized (ie the households given legal tenure to the land site they occupy). The Community Workers Training Programme is an important complimentary process to the Housing Loan Programme; people require both housing and basic services and infrastructure: the Housing Loan Programme provides credit to improve access to the former and the Community Workers Training Programme assists communities in negotiating the latter from the state authorities. In several communities, contact was first established through the Housing Loan Programme. The Community Workers Training Programme then became active, helping people to meet their other needs.

Historically the Catholic Social Services has not offered technical advice to households along with housing loans. However, through its work in Orangi, one of the largest informal settlements in Karachi, it has begun to work with the Orangi Pilot Project to increase the level of technical knowledge of both clients and local building manufacturers and construction workers.

HOUSING LOAN PROGRAMME

Introduction

During the 1950s and 1960s, mass low-income settlement took place in Karachi but neither formal nor informal loans for housing construction or improvement were easily available. Most people were able to invest little in their houses, especially in the period soon after settlement. After the mid-1960s, thallawalas (owners of building components manufacturing yards) became an integral part of the development of each settlement. Materials such as concrete blocks, reinforced concrete lintels and galvanized iron sheets for roofing became available. Credit was (and still is) normally available from the thallawalas and occasionally cash credit is offered. Social pressure is used to recover any monies owing and 'muscle power' is not considered to be necessary. However, this informal market is often expensive and may not be open to all of those in need.

Catholic Social Services began a programme of housing loans in 1981. At the time, Pakistan was under martial law and, in Karachi especially, there were many evictions from government land. In one community, Benaras Colony, 200 houses were demolished. The people approached Catholic Social Services who, at that time, operated very much as a welfare organization. Established in 1962 by the Cardinal for Pakistan, the purpose of the organization was to coordinate the activities of the congregations of local churches in Karachi. In immediate response to the request for assistance by Benaras Colony, tents were provided for the homeless people.

The community from Benaras Colony was given resettlement plots on land on the outskirts of Karachi, far from the site from which they were evicted. Without resources with which to build houses, the inhabitants remained homeless. Catholic Social Services provided loans to groups of households, with Rs 4000 (US$160) available for each household. The loans were interest free and to be repaid over 3 years with a monthly contribution of Rs 200 (US$8). The evictions programme was continued by the government and therefore it was agreed that the repaid funds should be 'revolved', with returned contributions being made available to other people in need.

In 1983, Bihari households from Bangladesh moved to Karachi. The families were offered resettlement plots by the government in Majeed Colony but only land was provided; there were no houses, no services and no site infrastructure. This initiated a second phase in the Housing Loan Programme with the Bihari households being included as a group eligible for help in the Revolving Loan Programme; in part, this was possible because the number of evictions had fallen. At this time, the size of loan available to a household was increased to Rs 6000 (US$240).

A third phase of the Housing Loan Programme was introduced once these families became established. Catholic Social Services recognized that there were many other low-income households in Karachi who needed some assistance. In many instances, they were living in accommodation of a poor standard or were renting overcrowded accommodation. The households needed credit to obtain access to housing but were too poor to be granted credit by banks or credit institutions because they did not have collateral. Commercial organizations were reluctant to lend because the poor often did not repay. The Housing Loan Programme was extended to include such families.

Over the last five years, Catholic Social Services has been experimenting with a number of different mechanisms for operating a revolving fund. The system they are now using is to give loans to an organization of creditors who collectively guarantee the repayment of individual loans. Since this system has been introduced, defaults have fallen to a small percentage.

Catholic Social Services presently has some 365 loans. Finance is given to both individuals and cooperatives. About 25 per cent of the loans are given to purchase land, the remainder to construct housing. The current value of the loan is Rs 15,000 (US$600), just sufficient to build a simple room about 10 by 12 feet. The experience of Catholic Social Services is that once a family has a permanent structure and their loan is repaid, additional income and savings are used to extend the property. Prospective participants are encouraged to organize themselves into cooperatives but loans are not restricted to cooperative members. Although there are up to 100 NGOs active among squatter areas in Karachi, few offer credit and Catholic Social Services is the only organization to offer loans for housing.

Obtaining a loan

If someone approaches Catholic Social Services with an enquiry about housing loans, they are encouraged to talk with other members of the community who are in a similar position to themselves. Staff may have a meeting with local community leaders. The community discusses its needs and may decide to form a cooperative. This process may take anything from two to seven months. The focus on cooperative action developed in order to promote the idea of self-reliance. The average size for a cooperative is 35 members. Many of those who approach Catholic Social Services would only like a loan and are not willing to go through the lengthy process of setting up a cooperative.

Once the cooperative organization has been formed, the community meets once or twice a month. These meetings are attended by a staff member from Catholic Social Services and provide an opportunity for discussing the problems faced by the community. There is a training programme for cooperative members with six components: history of the cooperative movement in Pakistan, religious concepts of cooperatives, how to manage finances, women's role in the cooperative, forming and working with cooperative rules and by-laws, developing a plan of action and evaluating activities. About six hours is allocated to each component but if the community has little time available this is reduced. The training programme takes six months to complete on average (additional training may be provided later if the community requests it). At the same time, a savings programme is started by cooperative members; each member has to save Rs 450 (US$18) a month for six months. Once the loan is sanctioned, all the savings are returned to assist in the costs of housing construction. Most members pay this amount; it is sufficiently low to enable even the very poor to participate in the Programme. The cooperative then recommends that the members receive a loan.

The application is made by each member in any language (Urdu, English, Sindhi, Punjab). Staff go to the cooperative to verify the details of each applicant. As only a small amount of funds are available, only the very poor are given access to the Revolving Fund. About 5–10 per cent of applicants are rejected for being too wealthy. The following groups are given priority access to loan finance: emergency cases, those with land but no other resources, those without land, those in need of additional accommodation and those whose homes are in need of repair. The average earnings of a low-income household are about Rs 1500 a month. Most families are currently renting accommodation and their monthly rent is almost certain to exceed the monthly instalments for the loan; the programme makes an immediate contribution to improving their situation. Once the loan has been agreed, the applicant must execute a promissory note, loan agreement, arrange a loan guarantor and deposit land documents (if the plot is in an authorized area) with the Catholic Social Services.

Once approved, the construction loan is paid in instalments. The maximum loan is for Rs 15,000 which covers the construction costs of a simple room plus toilet and boundary walls. Those who have no resources from which to purchase land must take two loans, the first to purchase land and the second to cover the costs of construction. Plots sizes vary from about 40 to 120 square metres.

Three quarters of those with loans are illegally occupying their sites. The other 25 per cent are building on plots allocated to them by the government (sometimes they pay the full price when they occupy the site, in other cases, they may pay in instalments). In general, government prices are less than market prices, especially since these are often considerably inflated by speculators. If the inhabitants of a site which was settled illegally are successful in being regularized, ie if they are given the legal right to the land by the government, they have to pay the government for the cost of the land.

The process of construction takes about 10–15 days. Blocks are used for the walls and asbestos sheets for the roof. All members of the cooperative live on the same site. The experience of Catholic Social Services is that once families have a permanent structure which they can call their own, they find additional resources to develop the site and the structure further. After the loan has been paid off, they can use the money which was being used for repayments for further rooms. By being supported in the initial critical step, households are enabled to provide themselves with better housing.

In the early stages of development, there may be no infrastructure or services provided by government. More developed sites may have piped water supplies and electricity connections. Even those who occupy an illegal site will have to pay something for the plot to the land developer. There are few facilities for the community in such settlements. One cooperative which was formed some six years ago has recently completed a community centre but this is an exception.

Where loans are provided to households who are illegally occupying land, these are occupying government land. Catholic Social Services staff ensure that the sites are not scheduled as amenity areas, and there are no particular dangers associated with the location, for example high tension power cables. In all other cases, the communities are relatively safe from eviction and will be likely to secure legal tenure in the future. To date, no homes built with loans from the Fund have been demolished in an eviction process.

The loans are for three years with a monthly repayment of Rs 450. In most cases, the repayment period increases to an average of 45 months. Some households have difficulties keeping up with repayments; after a visit by a staff member to verify their situation, they are generally granted an extension by the Board. If necessary, legal action is taken. Although each loan is guaranteed by another individual, this is only to increase social pressure to maintain repayments and the guarantors are not usually pressed to pay. In about 2 per cent of cases, the full value of the loan is not returned. In recent years, bad debts from some of the first loans have been recovered.

No interest is charged on the loan but each month an additional charge of Rs 35 (US$1.5) is made by Catholic Social Services to cover a small percentage of the costs associated with the programme. This charge was started in 1986 to encourage a sense of self-reliance by participants and to stress that the programme was not offering charity but an opportunity for self-help. An additional charge of Rs 50 (US$2) is made each month to the cooperative. This fund is used by the cooperative to give additional loans and to help in emergencies.

In several cases, cooperatives have broken up before the successful completion of a loan programme. The biggest problem has been ensuring the quality of leadership. In some cases, there is a problem of corruption, with the savings of the cooperative being taken by its executive. In such cases, the members normally become disillusioned with cooperative activity. However, once the loans have been repaid, cooperatives have continued to function. They go on collecting money from their members and may be joined by new households interested in obtain a loan for housing. Members from the different cooperatives meet up frequently and the more experienced cooperatives frequently support those who are starting. In the last year, as the original cooperatives have become increasingly able to support themselves, and new groups have been requesting support, Catholic Social Services has been encouraging several to become autonomous organizations. This will enable them to raise their own funds from new sources, and allow the revolving fund and Catholic Social Services to concentrate on newly formed or potential cooperatives.

Two of the cooperatives started under the Housing Loan Programme (including the Korangi Christian Cooperative Society described below) are now independent organizations registered with the authorities. These cooperatives are using their own capital to finance further activities. At present, Catholic Social Services is working with five cooperatives. It takes a minimum of four years before a group is able to consider being independent. But even the two independent groups maintain strong links with Catholic Social Services.

The current programme

Catholic Social Services offers about 100 loans each year. The demand for loans is much greater than they can hope to service. For this reason, they hope to double their present capital base of Rs 3.7 million, to be able to offer 200 loans a year. Their main donors agencies are Caritas and Misereor. Recently SELAVIP (Belgium) made an additional US$30,000 available, to permit an increase in each loan from Rs 10,000 to Rs 15,000. This increase was necessary because inflation had increased construction costs. Funding for staff costs is raized locally from Catholic churches, the general members and specific fundraising events. The programme is run by two members of staff and the loan records have now been computerized.

Catholic Social Services revolving fund (1981–92)

	Rupees (000)	US $ (000)
Total capital	3744	150
Fund disbursed	6754	270
Fund recovered	4155	166
Revolved from recoveries	3010	120
Outstanding (including not matured)	2597	104

Total number of beneficiaries:	830 families
	483 loans settled
	347 loans in operation

A profile of two cooperatives

Korangi Christian Cooperative Society was the first group with which the Society started work. The area is a resettlement site for those evicted from other parts of the city. The cooperative began with just 12 members in 1984; by June 1989, 45 members had purchased plots and most had completed the construction of houses with permanent roofs. In total, some 75 loans have been granted to this group. The group has also purchased land and built a community centre using the resources of their common fund. The Korangi Christian Cooperative Society was formally registered in 1989, and since then has begun to work autonomously, operating from its own resources and allowing Catholic Social Services to concentrate on newer groups.

Pahar Gunj Christian Cooperative Society was formed in 1985 and by 1988 had more than 150 members. By the end of 1990, the capital in their common fund amounted to Rs 200,000 and 70 loans had been granted to their members. In 1989, 30 members living in New Mianwali Colony left to form a new group. This group has recruited additional members, and during 1989 and 1990 has disbursed 30 loans. To improve the working and performance of the society, Catholic Social Services assessed the society and identified weak areas. It has been working with the society to strengthen and support its development.

Assessment

There are two problems with the current programme. First, there is a shortage of money in the revolving fund. In June 1990, for example, 17 members had loan applications approved but there were insufficient funds to grant their loans. Applications continue to arrive. Second, the size of the loan remains small. This amount has recently been increased so that it is now just sufficient to construct a basic single-room house, plus toilet and boundary walls. Within three years' residence, 70–80 per cent of households in illegal sub-divisions invests about Rs 30,000 (US$1430) in constructing a three-room house with a soak pit, kitchen and bathroom; the house is generally constructed of block masonry with a galvanized, sheet-iron roof. A variety of additional financial sources are used, including loans from friends and relatives, savings, sale of valuables, and loans from the local *thalla*.

However, two cooperatives (with 105 members in total) established under the scheme are now operating successfully with their own resources. And a further two cooperatives, with 130 members, may shortly become independent. Over 600 households have been supported in many housing investments.

Sources: Ghouri, Naeem Shahid and Hector Hihal (1993), 'The housing loan programme of the Catholic Social Services in Karachi', *Environment and Urbanization*, Vol 5, No 1, London; and Anzorena, Jorge (1990 and 1991), Assorted *SELAVIP* papers, Cebu City.

4

Comunidad Urbana Autogestionaria de Villa El Salvador* (CUAVES), Peru

Villa El Salvador
Lima
Peru

INSTITUTION

Background

The history of the Villa El Salvador Self-managed Urban Community, or CUAVES, is the history of the *Pueblo Joven* (squatter settlement) of Villa El Salvador (VES) in Lima, Peru. In 1971, this was one of the many *invasiones* (illegal settlements) of state land which have been the means by which low-income groups have found access to land and housing in the city. In the nine years between 1971 and 1980, the settlement grew from the original 180 occupying households to approximately 250,000 people. Villa El Salvador is distinctive because it emerged in a particular political context and, with the support of the military government, succeeded in establishing a community with a completely new form of organization.

The organization of CUAVES was based on the idea of creating a self-managed city in terms of production, services and commerce. VES had to be able to generate employment for its inhabitants. It was intended that development plans would be drawn up with the participation of the population. The structure that was to be created for this would be controlled by the neighbourhood organization. Thus Villa El Salvador was structured as a Self-managed Urban-Industrial Settlement, to be financed with the savings of the local community, organised by the Caja Comunal (Community Bank).[1] The first stage of the Development Plan included three Councils (Production, Services and Commerce) covering the different areas of CUAVES activity.

In 1983, VES was formally recognized as a district, a mayor was elected and there was an election for the Managing Council of CUAVES. This activity rejuvenated the settlement's organization and control which had deteriorated somewhat prior to this date. A municipal decree recognized CUAVES as the

* Villa El Salvador Self-managed Urban Community

legitimate neighbourhood organization, beginning a new stage of municipal-neighbourhood co-management directed at resolving the most urgent problems; for example, the resettlement of the population which had 'invaded' land intended for the community.

CUAVES was innovative in that it emerged as the result of a strong commitment on the part of the state to support the project and to initiate a totally different programme from that usually offered to squatter settlements. This endowed CUAVES with a rather unconventional dynamic, because, as it was initiated by the government, its history and evolution were marked by political events and the different political ideologies of the groups acting as official contacts. From its beginning in 1973, two years after the settlement was first established, the history of CUAVES has been the struggle of the VES inhabitants to achieve recognition and legitimacy for their neighbourhood organization and to achieve basic urban services.

Objectives

These include the following:

- Coordination between the government departments and private institutions operating in Villa El Salvador in order to serve the interests of the community as expressed in the Integrated Development Plan.
- The refinement and updating of the community organization.
- Establishment of close relations between CUAVES and other dynamic neighbourhood organizations, with the aim of jointly initiating neighbourhood movements.

Programme and activities

CUAVES' current activities are based on seven programmes which make up the Integrated Development Plan. The organization has to overcome the competition which exists between the District Municipality and the community organization, and to ensure that the government departments and private institutions operating in Villa El Salvador coordinate their work and channel their resources to serve the interests of the community. The seven programmes are:

1. Urban Development Programme, Housing and Services.
2. Programme for Education, Communication, Culture, Recreation and Sport.
3. Health Programme.
4. Food Production Programme.
5. Commercialization Programme.
6. Community Business Programme.
7. Industrial Park Programme.

Organizational structure

Villa El Salvador is divided into six sectors, of which sectors 1, 2, 3 and 4 are occupied under the Residential Groups scheme.[2] Each Residential Group is made up of 16 blocks, with 24 lots in each block positioned around a central square which is intended for the sector's facilities. Residential groups are surrounded by areas for productive use.

Every two years, adult residents in each block elect a Block Committee made up of five leaders. After these elections, there is an assembly for the residents of each Residential Group and eight members are elected for the Residential Group Central Management Council. Once the Central Management Council elections are over, the members meet at the Residents' Convention and elect the 11 members of the Community Executive Council, which is the highest executive level in CUAVES. The Residents' Convention also aims to evaluate what has been carried out, make agreements, approve the Development Plan and make other decisions as necessary. There are five Line Councils, each with a Management Committee, formed by members of the Residential Group Central Management Council. The five councils are: Health, Education, Production, Services and Commerce.

The General Assembly is the supreme decision-making body in CUAVES; made up of the 102 general secretaries of the Residential Groups, it meets at least once a month.

PROJECT FOR THE SUPPLY OF DRINKING WATER, SECTOR 2

Introduction

In 1986, the metropolitan agency responsible for water and sewerage in Lima began to approve plans for the extension of the water network and drainage to the *ampliaciones* in Sector 2. The *ampliaciones* are areas which were formed mainly between 1981 and 1983 by 'occupations' carried out in order to obtain housing. The occupied areas initially covered 65 hectares and were modelled on the typical layout of VES. By the beginning of 1988, it was estimated that the *ampliaciones* covered 300 hectares. The *ampliaciones* took up the areas set aside for communal facilities in sectors 1, 2, 3 and 4, and, in particular, 1560 lots in sector 2. All these occupied areas had a low level of urban services and infrastructure. However, as VES has access to general services such as electric light and drinking water, the problem of supplying the *ampliaciones* is not as acute as it was with previous settlements established on the margins. The project involved the improvement of 40 blocks with 912 lots in an area first settled in 1981.

Programme and activities

The company in charge of supplying drinking water and sewerage in Lima Metropolitana (SEDAPAL) is run by the state. It is responsible for approving technical projects and assessing the feasibility of services, as well as financing new works and administration. The most common means of financing joint projects between the company and local residents is through Banco de la Vivienda (BVP) (Housing Bank). BVP and SEDAPAL obtain money from their own resources, as well as additional loans. From 1985, public treasury funds and Fondo Nacional de la Vivienda (FONAVI) (the National Housing Fund) were also used.

The repayment of BVP loans includes an initial deposit (between 5 and 10 per cent) which residents pay before the works are undertaken. The rest of the loan is authorized once the work has begun. There is a large financial subsidy incorporated into this financing system. The approximate average cost for the networks and house connections is US$800 per lot and, for associated general works, US$300 per lot.[3] In 1984, after strong pressure from the residents of the squatter settlements, it was agreed that the cost of general works should be met by central government.

In 1986, the interest rate charged by BVP to the squatter settlements was sharply increased to 32 per cent, resulting in a fall in the amount of work undertaken. Faced with this situation, the residents protested and succeeded in bringing the interest rate down to 19 per cent.

Operational details

Signature of contract
Towards the middle of 1986, SEDAPAL began to approve plans for the water networks and drainage for Sector 2. In December, several areas in VES put forward their applications for finance to the BVP.

In 1988, there was a severe economic crisis with a 27 per cent fall in production and an annual rate of inflation of 2700 per cent. This meant that the total amount of the loan was reduced. Some works were provisionally halted and, for these to be resumed, the Bank required a new deposit or contribution totalling 30 per cent of the cost of work remaining. The residents could not easily afford these increased costs. As a result, they set up an Action Front which, with the support of the municipality of VES and CUAVES, negotiated a solution: the residents offered to take on 10 per cent of the works and the Bank agreed to meet the remaining 90 per cent.

The terms of the finance contract
The contract was to complete the water network and drainage for 912 beneficiary households. The allocation of costs is shown below:

Total value of the work	I/ 29,742,820
State funds	I/ 26,768,538
of which:	
BVP	I/ 9,874,914
FONAVI	I/ 16,893,624
Residents	I/ 2,974,282

The interest rate was 20 per cent. The repayment period was 60 months, starting from the month following the agreement or from the beginning of the works. The contract required that the borrowers (resident beneficiaries) should open a savings account in the BVP, with an initial contribution of I/ 2,974,282. It was also agreed that the municipality would ratify the agreement (in a municipal act) to guarantee that the term of the group management would not expire before the works had been finished. That is to say that the Municipality assumed the role of guarantor.

Construction stage of the work
After the contract was signed, a series of problems arose stemming from the Bank's refusal to make payments. In November, the Bank stopped payments and put forward a plan for the refinancing of the contract. By this stage, the cost of the work had risen by 1400 per cent. CUAVES and the Action Front organized a series of demonstrations for the work to begin again. The Bank agreed to restart payments but the construction companies notified the VES municipality that they could not begin work as they lacked funds; they had to apply for a temporary refundable loan.

In March of the following year, one of the contracted companies suspended work, alleging that the BVP had stopped payments. The construction company maintained that the BVP refused to make further repayments until the residents had agreed to accept the terms of the increased budget. Eventually the BVP established a refinancing contract with the following amounts to be paid by each party:

Total cost	I/ 1,171,946,978
Bank contribution	I/ 1,018,713,270
Residents	I/ 153,233,706

Since the signing of the first contract the cost had risen forty-fold (4000 per cent), and the residents had now to contribute 14 per cent of the total cost. The interest rate had risen to 330 per cent a year; although this involved a substantial subsidy as the rate of inflation was close to 3000 per cent and the commercial interest rate was over 1000 per cent a year.

Method of payment
The finance secretary was responsible for opening a savings account at the BVP in his/her name and for collecting payments from the neighbours once a week.

Residents' participation
There was little direct participation in the construction as the residents expected that all the work would be carried out by the company. Resident participation occurred only when some households were unable to make repayments because of lack of work or a steady income. As an alternative, they were allowed to contribute their labour instead. Their share of repayments to the Bank was reduced as this work was considered to be equivalent to a financial contribution.

Assessment

About six years passed between the beginning of the struggle and the completion of the project. This is a relatively short time when compared to the time normally taken for squatter settlements to obtain services, which can be from 15 to 20 years. A major reason for this is that existing areas already had general facilities which could be extended to the new areas. However, this generally meant that the same water source was shared among more families, the service provided was limited and water was rationed to certain hours of the day.

The BVP appeared to be trying to fragment the community. Had the residents acted in a more coherent manner with the Action Front, this might have been made more difficult. In this respect, the participation of CUAVES in supporting community organization and associated activities was fundamental. It was the leadership of the Residential Groups which were key in initiating and supporting the project and all the organizational work was directly related to the activities which CUAVES carried out. The residents' participation was fundamental in negotiations to reduce project costs and achieve accessible financing. The whole struggle was characterized by permanently tense relations with the BVP, as the Bank's policy was to adapt the credit system to a hyper-inflationary situation.

Other considerations which could have changed how the work was carried out and perhaps reduce costs were not considered by the residents. For example, there was no use of alternative technology and no direct participation involving the residents' labour. In general, the project was prepared by SEDAPAL. The regulations surrounding the installation of work of this type are inflexible and are designed to favour commercial companies.

The residents had no interest in community work, preferring the construction companies to carry out the work. There was the general feeling among the people that they were the only ones who could work efficiently, but they were not eager to offer their labour when they thought that this would not greatly reduce costs. Therefore the contribution of labour was confined to small groups of neighbours who were behind with their payments.

Notes:
1. However, the community bank project failed as it did not have the government's support. This together with poor and inefficient management led to its bankruptcy at the end of the 1970s.
2. Part of Sector 2 and all of 4 were developed through a project of lots with services run by the Empresa Publica de Edificacion de Inmuebles (ENACE) (Public Company for Building Construction). Sector 5 was not intended for residential use.
3. General works comprise of reservoirs, hydraulic systems, water pipes and drainage systems. In some cases they also include boring and building wells for the supply of drinking water.

Sources: Riofrio, G (1986) *Urban provision with popular participation*; and Espinoza, N and G Riofrio, (1990), *Service companies and popular urban consumers*. Additional information from: Peattie, Lisa (1990), 'Participation: a case study of how invaders organize, negotiate and interact with government in Lima, Peru', *Environment and Urbanization*, Vol 2, No 1, London.

5

Cooperativa de Vivienda Consume La Esperanza*, Buenos Aires

INSTITUTION

The Housing and Consumer Cooperative, 'La Esperanza' was initiated in December 1985 by 42 families who were then living in the Saldias district (in the Retiro district of Buenos Aires, Argentina). In 1983, a development project had been initiated in Saldias when technical workers from the parish of San Martin de Tours began to examine problems such as juvenile delinquency, illiteracy and poor nutrition. The first stage of this project culminated in the formation of a consumer 'precooperative' in 1985. With the establishment of some degree of community organization and after undertaking different participatory projects in health care, education and work, the inhabitants decided to initiate their own solution to their housing problem. They formed the La Esperanza Housing and Consumer Cooperative.

THE HOUSING PROGRAMME

Projects and activities

At the beginning of 1986, an interdisciplinary technical team was formed to provide technical support to the Cooperative. This team was made up of two architects, a social worker, a psychologist and a lawyer. Both the Cooperative and the technical team worked together to develop a integral community development programme which included the construction of a new district with 42 houses, a central square, a community centre, a consumer centre, a nursery and a football pitch.

At the end of 1985, the Cooperative applied to Caritas for a loan to buy the land on which to build the district. With this money, a plot of land measuring one and a half hectares was bought in the Del Viso area, still in the province of Buenos Aires but just under 50 kilometres from the centre of Buenos Aires.

In March 1986, the on-site planning for the project was begun. Within the

---

* La Esperanza Housing and Consumer Cooperative

year, the first four houses had been completed. In September 1988, the construction of the remaining 38 was started and by December 1990 the houses were handed over to the inhabitants. Work on community facilities and infrastructure and basic services had been started but not yet completed.

Each house covers an average area of 56 square metres. In order to reduce the cost, only part of the house was constructed in the first phase. Households build incrementally as additional finance becomes available. The construction system is an adaptation of the traditional system, carried out using self-construction methods with both communal assistance and individual efforts. Some external contractors are used for some specific jobs if none of the residents have the necessary skills (for example, water installation).

In addition to the physical construction of the district, a second important objective has been to form an organized and self-managed community to undertake further work on housing construction. In this respect, the formation and consolidation of the Cooperative has been important. Leaders are elected by the members once a year. The Cooperative is directed by a council made up of a president, secretary, treasurer, trustee, four members and four deputy members. Decisions are taken either by the council or by all the members in an Assembly, depending on their nature. The latter body is the highest authority. The council meets once a week to assess the project's progress (organization of work, timetables, finance, purchase of materials and equipment, etc) and particular problems encountered by members (such as payment of instalments, absences, personal and group problems).

Operational details

A number of institutions have provided support for the project, including: Caritas (financial and technical assistance), Fundación Vivienda y Comunidad[1] (see Case Study 12), Asociacion Vivienda Economica[2] and independent professionals (providing technical assistance), Fundacion Perez Companc, MISEREOR and private donors. The total cost of the project is US$230,000, divided as follows:

External resources

Loan subsidized by MISEREOR	20,000
Subsidy from Fundacion Perez Companc	20,000
Subsidy from Caritas San Martin de Tours	35,000
Private donations	15,000
Subtotal	*90,000*

Inhabitants' Resources

Payment of quota (US$15 per month per person)	40,000
Money raised (sales, raffles, etc)	10,000
Labour contributed (6 days a month per person)	90,000
Subtotal	*140,000*
Total cost of the project	*230,000*
Total cost per house	*5480*
Cost per square metre of housing	*97*

Assessment

An assessment of the work undertaken to date identified several measures which would improve the operation of the project:

* The length of time taken to complete the work makes it hard to maintain the enthusiasm and commitment of the group. Shortening this time might prevent the group from weakening.
* Technical assistance might be improved through better use of voluntary labour.
* The work should be reorganized to do away with closed work groups which seem to result in excessive competition.
* An increase in the number of contracted projects should be considered.
* A detailed evaluation of the way in which residents participate in housing design should be undertaken. This would enable better planning, and avoidance of designs which are technically unsuitable.
* The sources of financing should be diversified as much as possible.
* Residents should be encouraged to participate actively in the search for and management of funds for the project.

Notes:
1. Housing and Community Foundation
2. Low Cost Housing Association

6

Cooperative Housing in Ethiopia

Housing Coops Department
Ministry of Urban Development and Housing
PO Box 3386
Addis Ababa
Ethiopia

INSTITUTION

Background

Cooperative housing was introduced in Ethiopia after the 1975 revolution in order to help provide housing for those in urban areas. It received considerable government support as the government hoped that the cooperatives would bring together all those involved in house-building, and that the consequent pooling of resources, skills and labour would help to reduce costs. It was also hoped that the processes involved in working together would help to establish a sense of community. A second phase in the cooperative housing programme began in 1986, following the introduction of a new urban housing policy operated by the Ministry of Urban Development and Housing. The recent further revolution in 1991 has obviously changed the situation. Current indications are that the programme will remain but will be decentralized to local authorities.

The need for a new housing strategy was particularly acute because land ownership was highly concentrated before the revolution. Prior to 1975, only 7 per cent of urban land was lived on by those who owned it; the remainder was held by the imperial families, the church and feudal landlords. Between 1986 and 1989, 1424 cooperatives with a total membership of 37,129 were formed. Just under 1,500 houses were completed and a further 5000 were begun, with building on a further 4000 about to start. Between 1986 and the end of 1988, just under 500 cooperatives had land allocated to them in Addis Ababa and 17 other towns.

Associated projects and activities

The Ministry of Urban Development and Housing is responsible for the cooperative housing programme. Specific responsibilities include registering each cooperative, preparing and providing various types of approved housing design for different income groups, selecting and preparing sites, estimating loan repayment capacities, determining types and quantities of building materials, running training programmes, and coordinating government and NGO relations in this area.

Cooperatives must choose one of 25 different types of house plans. Efforts have been made to reduce costs by measures such as sharing party walls and septic tanks but many of the types are too expensive for those on low incomes. Just under 7 per cent of the programme is currently devoted to those on low incomes (defined as those with less than Birr 150 (US$75) a month).

HOUSING COOPERATIVES AND CREDIT

Introduction

Credit is essential for the successful completion of the housing projects. For most groups housing loans are provided through the Housing and Savings Bank. Some NGOs have become involved in the programme in order to help extend the programme to those in particular need who are not eligible for the conventional loan scheme. The first section below describes the process through which individuals can establish a cooperative and enter the programme; the second section looks at how credit is obtained.

Projects and activities

'Normal housing cooperatives' are the majority of those formed and these are eligible for Housing and Savings Bank loans. About 10 per cent of the total cost of each project must be met directly from the cooperative's own funds.

Individuals who are interested in obtaining a house through the programme have to form a cooperative with like-minded people. The group then contacts a regional office of the Ministry of Urban Development and Housing. After meetings to discuss the formation of a cooperative and the rights and obligations of members, the group forms an *ad hoc* committee until the cooperative is formally registered. The group then meets with the town planning and urban land adminstration (part of the Ministry) in order to select and sub-divide a site. The ability of each member to repay the loan, according to salary and age, is assessed by the Ministry. A suitable house plan is then selected. Generally all cooperative members have similar salaries and a single house plan is used throughout the site. At this stage, the cooperative can approach the local authority to obtain a title deed for the land and a building permit. The allocation of housing between the members of the cooperative is done through lots.

Each cooperative must have a General Assembly which meets monthly. Six sub-committees must be set up to oversee aspects of the construction process. The cooperative is the formal owner of the land (on leasehold) and the housing units. Members purchase their houses from the cooperative and, if they want to leave, they have to give the cooperative the option of buying back the house. The cooperative is then responsible for finding a new member to take over the house and loan repayments.

One of the biggest problems for the cooperatives is securing adequate supplies of building materials. The size of loans has been determined according to government prices which are considerably below those charged by private sector suppliers. Waiting for the materials supplied by the government may delay the project considerably and many cooperatives use other sources, paying higher prices. Free infrastructure is provided to housing cooperatives by the government.

There is also a second type of cooperatives called 'Pure self-help cooperatives' which include those whose members are not eligible for Housing and Savings Bank loans (see below) and who raise finance in other ways.

Operational details

The Housing and Savings Bank makes loans only to those who are in formal-sector employment. Detailed information about each cooperative member and the project is required before the Bank will authorize the loan. In some cases, the employer makes salary deductions for the loan repayments. In other cases, the cooperative collects the monthly repayments for the Bank. People taking out a loan have to pay for mortgage redemption and fire insurance. In addition to the interest charge, two per cent of the total value of the loan is paid to the Bank to cover supervision expenses during construction and loan adminstration costs.

The Bank charges an interest rate of 7 per cent for individuals and 4.5 per cent for cooperatives. The loans are repayable over 30 years. In 1989, inflation was running at 7–11 per cent, resulting in a negative interest rate for cooperative investments. This subsidy offered a considerable incentive to form a cooperative, although most of those receiving this advantage were in the middle-income bracket. Up to 1989, 70 per cent of Housing and Savings Bank loans had been allocated to the cooperative sector.

Loans are normally disbursed in four instalments: 15 per cent for foundation, 50 per cent for the structure, 15 per cent for doors and windows, and the remainder for completion. There is a grace period of one year after completion during which time only interest repayments need be made. Most cooperatives make repayments on time.

The Ministry and Bank offer a training and orientation programme for those receiving loans to ensure that they are familiar with the financial procedures. Such cooperatives usually use contractors to complete at least part of the building work and additional support is given in this area. The cooperative itself is responsible for overseeing the work and at least one member should be on site each day.

Whilst most cooperatives obtain loans from the Housing and Savings Bank, people with low and irregular incomes and those beyond retirement age are not eligible for credit and have to meet all the construction costs themselves. These self-help housing cooperatives are financed by a combination of members' contributions (either current income or existing savings), fundraising events, small-scale credit support such as special revolving funds, savings and credit associations and informal credit systems. Costs are reduced through the use of second-hand materials and self-help labour.

Some cooperatives have been funded by NGOs to benefit low-income groups or disadvantaged groups such as those with disabilities. In 1989, there were about ten such cooperatives.

Assessment

The following points have been made in respect of this programme:

- The supply of building materials in one of the greatest constraints.
  The Ministry is responsible for arranging for the supply of materials but
  there are often considerable delays. Cooperatives desire greater control
  both in this respect and in the design of their houses. Design
  specifications need to be reconsidered to make them less costly and to
  explore the possibilities for using cheaper local materials.
- The organizational approach has encouraged the formation of large
  numbers of small cooperatives (most with between 24 and 40 members)
  which operate relatively effectively. There is no formal structure through
  which the cooperatives can organize themselves in federations at a town,
  provincial or national level. However, one secondary union of 13
  cooperatives has been set up in Addis Ababa.
- Low-income groups are not well served by the present system as
  over 90 per cent of technical and financial resources are received by
  middle-income groups. There is a need for the Housing and Savings Bank
  to be more flexible in its approach. It should consider working with local
  government administrations and NGOs to offer loans for upgrading and
  rehabilitation, and should be willing to accept existing house titles as
  collateral in the case of low-income loan applicants.
- There is a need to ensure that more flexible ways of raising finance
  for housing are encouraged. Such means might be guarantees offered by
  NGOs, savings and credit societies and revolving loan funds.
- Building standards for low-cost housing need to be modified to
  match affordability. The use of low cost and locally-produced building
  materials should be promoted.
- There is concern that the government may become unable to provide
  resources for free infrastructure. It might therefore be useful to identify
  other methods of providing, maintaining and charging for the different
  types of infrastructure. In particular, higher-income groups could be
  charged for the services they receive, and cross subsidies between high-
  and low-income groups could be introduced.
- In respect of the management of cooperatives: small groups were
  considered to operate better; mixed income groups had not been
  successful as the members with lower incomes had not benefited equally;
  and more promotion of and training in self-help construction techniques
  would be helpful in bringing down construction costs for low-income
  groups.
- The scale and speed of the operation has been considered to be slow by
  the Ministry concerned; however, it has exceeded that of other
  cooperative programmes elsewhere in Africa.

Sources: Settlements Information Network Africa, Newsletter No 19, November 1989, Nairobi;
UNCHS (1990), *Co-operative Housing: Experiences of Mutual Self-Help*, Nairobi; and Lee Smith,
Diana (1991), 'Feasibility of SIDA aid to shelter and infrastructure through African NGOs',
unpublished report.

7

Equipo de Vivienda y Gestión Local*
(EVGL), Chile

Miguel Claro 2334
Nunoa Casilla 151
Correo 11
Santiago
Chile

INSTITUTION

Background

The Chilean Housing and Local Management Unit is a non-profit organization formed in 1983. Originally set up as a unit within the Centre for Environmental Research and Planning (CIPMA), it became independent in 1987. The Unit is currently made up of eight professionals (four architects, two economists and two social workers) and four administrative staff.

In recent years, the Unit has worked with poor urban groups to promote local development, participatory planning and self-management in the community. It seeks to reinforce the capacity of low-income communities by developing their own resources, coordinating these resources with others which are available and encouraging a democratic process of social development. The Unit has worked in three areas: housing and habitat; neighbourhood economy; and land management. Projects have been undertaken in different low-income districts in the metropolitan area of Santiago de Chile.

The institution's programmes and projects have mainly been funded by several international agencies including the Swedish Agency for Research Cooperation with Developing Countries, the Inter-American Foundation, NCOS (National Centrum Ontwikkelingssamenwerking), MISEREOR, EZE and CEBEMO.

Programmes and activities

The main current programmes and projects are listed below.

---

* Housing and Local Management Unit

- *Credit and Technical Assistance Programme for Housing Improvement (PCAT)* began at the end of 1987 as a result of a donation from the Dutch government to alleviate storm damage which had affected large sectors of the population at the time. The programme offers support to residents who want to extend, improve and/or finish their houses: a preferential credit system to obtain construction materials to carry out improvements, with sums ranging from US$150 to US$450, and professional technical assistance (social workers and architects) to form and strengthen credit groups and give training in the design and construction of the buildings.
- *Training Programmes for Small Businesses* have sought mainly to offer technical support to people running small businesses and provide technical management tools which allow business consolidation and strengthen the economic life of the district.
- *The Technical Consultancy Programme for Neighbourhood Councils* was set up in an agreement with the Municipality of La Florida and involves an initial stage in which training workshops will be set up in eight different Neighbourhood Councils to strengthen and improve neighbourhood organization and management. A second stage will have a neighbourhood assembly for all the participating organizations, held in order to combine and draw together the experiences and proposals of the different councils.
- *Andacollo Programme* is undertaken in coordination with the Municipality of Andacollo and sponsored by the Dayton Mining Company of Chile. An agreement was made to implement a programme in 1991 to promote a development plan for the city of Andacollo and its community with the technical assistance of the Unit. The objective of this programme is to design a management system which will: coordinate and strengthen the actions of different protagonists and organizations in the community; strengthen the different organizational and institutional bodies in existence (such as the municipality, Neighbourhood Councils and Community Centres); and set up a Development Fund (with resources from businesses, government and the community), an Information and Communication System and a Technical Assistance System.

CREDIT AND TECHNICAL ASSISTANCE PROGRAMME FOR HOUSING IMPROVEMENT

Introduction

The Credit and Technical Assistance Programme for Housing Improvement (PCAT) has been set up by the Housing and Local Management Team, with groups of families living in La Florida, a district in the city of Santiago, Chile. It aims to improve the self-help process which is how most of the residents build their houses. The Unit has carried out two previous projects which have served as an initial model:

1. A research project, carried out in 1982 and 1983, investigated how families with few resources built their houses, noting the possibilities and the limitations of the process.
2. With the results from the research project, the Unit carried out an action programme which attempted to overcome some of the limitations they had observed in their research. The programme consisted of setting up a Materials Bank in a settlement (Nuevo Amanecer Settlement) which gave credit for materials and technical assistance to families who connected their houses to the sanitary unit built by the government. The Bank was run by neighbourhood leaders and operated using a small amount of capital donated by the municipality, which was lent to the families for between one and four months. It made 846 loans, benefiting about 237 families.

On the basis of this experience, the Unit decided that it needed to involve an official body in the credit programme. Such an institution would need to be independent of the state (given that the residents do not repay the state, trusting in their previous experience of periodic loan cancellations). The Unit invited the Development Bank to participate and decided to set up a guarantee system among the beneficiaries of the loans as a means of assuring repayment. The Unit also undertook to coordinate the greatest possible number of institutions that might be able to offer support and benefits to the programme (financial bodies to authorize loans, private companies to provide materials at wholesale prices, NGOs for technical assistance, community organizations for support and initial organization of credit groups, and within the new democratic future, many government bodies).

The programme's general objective is to coordinate official resources from financial institutions with state resources and private resources from families, businesses supplying materials, and NGOs. The specific objective is to set up a system for credit and technical assistance to enable:

* a reduction in the period for self-help (from approximately 15–20 years to 2–5 years);
* by means of loans and savings, provision of resources for the traditional construction process;
* a reduction in the cost of housing of 15–20 per cent, by means of wholesale purchases;
* improvement in the quality and design of what is being built, through the provision of technical assistance; and
* facilitation of the formation of small self-help networks among residents to assist with housing construction.

Projects and activities

With the knowledge it had acquired, the Unit began a second project in 1987. It authorized loans through a commercial bank (the Development Bank) for groups of families acting as guarantors for each other, and established agreements with suppliers of materials. To begin with, the loans that the Bank gave were backed by a security fund equal to 100 per cent of the value of the loans, with the bank acting just as a formal intermediary for credit. Later, given the good record of loan repayment, the security fund required from the Unit was dispensed with, the bank risking its own funds.

The programme operates by forming groups of between five and eight people (heads of household), who have some previous knowledge of, and trust in, each other (neighbours, relations, friends) and who wish to join the PCAT. Each household opens a savings account with the Development Bank. Over a period of three months, they each have to deposit a monthly sum equivalent to the instalment that they will pay each month once the loan has been authorized. The members of the group each have to apply for the same amount of credit and repay it over the same period.

During this time, the Technical Advisory Team (made up of the Unit and another body) give technical assistance to enable each participant to develop their project, and to give the socio-organizational support aimed at consolidating the group. Once the initial amount has been saved and the formation of the group finalized, each person puts in a loan application to the Bank and makes a request to buy materials to the Technical Advisory Team. The Bank examines each member's background and the Technical Advisory Team checks the materials requested against the amount of the loan. Once both requests have been agreed, the group goes to the Bank. Each member places the initial amount saved in a long-term deposit account (the term being the duration of the loan), endorsing it in the Bank's name so that it can form a group guarantee. This guarantee represents 25 per cent of the loan.

The group members receive the money in the form of a promissory note which they make out to the Technical Advisory Team, which then buys and distributes the materials for each family. The households are given receipts for the purchases that have been made by the Technical Advisory Team and verify that these correspond to the request for materials which had previously been approved. Once they have the materials, the participants begin the construction (some do this individually, others with the help of other members of the group), with the support of the Technical Advisory Team.

The loans are repaid over a period of between 12 and 18 months. Once repayment is complete, the participants can automatically take out a new loan, or withdraw their contribution from the security fund, which is returned to them with adjustments corresponding to the commercial interest rate.

The challenge which the Unit set itself for 1991 was to carry out the PCAT on an extensive scale. To do this, they decided to set up a Technical Implementation Unit in conjunction with the Municipality of La Florida, in which both institutions contribute professional and administrative resources in order to carry out the so-called Pilot Phase II.

Phase II development has been in two stages. The first, carried out in 1991, was to implement the PCAT with about 2600 families. This group consisted of the Settlement Communities, made up of families with few resources who have properties on a plot of 160 square metres with a bathroom and kitchen. Most families also have provisional accommodation made of wood, in some cases connected to the sanitary units. The second stage, to be carried out from mid-1992, consists of extending the programme throughout the community to an estimated 32,000 families (40 per cent of the total population of the district).

Operational details

The programme aims to support the progressive improvement of housing through loans and technical assistance, starting with an urbanized plot with sanitary units. It targets the same population group as the Progressive Housing Policy Level 1, Stage 2 (to which the PCAT could be an alternative or a complement), which authorizes subsidies and loans to support the partial construction of the permanent housing which is connected to sanitary units.

The potential clients are families with monthly incomes of between US$175 and US$470. Families with an income of around US$175 can receive a loan amounting to approximately US$150, requiring monthly repayments of about US$15 over a year at an interest rate of 4 per cent a month. Families with incomes of about US$470 can receive a loan of approximately US$440, making monthly repayments of approximately US$47 for a year.

The PCAT requires an initial saving (which forms the Group Security Fund and is untransferable until the end of the term for repayment) equivalent to 25 per cent of the loan, which varies between a minimum of US$37 and a maximum of US$108. It does not authorize subsidies but offers a loan (received as construction materials) for the term of a year, for an amount which ranges from a minimum of US$147 to a maximum of US$441. The loan is renewable year by year, the applicant having access to between US$1176 and US$3528 over a period of eight years.

The loans are authorized by the Development Bank, and each group must begin its monthly repayments as soon as the loan has been received. Once repayment of the loan has been completed, the group decides whether or not to continue in the programme and renew its loan. If it decides not to continue, the Security Fund is returned (adjusted according to the consumer price index accumulated over the loan repayment period).

In the programme, the professional and administrative costs incurred by the Bank are charged to the user, but not the professional and administrative costs of the Technical Implementation Units.

Assessment

The impact of the PCAT was measured in three studies carried out at different stages of the programme (1987–1991). The main conclusions were:

- The programme provides, on average, 200 per cent more resources (materials, labour, other loans) than the total amount of credit authorized.
- A 15 per cent saving is achieved by buying materials in bulk, compared to the retail purchases made by the families on an individual basis.
- It provides access to technical assistance, rationalizing aspects of housing structure and construction, and improving its appearance.
- The period for the construction of permanent housing is reduced.
- For 30 per cent of the participants it facilitates mutual assistance (of particular benefit to women living alone).
- The self-esteem of participants is increased when they achieve concrete objectives through their own efforts.

- Households are integrated into a formal system for obtaining resources for housing.
- The programme is based on the traditional means of housing construction, with the families themselves providing labour, allowing the surplus (for example, savings as a result of no intermediaries being involved) to go to the people themselves.

One weakness of the programme is that those who do not meet the necessary financial requirements (among other things, insufficient monthly family income and/or a weak financial situation which is difficult or impossible to resolve) are excluded.

The implementation of the PCAT on a more extensive basis would depend on the following factors:

- Greater participation of financial institutions in the authorizing of loans: the current experience has shown the bank that it can obtain profits, with very little risk (there have been hardly any delayed payments), while making an improvement in people's living conditions.
- Capacity for family repayments, which requires certain stability in employment and earning opportunities.
- The formation of Technical Implementation Units which can be formed by municipalities, NGOs or similar institutions.
- Financial and technical resources (either from state funds, international aid or charging beneficiaries) to run the Technical Implementation Units in order to cover the professional and administrative costs.

Sources: This text has been based on the following documents: Saborido, Marisol (1991), 'Profile of Housing and Local Management Team 1991', Walker, Eduardo, 'Credit and Technical Assistance Programme for Housing Improvement – PCAT'; Banados, Ximena Concha, 'Steps or Stages of the PCAT.'

8

Fideicomiso Fondo Nacional de Habitaciones Populares* (FONHAPO), Mexico

Homero 203 y 205
Col Polanco
Mexico DF CP 11560

PROGRAMME

Introduction

Despite the challenges generated by the scale of Mexico City and its annual population growth and concentration of economic activities, there are instances that show that it is possible to implement large-scale programmes which are versatile, flexible and which reach low-income families and address the problems of the poor. One of these is a financing institution named FONHAPO which aims to provide for the housing needs of those whose income is less than 2.5 times the regional minimum wage (equal to US$272 in April 1990). As it developed the institution took into consideration the different experiences of low-income groups who had constructed dwelling units themselves. Thus, the specific needs and socio-economic characteristics of the beneficiaries have been determining factors in the formulation of mechanisms for the operation and adminstration of the financing programmes for the production of low-income housing and associated basic infrastructure and services.

Projects and activities

FONHAPO is a public institution established by the Federal Government in 1981 to finance housing programmes for low-income households. It has mainly been funded by the government although, following the earthquake in

---

* National Fund for Popular Housing

Mexico City in 1986, it also received funds from the World Bank.[1] FONHAPO developed from the direct experiences of NGOs working with the people in Mexico City. The government approached some of the staff of NGOs and asked for help in designing a national housing programme to assist low-income groups. The staff knew that one of the major constraints was a shortage of finance and a lack of interest among the commercial banks to service the credit needs of low-income communities. In response to this need, FONHAPO – a fund to give credit to the poor – was initiated. The credit system available through FONHAPO was designed by professionals with a long experience of working with the people. The Fund was established to:

- help low-income communities including those working in the informal sector in Mexico;
- respond to a need to double the housing stock between 1980 and 2000;
- finance the people's own housing construction processes and involve people in the process of housing finance;
- enable the financing of incremental development, not just new houses;
- redistribute national government funds to those with low incomes to reinforce principles of equity and social justice;
- support the development of democratic processes within and outside each community;
- locate financial support for people's urban development within the political process and ensure that government support was feasible and used efficiently;
- be decentralized; and
- institutionalize housing credit for low-income groups within government.

At the time that FONHAPO was initiated, there were many existing initiatives in Mexico but most were working with communities of between 100 and 200 households. One of the requirements of the fund would be that it would enable the scaling-up of such experiences. Communities applied for finance (loan and subsidy) from FONHAPO and implemented their projects with NGOs providing additional technical support where necessary.

This national fund provides the funding for public institutions, NGOs and community groups to undertake housing projects; it does not provide loans direct to individual households. Between 1983 and 1988, just over half its credits went to cooperatives, civil associations, urban and rural neighbourhood groups and other organized social groups. The Fund was designed to lend money only to communities who would then distribute the credit to individual households. One of the principles of the Fund's design was to support communities and their democratic principles – the organization of housing and neighbourhood improvement can be a powerful tool for community organization and the process of social consolidation. From the practical perspective, there were significant problems involved in the collection of individual repayments. If the Fund was to have an impact on the scale intended, the community would have to manage the individual accounts. When the Fund was fully operative, there were 800 accounts and 250,000 households.

FONHAPO provides credit for low-income households (in April 1990 for households earning the equivalent of less than US$272 per month) to purchase, build or improve their housing. Most of its credits have been provided in one of three credit lines: for acquiring a land site with services on which a shelter is then built; for acquiring a core housing unit with basic infrastructure and services from which the household can develop a larger unit; and for improving and enlarging an existing unit. This third credit line has also supported tenants in housing complexes suffering from physical deterioration to purchase collectively the units they rent and to improve the services and upgrade the structures. Support has also been given to the production and distribution of building materials and basic components for construction of low-income housing and support of self-help process.

Between 1983 and 1988, FONHAPO financed the construction or improvement of over 245,000 housing units throughout Mexico. Close to three quarters of these were new units in which the household taking the loan was responsible for much or all of the construction (ie the serviced sites or the core housing units). A quarter of the loans were for improving existing housing; 0.5 per cent were for the purchase of finished housing.

Operational details

The maximum size of loan is 1000 times the daily wage of the household head. The interest rates and repayment terms on its loans are tied to the 'minimum wage' which is regularly adjusted to reflect changes in living costs. A household taking on such a loan knows that its commitment is indexed to the minimum wage. In addition, the repayments cannot be greater than 25 per cent of the income of the household head at the time the loan is agreed. In rural areas, repayments are indexed to the price of the main commodity, rather than the minimum wage.

This system of calculating repayments was supported by the communities who recognized the need to maintain the capital value of the Fund and felt that their repayments were fair. Repayment rates average 93 per cent despite inflation of between 40 and 165 per cent and a reduction in the real value of earnings between 1982 and 1992. Although no interest charge was added at the beginning, Mexico had rapid inflation during this period and the linking of repayments to the minimum wage ensured that the real value of repayments kept pace (more or less) with inflation. An additional charge of 2 per cent was later added to repayments and passed on to the communities to cover their administration costs.

Loans are given for between seven and eight years. Communities which successfully repay their first loan can apply for a second loan. Land has been used as collateral, although, in a few cases, valuation has proved difficult. A subsidy is included in the programme and half the total value of this subsidy is earmarked for those with an income of less than 1.5 times the minimum monthly wage. Forty per cent of the total cost of a project is eligible for a subsidy; 25 per cent is given immediately and the remaining 15 per cent if the repayment schedule is maintained.

FONHAPO makes explicit the level of subsidy given by the government to the families and there are no preferential rates of interest. Repayment charges increase at a rate equal to the rates of increase in the minimum wage. If during one month there is no increase, then the payment stays the same as in the previous month. Families start repayments two months after the work is finished. In cases where the loan goes to buy a new house, it is after one month.

Assessment

FONHAPO's credit lines and programmes have given the institution an effectiveness seldom seen in governmental programmes. Probably its greatest achievement is the fact that, for the first time in Mexico, temporary workers and persons belonging to the informal sector, traditionally excluded from governmental financial mechanisms and from the formal financial system, make up a large proportion of the beneficiaries of the loans given by FONHAPO. Yet, its consolidation as a government programme cannot be explained without taking into consideration the past experiences of NGOs and community based groups in Mexico. In fact, the people who gave FONHAPO its creativity and flexibility in the first years of operation all had experience of low-cost housing in NGOs.

FONHAPO has succeeded in reaching the poor. Between 1983 and 1988, 50 per cent of loans were to families in which the head of household had an income of less than 1.5 times the minimum wage, the remaining 50 per cent was received by households where the household head earned between 1.5 and 2.5 times the minimum wage. In 1983, when the programme was first established, 25 per cent of all loans was given to communities and 75 per cent to other institutions such as local government departments. Within a few years, the structure of the programme had succeeded in shifting a much greater resource allocation to community development. Between 1985 and 1987, 66 per cent of the total number of loans was to community organizations.

Notes:
1. In 1986, the World Bank gave FONHAPO a loan for reconstruction of low-income housing damaged by the earthquake that shook Mexico in September 1985.

Sources: Ortiz, Enrique (1991), 'FONHAPO: Mexico's National Trust Fund for Popular Housing, 1983–88', Box 6 in *Access to Basic Infrastructure by the Urban Poor*, Aurelio Menendez, EDI Seminar Report No 28, The World Bank, Washington DC; Housing Finance Workshop (1993), MISEREOR/ACHR, Cebu City.

9

Fundación Carvajal, Columbia

Carrera 2, Norte
Apartado aereo: 6178 y 43
Cali
Colombia

INSTITUTION

Background

The Carvajal Foundation is a non-profit association which was set up in the city of Cali, Colombia, in 1961 to promote programmes for disadvantaged groups and to contribute to the development of the country. Its starting capital was provided by the transfer of 40 per cent of the shares from Empresa Carvajal y Cia, an important printing company.

From its inception until 1977, the Foundation worked in Popular Integration Centres which had been set up by the Archdiocese of Cali in various districts of the city. At the end of the 1970s, these Centres became autonomous and the Foundation began to implement community development projects among other underprivileged groups in the city of Cali.

The programmes are mainly carried out in Cali, which has a population of about 1.5 million. In particular, activities have focused on the district of Aguablanca, which has a population of approximately 300,000 and the highest concentration of poor people in the city. The training programme has had a broader focus and has extended to other areas of the city. As a result of their success in the programmes they have implemented, the Foundation has begun to work in other Colombian cities and in various Latin American countries, such as Chile, Ecuador, Venezuela and Brazil. This work has been implemented either through subsidiary foundations or through foundations which have been set up by the subsidiaries that the Carvajal Group has in these countries.

Programmes and activities

The Foundation's activities concentrate on a number of different issues including small-business development, low-income housing, popular education, basic health care and the development of basic community services. The last of these programmes includes: shopkeepers' suppliers, material banks (now integrated into the housing programme), health services and associated services such as the sale of household goods, loans from the Banco Central Hipotecario (the Central Mortgage Bank), telecommunications and post office branches.

The most innovative aspect of the Foundation's programmes is the emphasis placed on training; loans are reduced almost to an accessory component. The teaching materials which are produced are very important, particularly within the shopkeepers' and small-business programmes. A current project is the development of a construction handbook. The consultancy component is also important.

The objective in each of the programmes is to struggle against poverty through community development. The policy has been to help those who, according to the institution, want to help themselves. For this reason, all the programmes have mechanisms which support and complement (but do not substitute for) the efforts of the people and their communities. The Foundation uses its organizational experience to identify priorities, concerning itself with linking solutions to individual problems with solutions to the problems of urban life generally. This is exemplified in programmes such as refuse recycling, which help improve the urban environment.

Obtaining funds

The Foundation's main source of funds is its shareholding in the Empresa Carvajal y Cia. It also receives loans from international organizations such as the Inter-American Development Bank which has supported the small-business programme and the Ford Foundation which has supported the shopkeepers' programme. An agreement has been made with CARE in Ecuador for the development of a number of programmes for small businesses in the cities of Santo Domingo de los Colorados, Quevedo, Esmeraldas, Manta and Portoviejo. USAID has also pledged funds from its Regional Housing Office, as has the UNDP.

PROGRAMMES

Introduction

Information about three of the programmes of the Foundation is given below. The history of each of these programmes is different; the small business programme began its activities in 1977, the shopkeepers' programme nearly a decade later and the housing programme in 1982.

Projects and activities

Small businesses

The small business programme aims to improve the performance of existing small businesses, by providing administrative training, consultancy and loan finance. According to the definition of the Colombian programme, those with fewer than 10 employees are considered 'small businesses', but most have between two and four people working in them. Most small businesses do not have their own premises.

The programme carried out by the Foundation is centred around training and consultancy – essential requisites for access to loans. The training programme lasts for 72 hours and covers seven subjects, each forming the basis of a ten-hour workshop. The basic subjects included are: principles of administration, accountancy, costs, investment projects, marketing and sales. Specific teaching material appropriate to the different educational levels of the participants has been developed. A large percentage of those receiving training applies later for a loan. Consultancy is generally carried out in the workplace of the particular small business, the objective being to build on the knowledge acquired in the training courses.

The institution is currently devising new models for the development of the small business programmes which include:

*   *Support programmes in marketing and retailing:* annual exhibitions have been organized which are devoted to products from small businesses. In Cali, six exhibitions have been held with approximately 350 small businesses taking part in each one.
*   *Purchase unions:* groups of people who run small businesses in the productive sector join together to reduce the costs of inputs, making their products more competitive in the final market.
*   *Selling points:* merchandise from the Cali Small Businesses Association is distributed to large stores. The Foundation's programme helps small businesses promote their work, using the attributes of high quality, good design, reliability and low price.
*   *Support programmes in technical assistance:* in 1989 agreements were signed with the Servicio Nacional de Aprendizaje (SENA, the National Learning Service) and the Swisscontact Institution in Switzerland to support small businesses in the shoe and metal mechanics industries.
*   *Programmes for people running small and medium-sized businesses:* this programme was launched in 1989. It reflects the fact that the number of people successfully running small businesses had grown, the businesses have become larger and these enterprises have different requirements for administrative support.

Housing
The housing programme began in 1982 and includes both training in self-construction techniques and a materials bank. As with the other programmes, the emphasis is on training; in the present programme this is even more pronounced, as the Foundation does not provide loans for the construction of housing.

The programme works with a complex Land and Housing Programme which is jointly carried out by various institutions.[1] Between them, the institutions have divided up the tasks to be undertaken according to their specialist areas. Thus the Foundation contributes training and a materials bank, while others, such as the Banco Central Hipotecario, authorize loans. This joint effort with other organizations has been important in developing guidelines for subdividing land and construction work. The Foundation has been actively involved with government agencies in developing these guidelines.

The sub-programmes which make up the housing programme – training for self-help, training for completion of work and materials banks – are carried out independently. The present view of the specialists who coordinate this programme is that the housing sub-programmes need to be better coordinated both between themselves and with the other programmes.

The unusual aspects of this programme include: coordination with private and state organizations to develop a unified programme for land and housing; an emphasis on training for the different processes of housing construction and furniture-making; and encouragement to set up cooperatives to carry out projects such as surfacing roads or developing parks in public areas. The establishment of material banks which are linked to the small businesses that the Carvajal Foundation has promoted through training and loans is also important. Part of the materials sold by the bank are produced by small businesses, as the result of which the sale of their product is guaranteed and they can sell at lower prices than other businesses selling construction materials. This provides an important saving in the area of production prices, demonstrating that these can be lower than those of large businesses.

Shopkeepers' support programme
This programme aims to reduce food prices, particularly in the district of Aguablanca. The neighbourhood shopkeeper is the manager of a small commercial business and, like small industrial businesses, generally lacks managerial skills. The programme aims to provide the shopkeeper with the knowledge necessary to run the business efficiently. The programme has the same components as the small business programme. Since it was established it has trained 1,200 shopkeepers and supplied loans totalling approximately US$200,000 to 750 businesses. A shopkeepers' suppliers has been set up to act as a wholesale centre for the shopkeepers trained by the programme.

Operational details

Loans are an important component in the small business programme. They have been financed with resources from the Inter-American Development Bank and administered by financial intermediaries and the Foundation. In contrast to the training and consultancy, which are directly run by the Foundation, loans have always been administered by financial intermediaries. To begin with, the Foundation for Higher Education (FES) was the agent, but later the Banco Comercial Antioqueno and Financiacoop took over.

In 1989, the Inter-American Development Bank loan was about US$200,000. By 1989, the total of the Foundation's assets equalled approximately US$7.75 million. The shopkeepers' programme has obtained funds from the Ford Foundation. The housing programme does not yet have external financing. The people receive loans from the Banco Central Hipotecario for the construction of housing.

The beneficiaries have made it clear that they do not find the cost of the training courses excessive, considering the benefits. However, there is no information about the people who have not attended these programmes, and the problems that they have had in getting on to the programmes.

Assessment

In the small business programme, there is a very high return on capital investment; a job is created for every loan of US$1000. The people running small businesses who have received training and loans from the Foundation have generally gone on to form businesses with 20 employees and, in some cases, more than 30. Up to December 1989, about 15,000 managers of small businesses in Cali had taken part in training courses and 5000 business entrepreneurs had made use of credit amounting to more than US$2.5 million. Since 1984, the Colombian Government has adopted the small business programmes which currently forms part of the National Development Plan which is coordinated by the National Planning Department.

A study undertaken by the Centro de Investigaciones y Documentacion Socioeconomica (Centre for Socioeconomic Research and Documentatio) of the Universidad del Valle in 1989 showed that, among the many benefits of the shopkeepers' programme, was a reduction of between 15 and 20 per cent in the prices of essential items. The programme covered 20 per cent of the items in the family shopping basket in the residential area in which it was active, estimated to include 100,000 inhabitants in 1989.

There are as yet no assessments of the housing programme (FEDES-ARROLLO is currently carrying out a study) but it appears that the programme's results are very positive for the reasons which have already been mentioned. However, an analysis is needed of who the beneficiaries are and how many of those who could potentially benefit remain outside the programme because of the demanding construction schedule – the housing has to be completed within two months – and the costs involved.

Among the problems which have been noted (although without a comprehensive study of the Foundation) are that the programmes do not reach the poorest people; that fees are charged for the training courses; and that it is necessary to have a small amount of capital to begin a small business or to construct a house, because of the construction materials required and the period in which it has to be built. The Foundation has acknowledged that it does not support the sectors with the greatest needs in urban areas, but those sectors which have a capacity to save and who already have some small initial savings.

Notes:
1.   Participating in the agreement are the Banco Central Hipotecario; the Centro Nacional de Estudios para la Construcion (the National Centre for Construction Studies), CENAC; the Instituto de Vivienda de Cali (Cali Housing Institute), INVICALI, the Universidad del Valle; the Insitituto de Credito Territorial (the Institute for Land Credi), ICT; the Departamento Administrativo Nacional de Estadistica (the National Administrative Department of Statistics), DANE; the Corporacion de Recreacion Popular (the Corporation for Popular Recreation); SENA and the Carvajal Foundation.

Sources: Fundacion Carvajal (1990), *Informe anual 1989*, Cali; Fundacion Carvajal (1990), *Fundacion Carvajal de Cali y su tarea de desarrollo social*, Cali; Fundacion Carvajal, *Programa de Microempresas*, Cali; Fundacion Carvajal (1989), *Programa Intergral de Vivienda*, Cali; and material from interviews undertaken with the Foundation in 1990.

10

Fundación Promotora de Vivienda* (FUPROVI), Costa Rica

Apartado Postal 1231–1002
San Jose
Costa Rica

INSTITUTION

Background

The Housing Promotion Foundation is a private non-profit-making institution which was set up in 1987. The Foundation focuses on the problems of poor communities, particularly in relation to low-income housing and community development, and encourages the organization and participation of such communities in developing solutions to their problems. According to FUPROVI, it is the families and the communities that should carry out the work and provide the necessary direction, especially in public sector organizations: FUPROVI is an institution which facilitates and supports the action of such communities.

FUPROVI carries out national housing and community development projects and encourages a constant exchange of experiences at a regional level. It has focused on 'marginal' settlements in the metropolitan area of San Jose (the Costa Rican capital) and has recently begun to work with the residents of Limon Province, a region experiencing considerable social and economic deterioration and stagnation.

Programmes and activities

FUPROVI's action is based on family and community support. It aims to support people so that they can, either through assisted self-construction or their own efforts and/or mutual assistance, carry out projects and develop as a community. It also tries to identify solutions to community problems relating to such areas as health, employment opportunities, education and recreation. The Foundation provides technical resources, engineering, legal services, social support and financial resources to carry out these projects. The

---

* Housing Promotion Foundation

participating communities provide community organization and labour. The Foundation's general administrative costs are covered by charging for the financial administration of the resources that it manages. In order to encourage administrative efficiency, it has decided that administrative costs should not exceed 5 per cent of total programme costs.

HOUSING PROGRAMME FOR INFORMAL SETTLEMENTS IN THE GRAND METROPOLITAN AREA AND LESS DEVELOPED MUNICIPALITIES

Introduction

FUPROVI began work in July 1988 with the first programme, due to be completed in June 1991. A second programme was set up (1990–1991), taking up the components and objectives of the first and extending the geographical area of action.

The programme's objectives are to:

- carry out projects, with the participation of groups and municipalities, using self-help, mutual assistance and their own efforts;
- train community groups to identify solutions to housing and community problems;
- help with the management, support and supervision of groups interested in carrying out projects for the benefit of the community; and
- diversify sources of finance for FUPROVI and strengthen contacts at an international level (in order to disseminate these experiences).

The beneficiaries of the projects are families and communities in extreme poverty in Costa Rica. The work is carried out in neglected communities or informal settlements in the San Jose Metropolitan Area and also in some secondary cities which benefit little from existing programmes or policies. Special attention is given to vulnerable or disadvantaged groups, such as 'women-headed households', old people and refugee families. Other groups are also encouraged to participate in the programme (such as cooperatives, development associations, pre-housing committees and households which are not organized).

Projects and activities

The programme consists of the following areas of work:

- *Credit for construction materials, housing extension and improvements.*
  Funds are provided to families with few resources so that they can carry out projects using both self-help and mutual help. These are provided to families or communities with and without legal land tenure.
- *Assistance, training and support.* Three kinds of assistance are offered: technical, techno-legal and social. The first is mainly aimed at families and communities drawing up blueprints and plans for housing

construction, and applying for permission to carry out construction work, housing extension and improvement. The second is to help legalize property titles, possession or tenancy. The third, is given for the development of community organization necessary to carry out and administer construction work, and to help negotiate with public and private institutions to achieve the necessary support to resolve the community's most pressing problems.

- *Fund for basic services and projects of community and municipal interest.* This fund offers credit in materials used for the construction or improvement of basic infrastructure facilities and also supports projects of community and/or municipal interest.
- *Components for the acquisition of equipment and tools to facilitate community work.* This involves the loan of tools and machinery to community groups in support of their activities in housing improvement and construction and projects for community improvement. This is intended to facilitate such work, reduce the term and intensity of the processes, and the cost of carrying out the projects.
- *Institutional development.* The objective is to support the development of the executive body for the programme and other institutions participating in its implementation.

Operational details

Financial support for the programmes which FUPROVI undertakes comes from both national and foreign resources. Foreign resources come from:

- bilateral cooperation between governments (eg the Swedish International Development Authority);
- non-government organizations (eg DIAKONIA, Sweden); and
- funds from the United Nations Commission for Refugees, passed through the National Housing Bank, for refugee families.

National resources come from:

- the National Financial System for Housing;
- the beneficiary communities which give, among other things, their labour, material and intellectual resources during the process, and land (when it is in their possession);
- income generated by FUPROVI's financial administration from its capital resources; and
- private donations, private businesses and national institutions which identify themselves with the programme's objectives.

Financial needs
Financing limits have been established for different components of the programme:

- Loans for the construction of new housing and improvements include materials, tools, equipment and a small sum for labour (assigned to specialist work).

- Basic services: US$950 is the upper limit for loans to beneficiaries in Greater San Jose, which is equivalent to five basic services at US$190 per unit. In the Limon area, the maximum limit has been estimated as US$1140, the higher costs being incurred because of the location of the area.
- Funds for community projects: the average loan is US$5000. At least 30 families have to benefit from the work that is carried out.
- Assistance, training and support: the costs of these components are recovered through a fixed percentage applied to the full loan.
- Insurance policies and formalization costs: FUPROVI allocates an amount to cover the cost of insurance policies for delayed payments and for such items as fire insurance and solicitors' fees which are related to the formalization of the loan. These costs occur when the legalisation of the land is concluded and, due to the particular circumstances, the family cannot be party to a loan with the National Financing System for Housing (which is how the loan is recovered by FUPROVI).

Financing model

The relationship between FUPROVI and the household in relation to resources for housing, home improvements and work on infrastructure should be divided into two stages:

1. *Short term.* At this stage, the family is not usually the owner of the land it occupies. As the household does not yet own the land, the loan is authorized by guaranteeing it with a financing contract made in favour of FUPROVI, which comes to hold the executive title in the case of delayed repayments. During the construction period, which has been established by mutual agreement and during which time no interest is charged, technical and legal help and support are given to the household to enable it to legalize its tenure. If, a month after building has been completed, legalization has not been finalised, repayment by the beneficiary begins as specified in the repayment schedule in the signed financing contract. The sum received forms part of a rotating fund, which is used for the same programme.
2. *Long term.* The legalization of land aims to make the families who have loans become landowners and help them to join the National Financing System for Housing. This latter organization then becomes the lending agency and the programme recovers its investment and can then return the funds to a rotating fund for re-use.

If for some reason it is not possible for a household to obtain legal tenure or if the household is not accepted by the National Financing System for Housing, it will be debtor to the programme for the 15 year term of the loan and interest repayments. Once the loan has been authorized, the interest rate is fixed. To determine the interest rate, a scale is drawn up in which the interest to be charged is related to the family income, with those with a larger income paying more interest. Nevertheless, repayments at lower levels are increasing. The organization tries to ensure that the annual increase in repayment charges is lower than the percentage increase in the minimum salary.

Once the loan application has been accepted by the National Financing System, a subsidiary of this organization, the Mortgage Bank for Housing (BANHVI), offers a loan. By means of this system, a direct subsidy or 'family Bond' (FOSUVI) is authorized and a loan (FONAVI) for a 15 year term is granted. The size of the loan depends on the family's income. BANHVI stipulates the size of the bonds and the loans which each family can receive. By using this framework, FUPROVI knows from the beginning the amount which it can obtain for the families it assists.

In some cases an additional loan from FUPROVI is necessary, as the bond and the loan which have been authorized under the National Financing System are not sufficient to achieve a satisfactory solution.

Four groups are involved in FUPROVI's investment recuperation procedure through the National Financing System: BANHVI, FUPROVI, an authorized body (ie an NGO which is authorized to be a part of this programme), and the family which has received the loan. The procedure is as follows:

1. Each family's case is presented by FUPROVI to the authorized body, with the aim of obtaining the Family Bond and the loan on a long-term basis in accordance with the law for the National Financing System for Housing.
2. The authorized body considers the cases and presents them to the BANHVI for its approval via FOSUVI (family bond) and FONAVI (base loan).
3. The Bank approves the beneficiary's presentation, thus allowing the authorized body to formalize it.
4. The authorized body formalizes the loan individually with each beneficiary, granting the loan and the corresponding family bond. At this stage there are paper transactions only and none of the resources are transferred to the families.
5. Once the agreement between the authorized body and the beneficiary has been formalized, BANHVI transfers what corresponds to the family bond to the authorized body.
6. The authorized body, with the approval of the beneficiary family, repays FUPROVI the amount which has been invested up to this point.
7. The families then repay the loan on a long term basis to the authorized body.
8. All the sums repaid to FUPROVI are deposited in a rotating fund, which allows more families to be assisted.

Four kinds of assistance have been given to date within the programme:

1. *Relocations.* These occur when it is impossible to assist the group in the place where it is located for technical reasons, or when the group does not own the land it lives on and has asked for support to carry out a project on land which has been purchased, or the land is owned by a third party which has agreed to donate or sell it.

2. *Rehousing.* Groups of families which are located on the land on which the programme is to be carried out are rehoused.
3. *Assistance to individuals.* Assistance is given to individuals located on the periphery of the land where projects are carried out by the programme. The Refugee Programme also provides assistance on an individual, scattered basis with the resources from the United Nations Commission for Refugees.
4. *Reconstruction.* An emergency programme of reconstruction assisted families who were affected by the earthquakes of 22 December 1990 and 22 April 1991.

Assessment

The programme has provided housing, and has also developed human and material resources and services in the communities and institutions of the public and private sectors. In general, the first phase of the project was extremely successful in meeting the targets that were set. Where targets were not met, there were acceptable and understandable reasons for this.

Additional time was required to implement the first phase, in part due to the commitment to establish participatory planning processes for urban development. Initially many of the communities were sceptical and time was needed to demonstrate FUPROVI's willingness to develop an improvement programme. Time was also required because the public institutions took longer to undertake their role in the programme than was originally anticipated.

There have been other problems especially in the formation of the 'work team' and in the search for a working model which is able to show results and attract resources. Several measures have been taken to resolve this difficulty. A simple work structure has been designed which involves the families in the community in the execution of the project, resulting in very positive changes at an individual, family and community level. This also avoids an increase in personnel assigned to the projects. New plans avoid a separation between social work and technical construction.

Several important elements in the programme were identified as contributing to the success of Phase One. These include:

• careful monitoring of both quantitative and qualitative aspects;
• developing a training programme based mainly on national resources; and
• a support programme for the institution with short-term consulting services determined by need.

Sources: This text has been written based on the following documents: FUPROVI, 'FUPROVI: an example of community participation' and Stein, A (1990) 'Funding Community Level Initiatives: cases from Latin America', IIED-AL, Buenos Aires. Additional information has been taken from: Sevilla, Manuel (1993), 'New approaches for aid agencies; FUPROVI's community based shelter programme', *Environment and Urbanization*, Vol 5, No 1.

11

Fundación Salvadorena de Desarrollo y Vivienda Minima* (FUNDASAL), El Salvador

Calle L -B Nro 7 Reparto Santa Alegria
Ciudad Delgado
Apartado Postal 421
San Salvador
El Salvador

INSTITUTION

Background

FUNDASAL is a non-governmental organization which was originally set up in 1986 to provide relief for people affected by the flooding of the River Acelhuate in San Salvador, the capital city of El Salvador. FUNDASAL emerged from and operates within a national context characterized by rapid urbanization and a high population density, limited land and natural resources, little economic activity, a financially constrained public sector, an unequal distribution of income and wealth and a low level of organization among the poor. These difficulties are made more acute by the war taking place in the country and have also been made worse by natural disasters such as the earthquake of 1986.

Neither the private sector nor the government has been able to produce significant amounts of low-income housing. In part this is because of the scale of the problem: over 60 per cent of the population is classified as being of low income. At present, over half those with low incomes live in urban areas.

Working within such circumstances, FUNDASAL adopted the following objectives:

---

* Salvador Foundation for Development and Basic Housing

- to support the efforts of the poor to improve their housing and living conditions;
- to promote community organization and self-management, creating alternative models for community development; and
- to promote social and structural change.

FUNDASAL now has projects in each of the country's principal cities of San Salvador, Santa Ana, Sonsonante, Usulatan and San Miguel. It is a membership organization and its highest decision-making body is the General Members' Assembly, which elects an Executive Council, executive director and general manager. Administratively, the Foundation is structured into four divisions: operations, social action, finance and law.

There are several sources of finance for the institution's projects and activities:

- grants from Northern NGOs, eg CEBEMO and ICOO in Holland, MISEREOR in Germany – which provided more than 60 per cent of all institutional spending for over ten years – DIAKONIA and AIC in Sweden, OXFAM, CAFOD and Christian Aid in England, Catholic Relief Services and the IAF in the USA, Food for the World, Agro-Action and EZE in Germany;
- loans from multilateral and bilateral agencies, eg the World Bank (US$18 million), the Kreditandstalt fur Weideraufbau (KfW) of Germany (US$17 million) and the Inter-American Development Bank (US$0.5 million);
- loans from local financial institutions: Banco Hipotecario (Mortgage Bank, US$1.95 million), Financiera Nacional de Vivienda (National Housing Finance, US$0.13 million), and Direccion General de Tesoreria (General Budget Management, US$1.1 million);
- grants from multilateral and bilateral agencies: the Italian government through the UNDP (US$8 million); US-AID and the Organization of American States (OEA);
- private domestic donations, with an annual average equalling US$0.15 million from both companies and individuals;
- fees from the participating families, approximately 5 per cent of the institution's annual income; and
- financial benefits such as interest on long-term deposits (US$0.1 million per year).

Programmes and activities

FUNDASAL's main activity is to undertake housing programmes for low-income groups using a process involving mutual assistance and progressive development. Through these activities, it initiates social and economic changes for participants.

FUNDASAL's work made a quantitative and qualitative leap in 1974 and 1977 when the Foundation signed, with the support of the government, two loan agreements with the World Bank for US$18.7 million to construct 15,000 living units. Between 1974 and 1977, eight projects were carried out, containing 4719 units. This programme has shown that it is possible for an NGO to have a major impact in the construction of houses for low-income families through the large-scale reproduction of the mutual assistance and progressive development model.

FUNDASAL has carried out a range of secondary activities, mainly directed at the people involved in housing programmes. These have included the Educational and Cultural Programme, the Integrated Health Programme (primarily support for the establishment and operation of community clinics), the Socio-economic Development Programme (with financial, technical and social support for small businesses, support groups and cooperatives) and the Research Programme.

SANTA TERESA PROJECT

Introduction

The Santa Teresa Project is located in an area of approximately 42 hectares in the city of San Martin, Metropolitan Area of San Salvador, El Salvador. This project is within the framework of FUNDASAL's Housing Programme, which considers housing 'as a form of mediation bringing together social groups with few financial resources; thus enabling processes of education and analysis of their circumstances, which allows the beneficiaries to regain confidence in themselves and their potential and that of their social group to deal with the problems that affect them individually and collectively in a manner that is conscious and democratic'.[1] The fundamental aim is individual, family and community advancement for low-income communities.

The project primarily consists of preparing 2370 plots and equipping them with services, using a system of self-construction and progressive development (ie only a core unit is provided to allow families to complete the house as finance becomes available). The project is intended to facilitate self-management processes for the extension and improvement of housing, the resolution of other problems and the securing of basic infrastructure and services.

As with the other projects undertaken by FUNDASAL, the aim is to develop concepts and alternative working methods which may contribute to a social model beneficial to the majority of low-income groups. Additional components have been set up which are complementary to the main project, such as the Child Care Programme, the Archaeological Rescue Project, the Reforestation Project and others of interest to the community; 'carried out on the basis of new work perspectives ... that is, to enable the community to assume and internalize its responsibility for the conservation of the national heritage'.[2]

To be eligible, beneficiaries must have few financial resources, lack housing or any other land, be part of a family group, not have another housing loan, be able to participate in the processes of mutual assistance and earn 500 to 1300 colones (US$60 to 160) a month.

Projects and activities

The services supplied to the 2370 plots in the project are of two types:

1. services related to physical infrastructure such as individual services for drinking water, sewerage and drainage, electricity, roads and pavements; and
2. services for social infrastructure, areas for markets, ecological conservation, the conservation of places with archaeological interest, a place for the community centre and an area for future productive activities.

FUNDASAL's methodology involves combining the construction process (developed with community participation) with educational and organization processes fundamental to institutional work. It aims to maximize the labour beneficiaries contribute in order to maintain the project's level of financial accessibility, but without placing undue strain on participants. It also aims to achieve new sources of employment and maximize the quality and quantity of the work to be carried out with available resources (technical–professional capacity, construction market, unskilled labour, new sources of employment).

The work carried out can be classified in two categories:

1. projects carried out without community participation, ie those related to the preparation of the land, the structure of the plots, and work required for the implementation of basic services and community facilities; and
2. projects carried out with community participation, ie those related to the construction of houses and the provision of domestic facilities for drainage and sewerage, the construction of the community centre, and the implementation of programmes for reforestation and future productive activities.

Operational details

To date the Santa Teresa Project has the following sources of finance:

- *FUNDASAL* provides the land, the preliminary assessment, the overall design and part of the general administration.
- *The Italian government (through UNDP)* provides most of the financing of the projects for urban services, construction, housing materials and site administration, together with machinery and general administration. The total amount contributed is about US$8.3 million.
- *United Nations Development Programme* participates with its own funds, supporting construction projects of interest to the community (community centre and school) and funding the Training Programme.
- *Lay movement for Latin America* this Italian NGO participates in the project, using funds (donated by the Italian government) to provide four technicians working on contracts, the mutual assistance process, social infrastructure and the project's health programme.

The funds are spent in one of two ways. They are either assigned to the project in the form of subsidies (non-recoverable funds) or granted as loans (recoverable funds). The aim is to use the funds in a way which allows the project to be accessible to low-income households.

The potential beneficiaries are families whose income is between 500 and 1300 colones (US$60 to US$160) a month (the current minimum wage in the Metropolitan Area of San Salvador is 705 colones).

FUNDASAL sets down financial conditions in respect of the investment to be made in the project. It establishes a maximum investment and if this investment is exceeded through errors in the administration, the institution has to meet the excess without additional charges for the user; on the other hand, if the investment is less than the maximum investment then only the part which is invested is recoverable.

Loans made to beneficiaries in the Santa Teresa Project are for 20 years with an interest rate of 3.8 per cent a year. Payments are to be made monthly, and the maximum size of repayment is 80 colones (US$10) each month.

There are items which are subject to repayment (ie where the payment is taken on by the beneficiaries) and items which are considered non-recoverable (ie provided as a grant to beneficiaries). Among the recoverable costs are: land acquisition; the construction materials for housing (including foundations, walls, doors, windows, etc); and the on-site administration needed to carry out the project, plus a proportional share of FUNDASAL's administration costs, depending on the demands which each specific project makes of the latter. Among the non-recoverable costs are: the preparation of the land (including systems for the distribution of drinking water, sewerage systems, drainage systems, roads and pavements, preparation of land to form the plots and security systems); the installations needed to provide basic services (wells, pumping stations, water tanks, treatment plants, etc); networks for the distribution of electricity; the construction of permanent road surfaces for vehicular traffic; and the construction of community facilities, such as schools.

Assessment

FUNDASAL's Housing Programme (of which the Santa Teresa Project is an example) shows that it is possible to reproduce the mutual assistance and progressive development model adopted by the Foundation on a large scale and in a way which is meaningful in dealing with the country's housing problem. This is most evident when FUNDASAL's work is compared with the efforts of government institutions for the construction of low-cost housing over the same period. FUNDASAL also demonstrates that it is possible for an NGO to have a significant impact on the construction of housing for low-income families. And it demonstrates the potential of housing programmes as a means to produce psycho-social changes in the poorest population, encouraging a raising of their consciousness, improved organization and greater participation in national socio–political activity and their search for better living conditions.

However, certain conditions are necessary for an NGO like FUNDASAL to be able to make a significant contribution to the housing problem:

- The work must be begun and sustained through the efforts and initiative of the local community.
- It appears important to maintain the boundaries which separate social improvements from political activism.
- In projects for social improvement, qualified technical and professional personnel who also have a sense of social commitment are needed.
- Modern, flexible management is essential.
- In the scale of operations, the possibility for reproduction and relevance must be sought.
- International technical support and finance must be mobilized, thus preventing the NGO from coming under pressure from charitable agencies to go beyond its abilities, limitations and nature.

Notes:
1.   FUNDASAL (1991) *Proyecto Santa Teresa: Una experiencia de dotacion de viviendas a sectores de bajos ingresos economicos*, mimeograph.
2.   Ibid.

Sources: This text is, for the most part, a synthesis of internal documents written by FUNDASAL, in particular, the text *Proyecto Santa Teresa: Una experiencia de dotacion de viviendas a sectores de bajos ingresos economicos*. Additional information was obtained from: Bombarolo, F and A Stein (1990), *Las ONGs y su Rol en la Problematica Habitacional y en el Desarrollo Social de America Latina*, mimeograph, IIED-AL, Buenos Aires; FUNDASAL, Journal *Noticias de FUNDASAL*, various issues, El Salvador; FUNDASAL (1984), *Memoria de Labores*, mimeograph, Ciudad Delgado, El Salvador; FUNDASAL (1991) *Proyecto Santa Teresa: Una experiencia de dotacion de viviendas a sectores de bajos ingresos ecomonicos*, mimeograph, Ciudad Delgado, El Salvador; Silva, M and F Altschul (1986), *Programa de lotes con servicios y desarrollo comunal. FUNDASAL. El Salvador*, GTZ, Germany; Stein, A (1989), 'Critical Issues in Community Participation in Self-help Housing Programmes: the experience of FUNDASAL' in *Community Development Journal* Vol 25, No 1.

12

Fundación Vivienda y Comunidad* (FVC), Argentina

25 de Mayo 381
(1072) Buenos Aires
Argentina

INSTITUTION

Background

The Housing and Community Foundation is an NGO which promotes activities to improve the living environment of low-income urban communities.

During the period from its inception in 1971 until 1977, the Foundation carried out various programmes for the elderly. From 1977, objectives changed, and the Foundation began to support low-income groups, providing technical assistance for the self-help plans of the inhabitants in emergency housing areas in Buenos Aires.

The primary objective of the Foundation is to increase the level of organization and participation of the groups with which they are working, using as a basis a critical analysis of their circumstances and the implementation of initiatives designed to improve their lives.

Programme and activities

Among the projects completed or in progress are: house-building in four districts through technical assistance, self-help and mutual assistance (amounting to a total of 208 houses); participation in a programme, along with three other NGOs, for the provision of 4000 plots of land with services (286 now completed); consultancy services for communities and technical teams; and financing and support for 30 community micro-projects.

At present, the Foundation has a staff of 19 which includes architects, social workers, field workers, accountants, lawyers and administrative personnel. It works in the districts of Greater Buenos Aires and the Federal Capital. Main

---

* Housing and Community Foundation

sources of financing have been agencies in the North (including MISEREOR in Germany, IAF in the US, CEBEMO in Holland and Broederlijk in Belgium) and, to a lesser extent, private donations and contributions from the Argentine government.

PROGRAMME

Introduction

At the beginning of 1987, the Foundation began administrating a financial fund set up by MISEREOR to finance micro-projects in low-income communities. MISEREOR authorized 900,000 German Marks (approximately US$600,000) for this fund which aims to:

- respond to the needs of the underprivileged communities;
- reduce to an absolute minimum the administrative requirements for agreeing and dispersing funds;
- allow the decisions to be taken in the area where the projects are going to be carried out;
- allow for greater local control in establishing repayment schedules with beneficiary groups; and
- allow for the possibility to reinvest returned funds quickly in other local projects.

Projects and activities

The fund has financed projects in three main areas:

1. Neighbourhood improvement (eg nursery provision, first aid centres, water pumps, pavements, repairs and drains).
2. Work and income-generation (eg artisans' workshops, production of construction materials, consumer cooperatives, wholesale purchase of building materials and bakeries).
3. Popular education (eg schools, neighbourhood bulletins and equipment to print educational material).

Operational details

Community groups can obtain funding in a number of different ways, depending on what they want to do and the scale of resources available to them:

- *Full subsidy* the group commits itself to providing only 10 per cent of the total budget for the project, the remaining share being obtained from the fund.

- *Part subsidy and part loan* the group must return a part of what it receives to the fund, according to conditions agreed in each case.
- *Full loan* in all such cases, the loan must fall within the size limits established by the FVC (currently between 5000 and 22,500 DM).

The size of the loan and the associated terms and conditions vary depending on the type of project. In some cases where the loan is provided for income-generation activities, the size of repayments and of the capital loaned is adjusted according to either the anticipated increase in the goods produced, or the price which might be obtained for the new products or the cost of materials needed to carry out the project (for example, according to the price of bread in the case of bakeries, or according to the price of fabric in the clothing workshops). Repayments generally begin once the projects are established (for example, once the housing improvement is finished, a particular production process is set up or a retailing operation established).

At present, 31 micro-projects are in place: 13 productive projects, seven clothing workshops, seven nurseries, five warehouses for materials, four community centres and two training centres.

The procedure for approval of micro-projects involves several stages. The community group or cooperative first makes a presentation of the project to the staff administering the fund. The project is then evaluated by the staff and by an Approval Committee which is made up of a member of the Foundation, two local community residents and a member of the Bishopric of Quilmes. The Approval Committee considers each project and suggests amendments. Once the Committee is satisfied with the project, it makes a formal request to MISEREOR to agree with the proposed grant and loan. After this final approval has been granted, a contract is drawn up between the Foundation and those undertaking the project.

Assessment

In the current economic crisis, the rise in poverty, unemployment and a deterioration in the living conditions of large sectors of the country's population, this fund has directly or indirectly benefited many families in the low-income communities in the area of Greater Buenos Aires. In general, it has been able to distribute funding quickly and with greater flexibility than is often the case. Nevertheless, there are clearly some failings, among which the following have been identified:

- the need for a clearer definition of the roles of each of the parts involved in the programme (the Foundation, technical support team, community groups, etc);
- the need for more training for the members of groups borrowing money to help them carry out their projects successfully. This is particularly the case with micro-enterprise projects; and
- improved management of investments, to enable the fund to maintain the value of its reserves in an economy with high inflation rates.

13

Kenya Rural Enterprise Programme

P O Box 39312
Nairobi
Kenya

PROGRAMME

Introduction

The Kenya Rural Enterprise Programme was established in 1984 with the major objective of providing financial assistance to local NGOs involved in the promotion of small-scale enterprises. In 1987, the organization broadened its activities to include the direct provision of credit to groups and individuals seeking to fund innovative projects. At the same time, it set up a research unit to assess the relative impact and efficiency of the varying methodologies being used by the organizations that it was supporting, and to learn what is and what is not successful using participatory methods. In May 1990, the organization designed and implemented a credit model based on the Grameen Bank's lending programme to entrepreneurs, although modified to the Kenyan situation. This offered a basis for the organization to develop its own programme, lending directly to small-scale entrepreneurs. This programme was first started in Kibera in Nairobi and has now been extended to some other parts of Kenya.

Projects and activities

The Kenya Rural Enterprise Programme for individual entrepreneurs deliberately offers little support in addition to the provision of credit. An earlier programme had offered training and technical assistance as well as credit. However, research carried out by the programme showed that training was not a priority need for small-scale businesses, nor did it significantly improve their performance. The organization believes that research elsewhere in the world seems also to demonstrate little correlation between technical assistance and training, and loan repayments. The Kenya Rural Enterprise Programme now provides credit with little or no training, enabling it to reach large numbers of people at a low cost per loan. One NGO it supported was able to disburse more than 200 loans in less than three months using this approach (compared to only 57 loans in three years using the earlier programme). A number of NGOs supported through the programme are now using this approach.

Operational details

The Kenya Rural Enterprise Programme is currently providing financial and technical assistance to five NGOs in order to help them establish credit programmes. The main reason for wishing to establish a direct lending programme is to capitalize on its lending experiences to deliver a large volume of needed credit to the informal sector. A second reason is that the project offers a way of securing the organization's own financial stability. Originally established through USAID financing, the activity for which this funding was given will shortly be completed and the organization is seeking a new viable basis.

Sustainability is a major objective. The organization divides this into organizational and financial sustainability, the former referring to the organization's ability to ensure an adequate quality of staff, legal status and public acceptance of the organization and its goals; the latter, to the ability to continue to cover the real cost of delivering the services which are the main reasons for its existence.

Since its inception, the Kenya Rural Enterprise Programme has helped 12 NGOs to establish revolving loan funds, providing both working capital and investment finance for informal sector entrepreneurs. The organization was managing over KSh 260 million (US$11 million) by the end of 1990; and it was estimated that 2000 full-time jobs and 6000 part-time jobs had been either created or secured through the provision of this finance. It has been estimated that individual income increases by an average of 60 per cent as a result of participation in programmes operated through the scheme. The loan repayment rates of the different NGO programmes varies between 70 and 110 per cent; the loan repayment rate for the programme of direct lending to individuals is 100 per cent.

The success of NGO revolving loan schemes has been mixed. The NGOs with larger-scale networks who have used group formation techniques with group guarantees for repayment have generally been able to move relatively swiftly. NGOs which have dealt with clients on an individual basis have been slower to disburse loans.

The credit programme to individual entrepreneurs operates through the formation of *watanos*. These are groups of five entrepreneurs who already own small businesses. Any individual approaching the Kenya Rural Enterprise Programme is asked to identify four other similar entrepreneurs to establish such a group. Six *watanos* then join together to form a larger unit, called a *kiwa*, which is registered as a social and welfare group with the Ministry of Culture and Social Services.

Each *watano* elects a chair and treasurer. The group is responsible for reviewing loan applications and collecting loan repayments; it is also responsible for collecting savings contributions which form the loan guarantee fund. Members who leave the group are reimbursed their savings with interest, minus any loan repayments still owing. After each group member has saved KSh 50 (US$2) a week for eight weeks, three members of the group are eligible for loans. Following a further four weeks of successful savings and loan repayments, the remaining two members can also receive loans. Members' savings and loan repayments are deposited with local banks and post offices in the project area.

The minimum size of loan for first-time borrowers is KSh 10,000 (US$330); members receiving a second loan can borrow up to KSh 15,000 (US$500). Market rates of interest are charged; in 1990, 12.6 per cent a year (or 27 per cent on a reducing balance basis). This will be increased to 16.4 per cent (36.2 per cent on a reducing balance basis) over a seven-year period in order to raise sufficient funds to cover bad debts and to ensure that the programme can be self-sustaining. The loans must be repaid in weekly instalments within a year. Research undertaken by the organization on a sample of entrepreneurs has shown that about half were borrowing in the informal credit market at interest rates ranging from 5 to 20 per cent a month. The remaining half of the sample who had not been using the informal market said that the main reason for this was that they knew of no sources of finance. For this reason, lack of access to credit is believed to be a greater problem than the costs of borrowing, and the interest rates charged are not considered to be too high.

The *kiwa* group members are responsible for considering loan appraisals, disbursing loans and monitoring each group's savings. In this way, small-scale entrepreneurs learn to ensure that funds are used for the intended purposes. The members are supported by a network of staff, with each credit officer being responsible for about 300 individual clients.

The structure of the credit programme has meant that repayments rates of 100 per cent have been achieved. The large volume of loans disbursed has enabled the programme to cover its costs of operation. The organization estimates that it is possible to build up a sufficient number of loans after a three-year period to allow similar projects in new areas to be self sustaining.

Support for micro-enterprises specifically helps to increase the opportunities open to women. At present, 75 per cent of the individual beneficiaries of the programme are women.

Assessment

The experience has shown that, using group co-guarantee mechanisms and opportunities for further lending, it is possible to lend to the poor without conventional forms of security or collateral and have both the interest and principal repaid on time.

Source: Remenyi, Joe (1991), *Credit where Credit is Due*, Intermediate Technology; and Kenya Rural Enterprise Programme (1991), 'Project proposal submitted to ODA'.

14

Koperasi Kredit Borromeus, Indonesia

Jl Ir Haji Junada 100
Bandung
Indonesia

INSTITUTION

Introduction

The Borromeus Credit Union was established in 1972 in order to provide housing services to its members – employees of the Borromeus Hospital, Bandung, Indonesia. At present, there are 194 members with average individual savings of just under US$25. The aims of the organizations are to increase the welfare of its members, and in particular to:

* create capital through saving;
* provide cheap and quick loans;
* develop a wise attitude to money;
* strengthen the relationship between employees; and
* encourage self confidence among members.

The organization is funded by members' contributions, a private foundation at the hospital, private voluntary organizations based in the Netherlands and a loan from the National Savings Bank, a government organization.

Programmes and activities

Loans are primarily made for housing. The Credit Union offers three different programmes to members: they can borrow a fixed multiple of their savings for buying land or a house, or reconstructing or repairing their house; they can purchase a house constructed by the union; or they can benefit from a special scheme to provide housing for low-paid employees who are not currently home-owners.

Money may also be made available for transport, education and welfare services. The Educational Social Fund was initiated in 1990 by lending US$33 each to ten children for a year. In future, if this fund is successful, both the amount and the number of recipients may be increased.

Members are also asked to contribute to both voluntary and compulsory savings schemes.

CREDIT PROGRAMME

Introduction

The programme includes both the provision of credit for housing development and the building of houses. The Credit Union has been successful in raising funds to support its work in the provision of housing and/or housing finance to its members. The three types of support available, and the sources of funds, are described below. Many members of the Credit Union have only a limited capacity to make housing investments and the ways in which the union tries to support them are also detailed below.

Projects and activities

The houses built by the credit programme can be termed *rumah tumbuh*, or 'growing' housing. The initial building is simple and with limited facilities; thereafter the house can be developed according to family needs and resources. The houses are constructed in a 'team spirit' and using mutual cooperation between all those involved in the development of the settlement.

Operational details

The three types of support offered to members are described below.

1. *Housing loans.* Rapid loans equal to (or less than) five times current savings are available for buying land or houses, and repairing or reconstructing houses. The maximum value of these loans is US$1100 and they must be paid back within a year; the interest rate payable is 1.5 per cent a month.
2. *Housing Building Pilot Project.* The St Borromeus Foundation has provided a 'soft' loan (equivalent to just over US$100,000) for house-building. The loan is passed on to members without any interest charge. Additional finance has been made available by the government through the Housing Ownership Credit. To date, 142 housing units have been built with this money.
3. *Simple Housing Development Programme.* This is funded by the Netherlands Habitat Committee. Initial funding was only sufficient for ten units although the organization estimated that there were 40 low-paid members (employees) who did not currently possess a house. Additional funds (part grant, part soft loan) have recently been provided by ZERO-KAP (Netherlands) to allow for further development of the site acquired

for the Simple Housing Development Programme. It is estimated that a further 18 units can be constructed on the site.

To be selected to participate in this scheme an individual is required to be: a regular employee for at least five years, able to cooperate in a group, a good member of the Credit Union, in urgent housing need, and willing to obey rules and regulations. Those who are offered housing through this project are expected to participate in the project, helping to find a suitable site and working on site preparation and construction. About 20 per cent of the initial capital investment will be made by the Credit Union from its existing capital resources.

Conditions for obtaining credit

The Credit Union takes account of the specific needs of its members in a number of different ways. In both the Housing Building Pilot Project and the Simple Housing Development Programme, no down-payment is required as it is often difficult for low-income communities to accumulate savings, particularly if prices are rising fast. The price of the building, and the amount being spent on installation and construction, is agreed with the purchaser so that monthly payments are realistic. Mutual cooperation in construction helps to keep down costs. The chosen sites are located near to workplaces and schools in order to minimize travelling costs (although it is becoming increasingly hard to find such areas). Subsidies are sometimes given, but this delays the speed with which the revolving fund grows. Members are asked to take care of the environment around their houses, and to support an environmental programme. Attention is also given to possibilities of additional income generation by members of the household.

In order to qualify for a loan, recipients must occupy the houses within a month of signing the agreement letter, and must also begin making repayments by this date. Any alterations to the building construction should first be approved by the director of the Credit Union. Only those who continue to be employed by the hospital are entitled to be members of the Credit Union and in receipt of a loan.

Repayments are spread over 15 years, and each payment is automatically deducted by the hospital and forwarded to the Credit Union. Included in the repayments is a contribution to an insurance fund which guarantees repayment for the household if the loanee dies.

Source of funding

There are several sources of funding for the housing activities of the Credit Union. Members' savings contributions average just under US$25 each. The Borromeus Foundation, based at the hospital, has assisted the work of the union with a long-term loan of US$100,000 for which no interest is being charged. The Netherlands Habitat Committee has given a grant of US$26,000 for the programme in order to enable the Foundation to construct housing for those in urgent need and this amount has now been supplement by another

Dutch voluntary organization. The Housing Ownership Credit/National Savings Bank, a government organization, has given a loan of US$265,000 at 9 per cent interest.

Members repay the capital cost of houses built by the Credit Union. An additional interest rate of 6 per cent (based on 9 per cent charged by the Housing Ownership Credit and the interest-free loan from the Borromeus Foundation) is charged to all those who receive a loan. These repayments are paid into a revolving fund to enable further investments.

The total capital fund currently owned by the Credit Union is US$8730, and this is expected to increase by about US$1000 each month. Although apparently large, the organization does not think it is significant when compared to the scale of need.

Future plans

Through the use of cooperative action, opportunities can be made to increase the welfare of members including meeting their housing needs. The Credit Union hopes to continue to build up the revolving fund, either through the use of grants or soft loans. The Union believes that the local regional government has an important role to play in ensuring that it is simple to secure both the building construction allowance and the land certificate. The National Savings Bank should consider giving a special lower rate of interest in order to facilitate the work of such organizations. In the longer term, it is hoped to increase the range of facilities offered; in particular, extending into education (where a small programme has already been started), health and income-generation activities.

Sources: Assorted reports produced and published by Koperasi Kredit Borromeus, supplemented by Anzorena, Jorge (1990 and 1991), *SELAVIP* papers, Cebu City.

15

Local Initiative Facility for the Urban Environment, UNDP

United Nations Development Programme (UNDP)
One UN Plaza
New York, NY 10017
USA

INSTITUTION

Background

Established in 1965 as the central funding and development organization of the United Nations system, UNDP provides technical assistance and services to all Third World countries as requested. UNDP raises funds, coordinates the activities of the specialized agencies, and cooperates with host governments in identifying technical assistance requirements and strengthening national capacity to manage development programmes and projects effectively. With its staff of over 7000 working throughout a global network of over 125 country offices and at headquarters in New York, UNDP assists Third World countries in building self-reliance and achieving sustainable human development.

UNDP's approach to urban problems links human development to economic productivity. It encourages strategies that promote equitable growth, gender equality and participatory development. UNDP promotes human development in urban areas by focusing on five urban challenges: alleviating poverty; providing the poor with infrastructure, shelter, and services; improving the urban environment; strengthening local government and administration; and promoting the private sector and NGOs.

Programme and activities

UNDP-assisted urban development programmes are designed and implemented by governments and NGOs in Third World countries. At UNDP headquarters, the Urban Development Unit is responsible for providing technical, advisory support to the field offices and operational units; managing innovative urban programmes; and monitoring UNDP-funded and agency executed programmes.

As of the first quarter of 1993, UNDP, including the United Nations Capital Development Fund (UNCDF), was assisting over 270 ongoing urban development and human settlement projects at a total cost of over US$465 million. Many of the projects, 40 per cent, are in the area of infrastructure, shelter, and services; followed by local government, administration, and planning; environment; and poverty alleviation. One example of UNDP's programmes that targets grassroots-level initiatives for improving the urban environment is the LIFE Programme.

LOCAL INITIATIVE FACILITY FOR THE URBAN ENVIRONMENT (LIFE)

Introduction

Third World countries are faced with severe environmental problems rooted in rapid urbanization and the lack of local resources and ability to manage the urban environment. LIFE recognizes the critical role which local governments, NGOs (non-governmental organizations), and CBOs (community-based organizations) play in establishing development programmes to tackle the problems of the urban environment.

LIFE was launched in May of 1992 at the UNCED (United Nations Conference on Environment and Development) World Urban Forum in Rio de Janeiro. The LIFE Programme was formulated through consultations with mayors, NGO networks, cities' associations, bilateral donors and UN agencies. The following reasons and principles have guided the establishment of the LIFE Programme:

- locally-based organizations have inadequate access to international technical assistance for environmental improvement;
- past urban-development strategies have not strengthened partici-patory mechanisms, and there needs to be an emphasis on strengthening local government and promoting local dialogue;
- flexibility of programming technical assistance is needed to involve NGOs and communities effectively in programme implementation; and
- local government should be involved to ensure the 'scaling up' of community-based initiatives.

LIFE provides grants for small-scale projects by NGOs, CBOs, and local governments that deal with urban environmental problems. It assists Third World countries to generate replicable models of improving the living conditions of the residents in low-income urban settlements. In addition, it operates at the regional and inter-regional level to support NGO networks, cities' associations, and international agencies to promote the exchange of experience and innovative ideas for addressing the problems of the urban environment.

Programme and activities

The goal of LIFE is to promote local–local dialogue among municipalities, NGOs, and CBOs on ways of improving the urban environment, leading to sustainable development. The objectives are:

- to test and demonstrate strategies, processes, and small-scale projects based on local-level dialogue;
- to promote participatory approaches, drawing on the full complement of human energy in the city, especially the participation of women's organizations;
- to strengthen the capacity of CBOs, NGOs and local authorities in identifying and implementing local solutions to the urban environment; and
- to mobilize local resources to respond to urban environmental problems.

The pilot phase of LIFE has a budget of US$3.5 million. Activities to be funded include:

- *Community-based participatory activities.* Activities that work towards improving the urban environment and breaking the cycle of poverty, addressing some of the following environmental problems: inadequate provision of water supply and sanitation; inadequate solid and liquid waste management; air and water pollution; occupation of hazard-prone areas; poor environmental health; inadequate access to means of livelihood; lack of environmental education; environmentally unfriendly technologies; and lack of environmental considerations in urban planning.
- *Institutional strengthening and collaboration.* Strengthening the capability of NGOs, CBOs and local governments to identify and address local environmental problems.
- *Documentation and interchange.* Documentation and interchange of innovative responses to urban environmental issues; analysis of gender roles; exchange of information and experience among local organizations.
- *Transfer and replication.* Transfer and replication of successful environmental improvement activities at the country, regional, and inter-regional levels.

Operational details

Twenty-four pilot countries have been selected for the programme and eight of these will be used in the first phase. The pilot countries were chosen on the basis of two or more of the following characteristics: regional balance among countries; democratic processes and strong local authorities; a solid NGO base; successful small-scale environmental improvement activities likely to be replicated effectively in other areas; and local support for such programmes and activities.

The eight initial pilot countries are: Senegal and Tanzania in Africa; Thailand and Pakistan in Asia-Pacific; Egypt and Morocco in the Arab States; and Brazil and Jamaica in Latin America and the Caribbean. At the country level, consultations with NGOs, CBOs and local authorities, and the private sector, in the form of participatory workshops, will be arranged in order to set priorities and guidelines for the selection of the local project. A National Selection Committee will be formed, consisting of representatives of NGOs and CBOs, the private sector, the urban local authorities, a UNDP representative, and representatives of bilateral donors making contributions to the Facility. The selection committee will receive, review, and select applications for funding, and monitor the projects. At the regional and inter-regional levels, projects are submitted to a committee of UNDP representatives.

A National Coordinator with experience of working in the urban environment and with local actors will be recruited. He or she will be located either in a UNDP Field Office or in an NGO. For example, in Thailand the National Coordinator is based in the Grassroots Development Institute, an NGO working to improve living conditions in the slums of Bangkok. In Brazil the National Coordinator is based in the Institute of Technology for the Citizen, a private voluntary organization set up for the purpose of bringing science and technology to serve the interests and needs of the common citizen.

Assessment

As funding of country activities begins, LIFE is expected to promote the generation of local solutions to the urban environmental problems that directly affect urban residents, especially the urban poor.

Through its regional and inter-regional components, LIFE will encourage South–South dialogue and cooperation. LIFE is already supporting four global projects being undertaken by NGO networks: the 'Local Agenda 21' project by the International Council of Local Environmental Initiatives (ICLEI); a project on technical innovations of sanitation and water provision by Habitat International Coalition (HIC); a project on the linkage between poverty and the environment by the Mega-Cities Project and the 'People's Plan for the 21st Century' by the Asian Coalition for Housing Rights.

16

Microfund, Philippines

Kawit
Cavite
Philippines

PROGRAMME

Introduction

Microfund is a private development agency offering credit assistance to *katipunans* (organized economic units) in Kawit, Cavite. Cavite is a coastal province in the Philippines, located close to Manila; Kawit is the principal town with just over 9000 households. The organization also works in a number of other areas in the Philippines, although it is the programme in Kawit which is the focus of this study. The project has been operating for three years and the organization is still in the process of identifying the most effective working methods.

The programmes of Microfund have been specifically orientated towards helping small-scale entrepreneurs who were previously dependent on informal credit markets. The organization arose through the frustration of staff who were then operating another credit scheme within a larger institution.

Projects and activities

In addition to the credit programme, Microfund undertakes a number of other community development activities which are seen as essential to its effective operation. Loans are distributed through small groups of between five and ten members, called *samahans*, and these are organized into larger groupings in order to provide the necessary community base, and to allow for an autonomous savings and lending institution. Training is compulsory, both in order to support the community development structure and to ensure that the credit is used effectively.

Community organization
Katipunans are Microfund's main community-based structure, and each is composed of a number of *samahans*. Each *samahan* has a set of three officers

who are elected annually: a president, treasurer and collector, and five to ten members. Each member records their daily transactions, and the collector signs for the daily repayments. *Katipunans* each have four officers: a president, vice-president, secretary and treasurer. Members of each *samahan* make up the *katipunan* general assembly, from which a board of directors and the officers are elected.

The savings of all members are pooled and this forms the capital base for the *bangko sa bayan* (community bank). The Kawit *katipunan* was formed at Microfund's inception. Cavite's *bangko sa bayan* was formed in May 1987 with P5000 (US$235). The present capitalization (1990) totals P65,000 (US$3050), and an amount equivalent to this has been disbursed in loans. Two kinds of loans are offered: those required for emergencies or to meet the basic needs of families, and equity funds for business or cooperative ventures. Members are able to borrow an amount equal to twice their deposits in the bank.

One of the initial *samahans*, the Samasikap Alpha in Kawit, has completed the full loan and training cycle and has now become a 'graduate group'. Their businesses are now capitalized against their own savings in the *bangko sa bayan*. No longer eligible for Microfund loans, instead they can borrow from their own fund to meet their credit needs.

Each year there is a gathering of all the *katipunans*. In 1987, the first such convention was attended by 100 people: by the following year this had more than doubled. The convention decided to give awards for the best *katipunan* and the best *samahan*. In 1988, the Kawit *katipunan* came only fifth amongst eight. This promoted a re-evaluation of the demands made upon individual members and standards were increased. Delinquent members were 'purged', new members were expected to prove their commitment by regular attendance before loans were to be approved, and stricter checks on collateral were made.

Training programme
The training programme was designed by 1987. It has three components: self-development, community organization and development, and business management. Each component involves 18 lessons. The course is designed to take 18 months and coincides with the two-year loan cycle (ie four loans each for six months). Lessons within each component are divided into three grades and an oral examination is given at the end of each grade (this takes the form of a contest between two halves of each group with a cash prize of P10, or US$0.5, for successful answers). Although the training programme is given as one of the reasons why people leave the credit programme, those who have completed it recognize the value of what they have learnt. The process of weekly lessons and the group meetings are important for developing group solidarity. Many members continue to attend these meetings even after they have completed the training and loan cycle.

Operational details

In 1985, the current director of Microfund, Attorney Casas, then working at the Urban Financing Program of the Technology Resource Center, secured a

World Bank loan to promote credit assistance to the socially disadvantaged. The Technology Resource Center already had some experience operating loans within Metro Manila and Casas used this experience to develop a lending programme. With local agreement, a *samahan* of interested community members was formed in Cavite; this group was to be the route through which loans were disbursed. Each *samahan* was to be made up of 10–15 members (later reduced to 5–10), who would be able to offer loans of between P500 and P1000 (in 1990, equivalent to US$23.5–47) for a six-month period at an annual interest rate of 18 per cent. Four *samahans* were formed in the province.

As this programme began, Casas became frustrated with the limitations of working through government structures and decided to raise the finance for a private foundation to improve and develop the credit scheme operated by the Technology Resource Center. In June 1986, the Community Micro Enterprise Development Foundation, Microfund, was formed with an initial donation of P100,000 (US$4700).

Under the Technology Resource Center's credit scheme, contact with staff had been kept to a minimum; nor was there contact between members of the different community organizations. In determining its methods of working, Microfund took into account several factors. In particular, the community within which Microfund would be operating was already familiar with borrowing and many people already held debts from money lenders. The system initiated by the Technology Resources Center was adopted but was further refined.

In Kawit, it is mainly the women who work within Microfund. When a local *samahan* was asked to consider why, they identified three reasons: that many men were not patient enough to attend the training programme, or that they perceived the organization as being made up of mostly women and were reluctant to join such a group, or that women were naturally more industrious. A local US Navy base had provided a lucrative source of employment for the men and many were not interested in alternative employment.

As founder, Casas has been influential in the development of the organization. He has acted as a trainer, community organizer, fundraiser and financial advisor. Four types of loans were initially offered. The starter loan offered assistance of between P500 and P1000 (US$23.5–47), followed by three further developmental loans, the first ranging between P1000 and P5000 (US$47–235), the second between P5000 and P10,000 (US$235–470) and the third between P10,000 and P15,000 (US$470–700). The actual amounts offered in each category depend on an assessment of the business itself and the beneficiary's performance on past loans. Each loan is for 180 days and an annual interest rate of 24 per cent calculated on the declining balance is payable. Collective responsibility is enforced by making loans to the group rather than individual members. Each member has to wait until all the *samahan* loans have been paid back before receiving a further loan, and a default by one member constitutes a default by the group. One member of the *samahan* is responsible for collecting repayments on a daily basis and Microfund's area coordinator makes weekly visits to offer support and advice. Savings are encouraged within the group, all members' resources being pooled to act as collateral for the group.

A credit committee is responsible for approving all loan applications from each community. Before approval is given, there are site inspections, an examination of available collateral, interviews with the beneficiaries and a financial evaluation of each individual loan. There are ten staff members who serve as area coordinators, and each is developing expertise in nine specific subjects: community orientation and beneficiary interviews; site and collateral inspection; loan evaluation; documentation; disbursement orientation; field monitoring and credit supervision; comprehensive training; business monitoring; and *bangko sa bayan* (Microfund) audit.

Recent developments

In order to allow for the expansion of successful enterprises, Casas suggested that a fifth loan should be offered to members who had completed the two-year loan cycle. This loan, to be called the Graduates Entrepreneurial Loan, would range between P15,000 and P50,000 (US$700–2350). Due to difficulties with Microfund's board, a new foundation was set up to manage this loan scheme. The organization has been named the Sangsikap Foundation, after the *samahan* in Kawit.

Assessment

Since 1986, loans have been given to 816 micro-entrepreneurs in 132 *samahans* organized into eight *katipunans*. The total amount lent is just over P2 million (US$94,000), and a 100 per cent repayment rate has been achieved. Twenty eight per cent of loans have been given to micro-processing and manufacturing enterprises such as food items and furniture; just under 70 per cent to wholesale and retail merchandising; and the remainder to service enterprises (for example, beauty parlours and photographic outlets).

The values which are important to Microfund are stressed in their training course on self-development and community organization and development. These are self-reliance, determination, community sacrifice and responsibility, and self-discipline and trustworthiness. The development of such values is reinforced by the socio-economic components of the organization such as the credit mechanism, business training, monitoring and supervision, and by the socio–civic components such as the group organizations.

The following factors are believed to be important in understanding Microfund's success in operating their loan scheme:

- *Tier of loans*: the progression from small to large loans helps members develop confidence in their business abilities.
- *Tier of leadership*: responsibilities are not taken on solely by Microfund but are developed with each *samahan* and *katipunan*.
- *Dual supervision*: Microfund's staff member, acting as local area coordinator, complements, supports, and is supported by the officials within each local structure.
- *System of incentives*: the awards offered for course examination results

and the yearly conventions offer an incentive for individual and group achievements.

* *Group accountability and pressure*: the practice of group loans, collective collateral pools and shared accountability all emphasize the importance of the group over the individual. Each of these mechanisms provides valuable training in community organization.
* *Local area coordinators*: local staff mean that the accessibility of the informal money lenders is replicated for the benefit of low-income borrowers (more formal structures have traditionally excluded such individuals). Such accessibility does not only provide finance; it also allows for technical assistance and business advice.
* *Total training package*: the training programmes are important in helping participants gain self-confidence and self-awareness. In particular, the training package has assisted the development of opportunities for women. One advantage is that it uses 'action learning', drawing on the experiences gained through the lending process, to help the students learn.
* *Savings and capital accumulation*: each *samahan* member has to save a percentage of daily profits. For the first two loans, this amount equals 100 per cent; this figure falls to 75 per cent for the third loan, and to 50 per cent for the fourth loan. These savings prevent over-spending of the additional income and allow for the accumulation of future collateral.
* *Organizational learning*: Microfund sees its socialized credit scheme as something which must be open to change and development. In the course of its operation to date, amendments have already been made. Future plans include the strengthening of the *bangko sa bayan* structures, and the development of credit cooperatives.

Source: *Development Memo*, No 55, 1990. Published by the Centre for the Development of Human Resources in Rural Asia (CENDHRRA), PO Box 458, Greenhills Post Office, 1502 Metro Manila, Philippines. The description above is drawn from a study completed by CENDHRRA on 'Self-Help and Self-Reliant Processes' used by Philippine NGOs.

17

Research and Applications for Alternative Financing for Development (RAFAD)

3, rue de Varembe
Case postale 117
CH-1211 Geneva 20
Switzerland

INSTITUTION

Background

RAFAD works to support partner organizations in the Third World, particularly through providing loan guarantees which allow their partners to receive credit from local or national financial institutions within their own nation. It also offers additional support services to facilitate the successful operation of these loans. RAFAD is a new foundation which has been in existence for just over five years. From its inception, it has worked to enhance the autonomy and self-reliance of its partner organizations in the Third World. As such, its loan guarantees provide an alternative funding source to conventional grants from donor agencies in the North for Third World groups. The guarantees help to mobilize local capital for development as a complement and, in some cases, an alternative to aid.

RAFAD's objectives are:

- to obtain financial resources to promote all kinds of alternative financing in support of grassroots organizations and individuals from the Third World who have taken the necessary initiatives and risks to create and promote innovative activities favourable to their development;
- to strengthen the abilities and the efficiency of these organizations and their networks by giving them necessary support and training; and
- to encourage (through the Foundation's experiences and other similar initiatives) critiques, investigation and research which favour the promotion of alternative ways of financing development, and to disseminate the results to regional and international aid agencies.

RAFAD arose directly from the practical experience of a group of individuals from the North and rural partner organizations in French-speaking West Africa. The legitimacy for RAFAD comes from the South, with the local partner organizations becoming mobilized through their own resources and those of the local banking system. When RAFAD was initiated it was many years after national political independence but autonomy was only slowly being achieved. The partner organizations in West Africa wanted a method through which this autonomy could be encouraged and realized. The mechanism chosen was a guarantee scheme which seemed to offer an opportunity to gain access to greater local financing. Through RAFAD, these organizations have gradually established their own financial independence.

Following the drought in the mid-1980s, there was an increasing need for a fund which would offer partner organizations an alternative to having to negotiate continually for money from donors. The need for this was not only based on the pragmatic reason of reducing the time and cost of obtaining funds, but was also ideological. Those involved in the initiation of RAFAD saw a contradiction between the self-help movement using funds from the North and a desire for greater independence and autonomy. RAFAD was seen as a structure which would facilitate a productive relationship between these organizations and the local commercial banks. At the time RAFAD was established, there was very little contact between these two groups, although both are needed for development.

Programme and activities

RAFAD's main activity is the provision of loan guarantees to partner organizations to allow them to obtain credit from a local bank which refuses to grant loans without collateral.

The organization also offers a range of support services to its partner organizations. It now employs two advisors, one in Senegal and a second in Rwanda who advise local partner organizations in operating both the credit programme and the investments they undertake. Staff are also employed in Zaire and Zimbabwe. The particular support which each partner organization requires during the operation of the guarantee varies considerably and RAFAD tries to deal with each case individually, responding as appropriate.

In general, RAFAD wishes to decentralize its operations. Its capacity to employ staff in the Third World is limited, and it does not believe that this in an appropriate solution in many cases. In two countries, Sri Lanka and Thailand, it is developing an alternative; asking NGOs within the country to work first with groups interested in obtaining guarantees and then support these groups once a guarantee has been granted. Such NGOs are not responsible for the granting of the guarantees but they ensure that all the needs of participating organizations are met.

In order to offer a more general service, RAFAD has begun a programme of one-week workshops on access to credit. The workshops, all of which will be held in Africa, bring together representatives of a number of organizations: associations with practical experience of credit, groups wishing to obtain credit, local credit institutions (including banks, and savings and credit funds), and RAFAD staff. In 1990, four workshops, one each in Cameroon, Rwanda, Senegal and Zimbabwe were held; a further two were planned to take place in 1991, in Kenya and Zaire. One of the conclusions of the first workshops was that there is a large unmet demand for access to credit. At present, many organizations lack the necessary management and financial skills to manage credit but the opportunity to obtain credit helps stimulate them to overcome such problems. Those attending the workshops have requested a long-term follow-up programme to the workshops.

THE GUARANTEE FUND

Introduction

The paragraphs below describe the operation of the guarantee fund. The first sub-section describes the geographical and sectoral growth of the fund. The second sub-section summarizes the procedures followed in the issuing of guarantees. The final section identifies some strengths and weaknesses of the organization for the first six years of operation.

Projects and activities

RAFAD's operations have increased gradually since its inception. The table below gives the approximate number of new and renewed guarantees operating in each year. Following the interests of its founding members, RAFAD began work in francophone West Africa, gradually spreading its activities to central and east Africa, and then to Southern Africa in 1987 and involving groups from anglophone countries. The main reason for RAFAD's early expansion was a desire to respond to need. The main constraint on this expansion has been a lack of locally available support.

The number of new or renewed guarantees

1984	4
1985	5
1986	10
1987	12
1988	12
1989	15
1990	26
1991	30 (estimated)

Once again driven by demand, RAFAD extended its operations into Sri Lanka in 1987, and into Thailand in 1988. In 1989, it began to work in Latin America. RAFAD's Latin American programme has since grown slightly to include partner organizations working in Ecuador, Chile and Peru. Finally, in 1990, it extended its operations into north Africa.

There are two main areas of activities receiving RAFAD guarantees. The first activity is marketing; generally peasant or craft organizations which believe that they could greatly expand sales through undertaking specific activities such as publicity and advertising, improvements in transportation and the identification of new markets. (In these cases, little credit is given for direct investment in production equipment.) The second main area for which credit is given is investment in permanent job creation, perhaps using the funds to purchase capital equipment or raw materials. A third and smaller category of funds are those allocated to help with cashflow problems, for example an NGO working with such groups may wish to expand its activities but lacks the finance to start such operations. Since its first years of operation, the types of project funded by RAFAD have broadened, reflecting changes in demand.

The most common types of project rejected by RAFAD are requests for guarantees to undertake building or major capital investment. These are mainly turned down because the maximum repayment time for a RAFAD guarantee is two years. Some groups receive a further guarantee after the two-year period if they have successfully completed their first programme within this time. Among other new areas for guarantees, RAFAD is currently considering an application from a cooperative in Douala, Cameroon, which would like to build houses for its members on a new site but which has only limited opportunities to obtain credit at a reasonable rate of interest.

In recent years, RAFAD has supported partner organizations in determining a new relationship with donor agencies. RAFAD suggested that the partner organizations approach their major funders saying 'you currently support us in a number of ways; please continue to give us grants for training and institution building, but transfer the funds you allocate to us for credit to RAFAD to enable us to set up a guarantee programme'. This scheme has been successful for some partner organizations looking for an alternative to grant aid.

Description of the credit programme

The guarantee-granting process begins with an application which can take some months to complete. Once the decision is taken, the release of funds is immediate as the guarantee is a simple notification from bank to bank. Although RAFAD has a standard application form, this is rarely used because RAFAD's board have an intimate knowledge of many of the groups with which it is likely to work; this means that the type of information required is often specific to each organization. In addition to any extra information required, all potential partners have to present their latest balance sheet, recent accounts and documentation relating to the long-term economic viability of the organization. RAFAD's staff are responsible for collecting the information and for presenting the proposals for the Board's consideration. The type of factors which are important in deciding whether or not to grant a guarantee include the extent to which the organization's own savings have been collected and committed to the project, and the expertise available to the partner organization.

The demand for access to credit by popular organizations is increasing all the time and it is not possible for RAFAD to accept all applications for support. Some applications are rejected as unsuitable, either because of the type or duration of project, or because RAFAD lacks the necessary support structure to complement the guarantee within the country or area in which the partner organization is working.

Once the Board has agreed to grant the guarantee, staff prepare a draft letter of guarantee. Each of these is drawn up individually to take account of the group's particular circumstances. Once this text has been approved by both the partner and the local bank, RAFAD's bank is instructed to proceed. The bank used by the partner organization is generally selected by them or, if they do not know of a suitable partner, it will be identified through common research. The average time from the Board's agreement to the partner organization receiving the money from their local bank is five months – although, in some cases, very much shorter times have been achieved.

Strengths and weaknesses of the programme

On reflection, RAFAD does not believe that it fully recognized all the obstacles to the effective operation of a credit guarantee fund before it started its work. In particular, perhaps too little consideration was given to the difference in working methods between the partner organizations and the banking system, and how much time would be needed to familiarize these two partners with each other.

RAFAD is confident that the partner organizations with which it works are creditworthy – to date its losses have been less than 1 per cent of the total amount guaranteed, thus demonstrating that the poor can be creditworthy and that they should have better access to credit. However, it is important that the amount of credit extended suits the capacity of the organization. RAFAD believes that one reason why so many previous credit schemes have failed is because the groups borrowing money had to match the expectations of the lending programme and not the other way around.

The organization both benefits and suffers from its smallness and flexibility. RAFAD's greatest advantage arises because it has located itself at the intersection of the partners with which it works and the banking system. Many donors and NGOs have been exploring the possibility of setting up their own credit guarantee funds, and there is much interest in RAFAD's work.

Due to its small size, RAFAD believes that it has an important role in setting examples and showing how things might be done. Starting in West Africa, which has a relatively under-developed credit market compared to Asia and Latin America, RAFAD has shown that it is possible to give self-help groups and the NGOs who support them access to formal banking systems. The relevance of RAFAD's experience can only be seen after becoming involved with its work and assessing the value of the result.

An ongoing problem for RAFAD is the funding of its own operations in Geneva. In 1989, for example, the total cost of RAFAD's operation (not including the capital invested in the guarantee fund) was just over 400,000 SF (US$267,000); this sum includes the cost of staff and associated office costs; legal fees incurred in granting guarantees; meetings, workshops and seminars; missions to partner organizations; and associated support and counselling costs. Despite much support for the work it is doing, many donors are reluctant to fund an office based in the North. To date, RAFAD has been heavily dependent on support from the Swiss Development Cooperation. Whilst this organization retains its interest in and support for RAFAD's work, it may be reluctant to continue to remain their main funder on an indefinite basis.

Source: RAFAD (Recherches et Applications de Financements Alternatifs au Développement) (1991), *Environment and Urbanization*, Vol 4, No 1, London.

18

Uvagram Foundation, Sri Lanka

Padmalaya
Welimada Road
Bandarawela
Sri Lanka

PROGRAMME

Introduction

The Uvagram Foundation was founded in 1984 by Chandra de Fonseka, an ex-UN official who retired to his original home. The Foundation is non-profit-making and sees itself as a combination of a voluntary development organization, a local development institute and a small private-sector business. Its main focus is on the provision of credit for income-generation. In 1989, it had a staff of ten and about 30 supporting members, and it operates on the basis that 'small is effective'.

The Foundation operates in Uva, one of Sri Lanka's least-developed provinces located in the south of the country. The government owns much of the land, which was previously held as large private tea estates. There are many peasant families who grow vegetables and tea on small amounts of land. The name of the Foundation derives from the province and *gram*, meaning village or rural area.

Many of the local farmers are dependent on local money lenders who charge high rates of interest. In some cases, farmers have to sell their produce to the money lenders, who offer them prices well below the market rate. Although there are nine regional rural development banks and 977 rural cooperative banks, Fonseka believed that these fail to support the poor. In order to assist low-income communities, he believed that there was a need to establish a structure of people's institutions in rural areas which would parallel more formal government initiatives. Uvagram's aim is to teach communities the principles of self-management, and to introduce them to structures which might enable them eventually to become self-sufficient. Since its inception, the Foundation has managed to convince many farmers of the advantages of such group initiatives, especially for managing loans and establishing revolving funds.

Projects and activities

In addition to the main credit programme, a number of other, related initiatives have been developed.

- *Self-help revolving funds.* The small groups established for guaranteeing repayment of loans have begun to set up their own revolving funds. One group has accumulated US$18 from collective savings; this money is now lent out to members of the group at 2 per cent interest a month.
- *Distribution systems.* Uvagram has supported villagers in developing an alternative distribution system to that offered by either the government or the *mudalali* (the agent who controls local markets). A marketing programme has been established which transports vegetables direct to consumers in Colombo (the capital). The main aim of the project is to be illustrative, showing farmers what can be achieved, and the Foundation does not intend to become a major operator in this area. The *mudalali* are trying to pressurize farmers into continuing to use their services, and in 1989, one year after having been established, the marketing programme still required a subsidy.
- *Training.* The Foundation also offers agricultural training in such skills as the use of fertilisers and pesticides, nursery-keeping and compost-making.

Operational details

In their search for finance to establish their lending operation, Uvagram Foundation approached RAFAD who offered a dollar guarantee of US$3500. The local branch of the Bank of Ceylon agreed to open an account, supported by the guarantee, which would allow the Foundation to lend the equivalent of US$2666. After consultation with the farmers, an interest rate of 2 per cent a month was agreed, and procedures for borrowing money were simplified as much as possible.

In order to secure a loan, members had to form a group. Although loans were given to individuals, the group was responsible for guaranteeing repayment to the Foundation. Individual members must repay the group leader, who then repays the Foundation which in turn repays the bank. This reduces the latter's administration costs to a minimum. As an extension of this system, Uvagram has recently started encouraging local groups to pool their savings, using this money as a small revolving fund for emergencies.

RAFAD recently agreed to raise the amount of the dollar guarantee to US$14,000. Part of this guarantee is now held with the Seylan Trust Bank which became interested in the work of the Foundation and which offered more favourable terms. About half of the value of this guarantee has been allocated to work with tea smallholders who are in particular need of support and technical advice.

Although there have been some defaulters, the repayment rate for the first years was 92 per cent, substantially higher than that achieved by banks with direct personal loans.

The Foundation identifies and supports 'change agents', who are group leaders. These individuals are taught how to gather the information they need and to motivate villagers into forming small groups. In some cases, these people have been previously trained by a government programme. The first task of the group leaders is to survey a potential village to identify the social and economic profile of the people living there, and to explore their need for credit.

For example, in 1985, in the village of Piyarapadora, one small group of four women and one man applied to the Foundation for help. Together they borrowed US$1212 at 2 per cent interest a month for two months. After the harvest, they were able to repay the money. Thirteen different groups were formed in the village. In 1988, 54 farmers each borrowed about US$30. This time there were some difficulties with repayment as political disturbances disrupted farming; three of the farmers were unable to repay their loans.

Most of the funding has been for agricultural work but a further project has recently been started with local potters in the province who are often forced to use money-lenders in order to purchase the clay and other materials they need. In 1989, the equivalent of about US$65 capital was required for each batch of pots. Through using a loan provided by the Foundation, the women doing this work in Rathpahagama have been able to reduce the interest charges they had been paying, and accumulate enough capital to invest in more efficient equipment and techniques.

Future plans

The Uvagram Foundation expects the village-level system they have established to change and expand in future years. They expect the groups to become increasingly self-reliant, learning to deal directly with the banks. Revolving funds established through their own savings can be used to meet small credit needs. Such groups might provide the basis for producer cooperatives, marketing cooperatives or joint wholesaling operations.

Source: Wanigasundara, Mallika, (1989) 'Sri Lanka: Escaping the clutches of the moneylenders' in Bakhoum, Ibrahima et al, *Banking the Unbankable*, Panos Institute, London.

Bibliography

Adrianza, B.T. and G.C. Graham (1974) 'The high cost of being poor: water' *Architecture and Environmental Health No. 28*, pp. 312–315.

Aina, Tade Akin (1989) *Health, Habitat and Underdevelopment – with Special Reference to a Low–Income Settlement in Metropolitan Lagos*, IIED Technical Report, IIED, London.

Albert, Ramon (1991) 'The community mortgage programme' in Aurelio Menendez (ed), *Access to Basic Infrastructure by the Urban Poor*, EDI Seminar Report No. 28, the World Bank, Washington DC.

Anheier, Helmut (1990) 'Themes in international research on the non-profit sector', *Nonprofit and Voluntary Sector Quarterly*, Jossey-Bass Inc., pp. 371–391.

Anzorena, Jorge (1988) 'The Grameen Bank (GB) housing loan', *SEVAVIP* (Latin American and Asian Low Income Housing Service), March.

— (1989) 'The Grameen Bank (GB) and its housing activities', *SEVAVIP* (Latin American and Asian Low Income Housing Service), March.

— (1989) 'Community Mortgage Program', *SEVAVIP* (Latin American and Asian Low Income Housing Service), September.

— (1990) 'Community Mortgage Program', *SEVAVIP* (Latin American and Asian Low Income Housing Service), March.

— (1990) 'Grameen Bank (May 1990)', *SEVAVIP* (Latin American and Asian Low Income Housing Service), September.

Asian Coalition for Housing Rights (1989) 'Evictions in Seoul, South Korea', in *Environment and Urbanization* Vol. 1, No. 1, October, pp. 89–94.

— (1994) *Housing Finance Seminar – October 1993* (draft report), MISEREOR/ACHR, Bangkok.

Ba, Hassan with the collaboration of Cristophe Nuttall (1990) 'Village associations on the riverbanks of Senegal: the new development actors', *Voices from Africa Issue no. 2*, NGLS, pp. 83–104.

Balista, Jose (1981) *'La participacion en los programas de autoconstruccion con asistencia tecnica en la Provincia de Buenos Aires'* CONICEYT-SVOA, Buenos Aires, Argentina.

Belmartino, Susana, Carlos Bloch, Jorge E. Hardoy and Hilda Herzer (1989) *Urbanization and its Implications for Child Health: Potential for Action*, World Health Organization, Geneva.

Berger, Peter L. and Richard John Neuhaus (1977) *To Empower People: The Role of Mediating Structures in Public Policy*, American Enterprise Institute for Public Policy Research, Washington DC.

Bird, Richard (1978) *Inter-Governmental Fiscal Relations in Developing Countries*, World Bank Staff Working Paper No. 304, the World Bank, Washington DC.

Black, Maggie (1986) *The Children and the Nations: The Story of UNICEF*, UNICEF, New York.

Bombarolo, Felix and Alfredo Stein (1990) *Las ONGs y su Rol en la Problematica Habitacional y en el Desarrollo Social de America Latina*, IIED-AL, Buenos Aires, mimeo.

BRAC (1990), *Annual Report 1990*, Bangladesh Rural Advancement Committee, Dhaka.

Bradley, David, Carolyn Stephens, Sandy Cairncross and Trudy Harpham (1991), *A Review of Environmental Health Impacts in Developing Country Cities*, Urban Management Program Discussion Paper No. 6, the World Bank, UNDP and UNCHS (Habitat), Washington DC.

Brenton, M. (1985) *The Voluntary Sector in British Social Services*, Longman, London.

Brown, L. David and David C. Korten (no date) *Voluntary development organizations: what makes this sector different?* Institute for Development Research, Boston.

Cairncross, Sandy (1990) 'Water supply and the urban poor' in Jorge E. Hardoy et al. (eds), *The Poor Die Young: Housing and Health in Third World Cities*, Earthscan Publications, London.

Cairncross, Sandy, Jorge E. Hardoy and David Satterthwaite (1990) 'The urban con text' in Jorge E. Hardoy et al. (eds), *The Poor Die Young; Housing and Health in Third World Cities*, Earthscan Publications, London.

Cassell, Michael (no date) *Inside Nationwide: One Hundred Years of Cooperation*, Nationwide Building Society, London.

CCU (1985) 'El cooperativismo y la ayuda mutua en el Uruguay', in *CCU Journal*, Montevideo, Uruguay.

CENDHRRA (1990), *Development Memo, No. 55*, the Centre for the Development of Human Resources in Rural Asia, Metro Manila, Philippines.

Clark, John (1991) *Democratizing Development – The Role of Voluntary Organizations*, Earthscan Publications, London.

Cochrane, Glynn (1983) *Policies for Strengthening Local Government in Developing Countries*, World Bank Staff Working Paper No. 582, the World Bank, Washington DC.

Cointreau, Sandra J. (1982) *Environmental Management of Urban Solid Wastes in Developing Countries: a Project Guide*, Urban Development Technical Paper, No. 5, the World Bank, Washington DC.

Cooper Weil, Diana E., Adelaida P. Alicbusan, John F. Wilson, Michael A. Reich and David J. Bradley (1990) *The Impact of Development Policies on Health: A Review of the Literature*, World Health Organization, Geneva.

Cousins, William J. (1989) *Unicef in the Cities: a History of Urban Basic Services Programme*, Monograph, UNICEF, New York, December.

Cuenya, Beatriz, Diego Armus, Maria Di Loreto and Susana Penalva (1990) 'Land invasions and grassroots organization: the Quilmes settlement in Greater Buenos Aires, Argentina', *Environment and Urbanization* Vol. 2, No. 1, April, pp. 61–73.

Dichter, Thomas W. (1988) 'The changing world of northern NGOs: problems, para-doxes and possibilities' in John Lewis (ed), *Strengthening the Poor: What Have we Learned?*, Transaction Books, New Brunswick.

Dieng, Isidore M'Baye (1977) *Relogement de Bidonvillois a la Peripherie Urbaine*, ENDA, Dakar, 1977.

Dobkin Hall, Peter (1987) 'A historical overview of the private nonprofit sector' in Walter W. Powell (ed), *The Nonprofit Sector: a Research Handbook*, Yale University Press, New Haven and London.

Environment and Urbanization (1989) special issue on 'Environmental Problems in Third World Cities', Vol. 1, No. 1, April.

— (1991), special issue on 'Rethinking Local Government: Views from the Third World', Vol. 3, No. 1, April.

Esrey, S. A. and J. P. Habicht (1986) 'Epidemiologic evidence for health benefits from improved water and sanitation in developing countries', *Epidemiologic Reviews*, Vol. 8, pp. 117–128.

Falu, Ana and Mirina Curutchet (1991) 'Rehousing the urban poor: looking at women first', *Environment and Urbanization*, Vol. 3, No. 2, October, pp. 23–38.

Flintoff, F. (1976) *Management of Solid Wastes in Developing Countries*, WHO (SEARO), New Delhi.

Fundacion Caravajal (1989) *Programa Integral de Vivienda*, Cali,
— (1990) *Fundacion Caravajal de Cali y su tarea de desarrollo social*, Cali.
— (1990) *Informe anual 1989*, Cali.
— (1990), *Fundacion Caravajal 1990: Programa de Microempresas*, Cali.
FUNDASAL (1984) *Memoria de Labores*, Ciudad Delgado, El Salvador, mimeo.
— (1991) *Proyecto Santa Teresa: Una experiencia de dotacion de viviendas a
sectores de bajos ingresos ecomonicos*, Ciudad Delgado, El Salvador, mimeo.
Gakenheimer, Ralph and C.H.J. Brando (1987) 'Infrastructure standards' in Lloyd
Rodwin (ed.), *Shelter, Settlement and Development*, Allen and Unwin, Boston.
Garcia-Guadilla, Maria Pinar and Jutta Blauert (eds) (1992) 'Environmental social
movements in Latin America and Europe: challenging development and
democracy', *International Journal of Social Policy*, Vol. 12, Nos. 4–7.
Godofredo, Sandoval (1988) *Organizaciones no Gubernamentales de Desarrollo en
America latina y El Caribe*, UNITAS, Bolivia
Goethert, Reinhard and Nabeel Hamdi (1987) *La Microplanificacion. Un proceso de pro-
gramacion y desarrollo con base en la comunidad*, MIT, Boston.
Gorman, Robert F. (1984) *Private Voluntary Organizations as Agents of Development*,
Westview Press, Boulder and London.
GTZ (1988) *Planificacion y Gestion de Proyectos de Mejoramiento Urbano*, prepared by
the German Agency for Technical Cooperation, Eschborn.
Guarda, Gian Carlo (1990) 'A new direction in World Bank urban lending in Latin
American countries', *Review of Urban and Regional Development Studies* Vol. 2, No. 2,
July, pp. 116–124.
Habitat International Coalition Women and Shelter Network (1991) NGO Profile in
Environment and Urbanization Vol. 3, No 2, October, pp. 82–86.
Habitat International Coalition (1990) NGO profile in *Environment and Urbanization*
Vol. 2, No. 1, April, pp. 105–112.
Hardoy, Ana, Jorge Hardoy and Richard Schusterman (1991) 'Building community
organization: the history of a squatter settlement and its own organization'
Environment and Urbanization, Vol. 3, No. 2, October, pp. 104–120.
Hardoy, Jorge and David Satterthwaite (1981) *Shelter, Need and Response; Housing,
Land and Settlement Policies in 17 Third World Nations*, John Wiley and Sons,
Chichester.
— (1987) 'Laying the foundations: NGOs help to house Latin America's Poor',
Development Forum, October (part 1) and November (part 2), New York.
— (1989) *Squatter Citizen: Life in the Urban Third World*, Earthscan Publications,
London.
— (1991) 'Environmental problems in Third World cities: a global issue ignored?',
Public Administration and Development, Vol. 11, pp. 341–361.
Hasan, Samiul, George Mulamoottil and J.E. Kersell (1992) 'Voluntary organizations
in Bangladesh: a profile', *Environment and Urbanization* Vol. 4, No. 2, October, pp.
196–206.
Hurley, Donnacadh (1990) *Income Generations Schemes for the Urban Poor*, Oxfam,
Oxford.
IFAD (1988) *International Seminar on Credit for Rural Women*, IFAD, Rome.
IIED-AL (1991) *El rol de las ONGs en America Latina*, mimeo, Buenos Aires,
Argentina.
Ingersoll, T.G. and P.W. Ingersoll (eds) (1990) *Towards Partnership in Africa*,
Interaction and FOVAD, Massachusetts.
Inter-American Foundation (1990) *A Guide to NGO Directories*, Virginia, USA.
— (1991) *1990 Annual Report*, Washington DC, USA.
Interaction (1985) *Diversity in Development*, Interaction, New York.
Jorgensen, Steen, Margaret Grosh and Mark Schacter (eds) (1992) *Bolivia's Answer to*

Poverty, Economic Crisis and Adjustment: The Emergency Social Fund, the World Bank, Washington DC.

Kasarda, John D. and Edward M. Crenshaw (1991) 'Third world urbanization: dimensions, theories and determinants', *Annual Review of Sociology*, Vol. 17, pp. 467–501.

Korten, David C. (1990) *Getting to the 21st Century: Voluntary Action and the Global Agenda*, Kumarian Press, Connecticut.

— (1991) 'The role of non–governmental organizations in development: changing patterns and perspectives' in Samuel Paul and Arturo Israel (eds) *Non Governmental Organizations and The World Bank*, the World Bank, Washington DC.

Landim, Leilah (1987) 'Non-governmental organizations in Latin America', *World Development* Vol. 15 supplement, Autumn, pp. 29–38.

Lee Smith, Diana (1991), *Feasibility of SIDA aid to shelter and infrastructure through African NGOs*, paper prepared by Mazingira Institute for SIDA, Nairobi, mimeo.

Limuru Declaration – Declaration by representatives of 45 Third World NGOs and 12 international NGOs after a seminar in Limuru in April 1987, published in Bertha Turner (ed) (1988) *Building Community, a Third World Case Book*, Habitat International Coalition, London.

Max-Neef, M., A. Elizalde and M. Hopenhayn (1986) *Desarrollo a escala humana, una opcion para el futuro*, CEPADUR, Santiago de Chile.

McKeown, Thomas (1988) *The Origins of Human Disease*, Basil Blackwell, Oxford and New York.

McLeod, Ruth and Diana Mitlin (1993) 'The search for sustainable funding systems for community initiatives' *Environment and Urbanization*, Vol. 5, No. 1, April, pp. 26–37.

Mendez, Lopezllera (1988) *Sociedad civil y pueblos emergentes*, PDP, Mexico.

Mitlin, Diana and David Satterthwaite (1992) *Reaching Summit Goals in Urban Areas: New Means and New Partnerships*, Urban Examples No. 18, UNICEF, New York.

Moser, Caroline O.N. (1989) 'Community participation in urban projects in the Third World', Progress in Planning Vol. 32, No. 2, Pergamon Press, Oxford.

— and Linda Peake (eds) (1987) *Women, Housing and Human Settlements*, Tavistock Publications, London and New York.

Murphy, Denis (1990) *A Decent Place to Live – Urban Poor in Asia*, Asian Coalition for Housing Rights, Bangkok.

OECD (1988) *Voluntary Aid for Development: the role of Non–Governmental Organizations*, Organization for Economic Cooperation and Development, Paris.

— (1989) *Development Cooperation: Efforts and Policies of the Members of the Development Assistance Committee – 1989 Report*, Organization for Economic Cooperation and Development, Paris.

— (1990) *Development Cooperation: Efforts and Policies of the Members of the Development Assistance Committee*, Organization for Economic Cooperation and Development, Paris.

Oruwari, Yomi (1991) 'The changing role of women in families and their housing needs: a case study of Port Harcourt' *Environment and Urbanization*, Vol. 3, No. 2, October, pp. 612.

Padrón, Mario (1982) *Cooperación al Desarrollo y Movimeinto Popular: las organizaciones privadas de desarrollo*, DESCO, Peru.

— (1987) 'Non–government development organizations: from development aid to development cooperation', *World Development* Vol. 15 supplement, Autumn, pp. 69–78.

Patel, Sheela and Celine d'Cruz (1993) 'The Mahila Milan crisis credit scheme: from a seed to a tree', *Environment and Urbanization*, Vol. 5, No. 1, April, pp. 9–17.

Paul, Samuel and Arturo Israel (eds) (1991) *Non-Governmental Organisations and The World Bank*, the World Bank, Washington DC.

Portes, Alejandro (1979) 'Housing policy, urban poverty and the state: the favelas of Rio de Janeiro', *Latin American Research Review* No. 14, Summer 1979, pp. 3–24 and *Revista Interamericana de Planificacion* No. 13, March 1979, pp. 103–124.

Private Agencies Collaborating Together (1990) *Steps Toward a Social Investment Fund*, PACT, New York.

Remenyi, Joe (1991) *Where Credit is Due*, Intermediate Technology Publications, London.

Renaud, Bertrand (1981) *National Urbanization Policies in Developing Countries*, Oxford University Press, Oxford.

Roth, Gabriel (1987) *The Private Provision of Public Services in Developing Countries*, Oxford University Press, Oxford.

Salamon, Lester and Helmut K. Anheier (1992) *In Search of the Nonprofit Sector 1: The Question of Definitions*, Working Paper 2, The Johns Hopkins Comparative Nonprofit Sector Project, Johns Hopkins University Institute for Policy Studies, Baltimore.

Salmen, Lawrence F. and A. Paige Eaves (1991) 'Interactions between Non-governmental Organizations, Governments and the World Bank' in Samuel Paul and Arturo Israel (eds), *Non Governmental Organizations and The World Bank*, the World Bank, Washington DC.

Sanin, Hector (1989) *Manual de Administracion de Proyectos de Desarrollo Local*, pre pared at the request of the IULA Latin American office, Quito.

Schmidt, R. H. and Erhard Kropp (1987) *Rural Finance: Guiding Principles*, GTZ and DSE, Bonn/Eschborn/Berlin.

Sevilla, Manuel (1993) 'New approaches for aid agencies; FUPROVI's community based shelter programme', *Environment and Urbanization* Vol. 5, No. 1, April, pp. 111–121.

SIDA (1990) *Development Cooperation; Sida Infrastructure Division*, Stockholm.

Silas, Johan (1992) 'Environmental management in Surabaya's Kampungs', *Environment and Urbanization*, Vol. 4, No 2, October, pp. 33–41.

— and Eddy Indrayana (1988) 'Kampung Banyu Urip' in Bertha Turner (ed.), *Building Community, a Third World Case Book*, Habitat International Coalition, London.

Silva, M. and Altschul, F. (1986) *Programa de lotes con servicios y desarrollo comunal. FUNDASAL. El Salvador*, GTZ, Eshborn, Germany.

Silva, Mauricio (1986) 'La participacion comunitaria en Programas Sociales', *Revista Interamericana de Planificacion*, SIAP.

SINA (1987) *NGOs and Shelter*, Settlements Information Network Africa, Mazingira Institute, Nairobi.

Sinnatamby, Gehan (1990) 'Low cost sanitation: in Jorge E. Hardoy et al. (eds), *The Poor Die Young: Housing and Health in Third World Cities*, Earthscan Publications, London.

Society for Participatory Research in Asia (1989) *NGO–Government Relations: A source of life or a kiss of death* PRIA, Delhi.

Stein, Alfredo (1989), 'Critical Issues in Community Participation in Self-help Housing Programmes; The experience of FUNDASAL' *Community Development Journal* Vol. 25, No. 1.

Stein, Alfredo (1990) *Funding Community Level Initiatives: cases from Latin America*, IIED-AL, Buenos Aires.

Stephens, Carolyn, Trudy Harpham, David Bradley and Sandy Cairncross (1991) *A Review of the Health Impacts of Environmental Problems in Urban Areas of Developing Countries*, Paper prepared for the Panel on Urbanization for the WHO Commission on Health and the Environment, London School of Hygiene and Tropical Medicine, London.

Streeten, Paul (1988) 'The contributors of non-governmental organizations to development' *Asian Institute of Economics and Social Studies* Vol. 7, No. 1, pp. 1–9.

Stren, Richard E. (1989) 'Urban local government' in Richard E. Stren and Rodney R. White (eds), *African Cities in Crisis; Managing Rapid Urban Growth*, Westview Press, Boulder.
— (1989) 'Administration of Urban Services', in Richard E. Stren and Rodney R. White (eds), *African Cities in Crisis; Managing Rapid Urban Growth*, Westview Press, Boulder.
— and Rodney White (eds) (1989) *African Cities in Crisis: Managing Rapid Urban Growth*, Westview Press, Boulder.
Theunis, Sjef (ed.) (1992) *Non-governmental Development Organizations of Developing Countries: And the South Smiles*, Martinus Nijhoff, Dordrecht.
Turner, John F.C. (1988) 'Issues and conclusions' in Bertha Turner (ed.), *Building Community, a Third World Case Book*, Habitat International Coalition, London.
— (1988) 'Introduction' in Bertha Turner (ed.), *Building Community, a Third World Case Book*, Habitat International Coalition, London.
UNCHS (no date) *The UNCHS (Habitat) Community Development Programme*, Nairobi.
— (1987) *The Global Report on Human Settlements 1986*, Oxford University Press, Oxford.
— (1987) *IYSH Bulletin* Tenth Issue, July.
— (1990) *Co–operative Housing: Experiences of Mutual Self–Help*, Nairobi.
UNICEF (1983) *UNICEF and Non-Governmental Organizations* – a Report by Martin Ennals, United Nations Economic and Social Council document no E/ICEF/NGO/209, New York.
— (1988) *Improving Environment for Child health and Survival*, Urban Examples 15, UNICEF, New York.
United Nations (1991) *World Urbanization Prospects 1990; Estimates and Projections of Urban and Rural Populations and of Urban Agglomerations*, United Nations, ST/ESA/SER.a/121, New York.
van Til, J. (1988) *Mapping the Third Sector: Voluntarism in a Changing Social Economy*, Foundation Center.
Verhagen, Koenraad (1987) *Self–help Promotion: a Challenge to the NGO Community*, CEBEMO/The Royal Tropical Institute, Amsterdam.
Wanigasundara, Mallika (1989) 'Sri Lanka: Escaping the clutches of the moneylen ders' in Bakhoum, Ibrahima et al (eds), *Banking the Unbankable*, Panos Institute, London.
World Bank (1988) *World Development Report 1988*, Oxford University Press, Oxford.
— (1990) *World Development Report 1990*, Oxford University Press, Oxford.
— (1991) *Cooperation between the World Bank and NGOs*, the World Bank, USA.
— (1991) *Urban Policy and Economic Development: an Agenda for the 1990s*, the World Bank, Washington DC.
— (1991) *The World Bank and Non Governmental Organizations*, Washington DC.
World Commission on Environment and Development (1987) *Our Common Future*, Oxford University Press.
World Health Organization (1987) *Housing and Health, a Programme for Action*, Geneva, Switzerland.
— (1990) *Environmental Health in Urban Development* – report of a WHO Expert Committee, Technical Report Series 807, Geneva.

Index

Index compiled by Frank Pert

Relevant publications from Earthscan

Environmental Problems in Third World Cities
Jorge E Hardoy, Diana Mitlin and David Satterthwaite

It is rare to encounter a work as authoritative and accessible as this. It is a mine of useful information from cities in every part of the Third World, which does not shy away from the immensity of the problems but says much about the solutions to them as the problems themselves.

Jonathon Porritt

Environmental Problems in Third World Cities is not just a masterly analysis. It shows how to manage issues which have often proven unmanageable.

Sir Crispin Tickell

This well-written and lucid book is a useful primer on the complex environmental problems facing cities in the south.

Peter Oakley, Save the Children in *Health Action*

This book describes environmental health problems in Third World cities and how they affect human health, local ecosystems and global cycles. It analyses the causes of the problems, and reveals their political roots – such as the failure of governments to implement existing environmental legislation and land owning structures which force poorer groups to house themselves on illegal and often dangerous sites. The authors show that practical solutions to many of the problems can be found: above all, cities need to have competent local government, giving those whose health or livelihood may be threatened more control over their environment.

The Poor Die Young: Housing and Health in Third World Cities
Jorge E Hardoy, Sandy Cairncross and David Satterthwaite (eds)

The authors concentrate on detailed analyses of the cities... they consider innovative schemes for dealing with the problems, the needs of the people and how they could be met. In a fascinating chapter, they peer into the future and see what might happen if no changes are made in governmental and aid agencies' approaches and what could be achieved if lessons are drawn from present failures.

John Vidal, *The Guardian*

This volume shows hundreds of examples of self-help, in cities as diverse as Allahabad, Rio de Janeiro and Khartoum. There, more people are improving their health by upgrading their neighbourhoods, in ways that are far cheaper and more enduring than any of the large-scale projects advocated by planners and engineers trained in the Western mode.

Jeremy Seabrook, *New Statesman and Society*

Considers the scale of ill health, disablement and premature death in Third World cities and examines their links with housing and living conditions. The authors highlight the extent to which such problems can be prevented, even within constrained investment budgets.

Squatter Citizen: Life in the Urban Third World
Jorge E Hardoy and David Satterthwaite

... a book which should enjoy wide appeal: as a plea for adoption of the 'popular approach'; as a text for student use; and as an accessible and stimulating guide to the urban problems of developing countries.

Ann Varley, *Progress in Human Geography*

... one of the best contemporary statements of what is occurring in the growth of urban places in the Third World.

T G McGee, *Environment and Planning A*

... a very readable book, containing a lot of well documented information. The book is especially relevant for interested lay people, but many a professional can also benefit by having it on the bookshelf.

Jan van der Linden, *Third World Planning Review*

Describes the vast and complex process of urban change in the Third World and considers its impact on the lives of its poorer citizens. Boxes intersperse with the text to illustrate points made and also tell stories of how a squatter invasion was organized or how communities in illegal settlements organized their own defence or worked together to improve conditions.

Available from bookstores or by mail from Earthscan Publications Ltd, 120 Pentonville Road, London N1 9JN (Tel: 071 278 0433, Fax: 071 279 1142) or from IIED Bookshop, 3 Endsleigh Street, London WC1H 0DD (Tel: 071 388 2117, Fax: 071 388 2836)